AF395539

OPERATION SPIDER'S WEB

OPERATION SPIDER'S WEB

Ukraine's Devastating Drone Attack on Russia's
Long-Range Aircraft and its Aftermath

CHRISTOPHER A. LAWRENCE
THE DUPUY INSTITUTE

FRONTLINE
BOOKS

OPERATION SPIDER'S WEB
Ukraine's Devastating Drone Attack on Russia's Long-Range Aircraft

First published in Great Britain in 2026
by Frontline Books
An imprint of
Pen & Sword Books Ltd
Yorkshire - Philadelphia
Copyright © Christopher A. Lawrence
ISBN 9781036196738

Typeset by Lapiz Digital
Printed and bound in the UK by CPI Group (UK) Ltd,
Croydon, CR0 4YY.

Printed on paper from a sustainable source by
CPI Group (UK) Ltd, Croydon, CR0 4YY

The Publisher's authorised representative in the EU for product safety is
Authorised Rep Compliance Ltd., Ground Floor, 71 Lower Baggot Street,
Dublin D02 P593, Ireland.
www.arccompliance.com

For a complete list of Pen & Sword titles please contact
PEN & SWORD BOOKS LTD
47 Church Street, Barnsley, South Yorkshire, S70 2AS, England
E-mail: enquiries@pen-and-sword.co.uk
Website: www.pen-and-sword.co.uk
or
PEN & SWORD BOOKS
1950 Lawrence Rd, Havertown, PA 19083, USA
E-mail: uspen-and-sword@casematepublishers.com

DEDICATION

This book is dedicated to my son
Sasha Lawrence
University of Virginia School of Medicine
He has worked hard. Deserves another dedication.

CONTENTS

MAPS

ACKNOWLEDGEMENTS

First, I want to thank John Grehan and the managing director Charles Hewitt over at Pen & Sword in the UK for suggesting this idea to me.

I also want to thank those people who helped me a little with research and analysis. This includes Dr. Julian Spencer-Churchill of Concordia University in Quebec, Stefan Korshak of the *Kyiv Post* and co-author of *The Siege of Mariupol* and *The Battle for the Donbas*, and Carl Larson, a former deployed combat veteran for Ukraine, still an active supporter and heads the Ukraine Defense Support.[1] War Mapper has continued to be a supporter by graciously providing us with all his excellent maps. Jay Karamales made five maps and three graphs for this book. His professional-quality work was done for free. He was my co-author for the book *The Hunting Falcon*, about the World War I German ace Hans Buddecke.

Finally, I want to thank all the people on Twitter (now known as X), Telegram and other social media sites, all the people who blogged about this war, and all the reporters who reported on this war. There has been a plethora of day-to-day accounts of each action, each raid, and many of the strikes and explosions. There often been useful follow-up of these strikes. These large collection efforts done by hundreds of people have made this book possible. The social media posts, blog posts and newspapers articles provide the data that this book is based upon. I could not have written this book without their help. Many of their names are in the 400 footnotes to this book.

---

1   See: Home Page – Ukraine Defense Support.

PREFACE

This book came about at the request of Pen & Sword. I was systematically working my way through a series of books that was tracking the military history of the war in Ukraine in the uncertain research environment of an ongoing war. These are *The Battle for Kyiv* covering the first six weeks of the war; *The Siege of Mariupol*, covering the three-month siege of that city; and the currently in process *The Battle for the Donbas*, covering the Russian operations against the cities of Severodonetsk and Lysychansk in the spring and summer of 2022.

I was trying to write a series of serious military histories of the war and ended up enlisting Kyiv-based Stefan Korshak to help with these. On 1 June 2025 Ukraine executed Operation Spider's Web. That week, Pen & Sword contacted me and asked if I could write a book on the air strike right away. Well, I had done my initial work on *The Battle for the Donbas* and had passed the manuscript over to my co-author. I was well ahead of schedule on my latest Battle of Kursk book, *The Battle of Tolstoye Woods*. I was on track to complete it by the end of September. So, I was kind of looking at a quiet summer. They asked, I accepted, and this book was written.

This is an attempt to create the complete story of the strike. As it was an intelligence operation, we will probably never have the complete story. So this is as complete of a story as could be done in the summer of 2025. Later writers may have better sources. Still, much of the story can be told.

The rest of book puts the events in context, as there were multiple aspects to this operation, strategic, political, and social. The Ukrainians continue to creatively show what dramatic effects they could obtain with their rather limited resources.

This book also allows us to explore the drone and missile campaign against infrastructure and cities. These are not addressed in depth in any of our other books.

Chapter 1

THE STRIKE

"A brilliant operation was carried out. It took place on enemy territory and was aimed exclusively at military targets – specifically, the equipment used in strikes against Ukraine. Russia suffered truly significant losses – entirely justified and deserved."

President Volodymyr Zelenskyy
1 June 2025[1]

It was a lazy Sunday morning in Russia on 1 June 2025. The war with Ukraine had been going on now for over three years. That morning 117 Ukrainian drones rose up from the back of four trucks inside of Russia and started flying towards their targeted Russian air bases.[2] They were Ukrainian-made Osa ("Wasp") quadcopters.

They were packed in crates of at least 27 drones each and driven across the country in the back of cargo trucks. The unsuspecting Russian truck drivers thought they were delivering materials for pre-fabricated houses. Instead, several of the drivers were asked to pull over at a local gas station or parking lot, and then suddenly the cover of the cargo container came off and more than two dozen drones took off towards a nearby air base. The drivers were taken completely by surprise.

---

1   From President Zelenskyy's address to Ukraine, 1 June 2025 at https://www.americanrhetoric.com/speeches/volodymyrzelenskyoperationspiderweb.htm.

2   The count of 117 comes from Ukrainian government public statements. See "The Economic Lessons from Ukraine's Spectacular Drone Succes," *The Economist*, 12 June 2025.

The drones then attacked the Russian bombers at four air bases across the vast expanse of Russia, from a base above the Arctic Circle near Murmansk, to the heart of European Russia, and out to the middle of Siberia, near Lake Baikal. Large old Russian strategic bombers, like Tu-95s and Tu-22s, came under attack, along with Russia's valuable Airborne Early Warning and Control (AEW&C) Beriev A-50s.[3] Maybe two dozen planes were attacked by the drones on three of the airfields, and it appears that over a dozen were destroyed.

This attack stunned Russia, as this was their strategic bomber force. Not only was it being used to regularly strike at Ukrainian infrastructure and cities, but these were the nuclear-capable strategic bombers that were an important part of their Strategic Deterrent Forces. Some Russians, in shock, equated it to a Russian Pearl Harbor.[4]

This was the strike back at the Russian bomber force which had been regularly firing cruise missiles at Ukrainian cities. It was organized by the Security Services of Ukraine (SBU), in an attempt to take action against the nominally invulnerable Russian strategic bombers that had been striking at them for over the last three years.

The attacking weapons were the Ukrainian-designed and manufactured small four-propeller drone, call the Osa or "Wasp."[5] The Osa was a small FPV (first person view) drone with a take-off weight without payload of 11 pounds (5 kilograms). It was manufactured by the Ukrainian company First Contact, which was originally Kyiv-based but has now moved to an undisclosed location. The drones are capable of carrying a payload of 7.3 pounds (3.3 kilograms) giving is a fully loaded weight of 18.3 pounds (8.3 kilograms). Twenty-seven or more of these drones loaded into a crate would weigh at least 494 pounds (224.1 kilograms).

---

3   AEW&C is a newer term for AWACS – Airborne Warning and Control System. It means the same. AWACS is the specific name for the system mounted on the U.S. Boeing E-3 Sentry plane. AEW&C is the newer term, only becoming common in the last two decades.

4   This is clearly a gross overstatement on the part of the Russians. To start with, this was an attack by a country they had already been at war with for over three years. See: "Russia's 'Pearl Harbor': Putin Dealt 'Serious Loss' in stand off with NATO," *Newsweek*, 2 June 2025.

5   "First Contact Osa were the Ukrainian FPV drones that destroyed Russian Tu-95MS, Tu-22M3, and Tu-160 Strategic Bombers," *Defence Express*, 2 June 2025 at https://en.defence-ua.com/weapon_and_tech/first_contact_osa_were_the_ukrainian_fpv_drones_that_destroyed_russian_tu_95ms_tu_22m3_and_tu_160_strategic_bombers-14721.html.

One source states that each drone consisted of two warheads each weighing 800 grams. This would give them a combined explosive weight of 3.5 pounds (1.6 kilograms). It is claimed that they are "…shaped charge explosive devices. They are designed to burn through the aircraft's fuselage and cause an explosive blast inside, followed by ignition, which we have already seen later as the burning of aviation fuel stored in the aircraft's fuel tanks."[6]

The drone's top speed is around 93 mph (150 km/h) and it has an airtime of up to 15 minutes. This means that its operational range is effectively no more than 23 miles (37.5 kilometers). Various public stat sheets state that they have a control range of up to ten kilometers and a maximum combat radius of 25 kilometers. They cost less than $500 each.[7] The drones took off from less than six miles (ten kilometers) from the bases.

These drones were smuggled into Russia. They were collected in a SBU facility in Chelyabinsk and loaded onto trucks there. The drones were packed in large boxed containers with around 27 or more drones per box (see photo section). The cargo container or cargo box of each truck was rigged so their roof panels could be lifted off by a remote activated mechanism. This would then allow the drones to fly out.[8] We suspect each container held 30 drones each, resulting in 120 drones set up for launch from the four activated containers and only 117 launching (97.5% launch).

They were driven across the county by unsuspecting Russian drivers in flatbed or cargo trucks. In at least two cases, the drivers were instructed to stop on the side of the road, at a gas station or parking lot. The covers of the cargo containers were then activated, flipped open and

---

6   "Ukraine's Operation Spiderweb: Security Service chief reveals details," *RBC-Ukraine*, 12 August 2025. Quote is from Lt. General Malyuk. Also see Kateryna Zakharchenko, "'117 Drones and 2,200 kg of Explosives': SBU Chief Unveils Ukraine's Secret Ops," *Kyiv Post*, 23 June 2025, which specifically states that "The warhead inside each drone consisted of two components – 800 grams and 800 grams – making a total of 1.6 kilograms of a special shaped-charge high-explosive."

7   See https://osa-drone.com/en. They provided stats for the OSA B7 and OPSA K7. First Contact provides drone stats here: https://firstcontact.biz/en/projects/hihg-acrobatic-uav-osa/.

8   The truck that attacked Olenya appears to have been a typical cargo truck. The truck that attacked Belaya was a flatbed truck with two cargo containers sitting in the bed and was the truck that blew up near Ukrainka. See photo section.

more than two dozen drones came flying out. The unsuspecting Russian drivers got to watch the drones fly off.[9] The roof panels of the truck's cargo containers were seen lying on the ground next to the truck.[10]

It was later stated that each of the drivers left Chelyabinsk heading towards the designated airfield. Each driver was given a specific location where they were to arrive and deliver their house. Supposedly, a buyer was to come there, pay for the house, and pick it up.[11] This would explain why if called by a stranger and asked to pull over at a gas station or near a coffee shop, the drivers would respond without suspicion.

Both Russia and Ukrainian social media provided confirmation of parts of this story. The Ukrainian SBU said this was all done remotely. It is more likely that there were SBU operators in the launch area to activate the opening devices on the cargo containers and to activate the drones.

This started the attack. It was done mid-morning. The photos show a daylight attack and doing it in the morning when most of the planes were still on the ground makes perfect sense. The drones then took off, hitting their targets maybe five minutes later. Any SBU operators were able to discretely leave the area.

The operators were probably a mix of SBU agents from Ukraine and local Russians of Ukrainian descent. They clearly could do this with small teams of two to six people. It would take five teams. It is claimed that the SBU had already withdrawn all of their people to Ukraine before the day was over.[12] This is possible for the three bases that were near international borders. Two of these locales were far from the Ukrainian border, Dyagilevo and Ivanov Severny. Most likely these teams were in the area until the firing, so they could witness and confirm they had been launched and then took off to hide is a safe location inside of Russia. Some of these agents might still be in Russia now.

The SBU agents in Chelyabinsk supposedly left on Thursday, 29 May. The trucks reportedly departed Chelyabinsk on that day, and

---

9   "James Marson, Jane Lytvynenko, Brenna T. Snith, Serhii Bosak, "Inside the Ukrainian Drone Operation That Devastated Russia's Bomber Fleet," *The Wall Street Journal*, 3 June 2025.

10   "To attack Russian air base, Ukrainian spies hid drones in wooden sheds," *NewsMaxWorld*, 1 June 2025.

11   From an interview by Lt. General Malyuk given on 12 August, 2025. See: "Ukraine's Operation Spiderweb: Security Service chief reveals details," *RBC-Ukraine*, 12 August 2025.

12   From President Zelenskyy's speech on 1 June 2025.

then the agents left under the pretense of going on vacation. Therefore, when the operation took place on Sunday morning, 1 June, the agents that were in Chelyabinsk were already back in Ukraine. The agents were back at their headquarters in Kyiv on Sunday and were able to monitor their drivers in phone conversations.[13]

Five Russian airfields were targeted: Dyagilevo, Ivanovo Severny, Olenya, Belaya and Ukrainka.

The closest base to Ukraine was Dyagilevo. The Dyagilevo air base is located in the Ryazan Oblast, two miles (three kilometers) west of Ryazan (pop. 528,599 in 2021). Its concrete runway is 3,000 meters (9,843 feet) long. It is a training center for Russia's Strategic Bombing Force. It is also the home of Ryazan Museum of Long-Range Aviation.

The city is 122 miles (196 kilometers) southeast of Moscow and 290 miles (467 kilometers) northeast of Ukraine. The original Ryazan was an old settlement, which existed since at least 1095. It was conquered by the Mongols in 1237 and razed. The capital of the Principality of Ryazan was moved around 55 kilometers to the northwest to a town called Pereyaslvl. The town was renamed Ryazan in 1778 by order of the German-born Russian Empress Catherine the Great.

It is the closest to Ukraine of the five attacked air bases. Located at the base is the 203rd Guards Aircraft-refueling Aviation Regiment with Ilyushin Il-78s and 78Ms, and the 49th Instructor Heavy Bomber Aviation Regiment.

The base first received Tu-22 aircraft in 1973 and has regularly supported Tu-22s and Tu-95s. On 5 December 2022, in the first year of the war, the base was attacked by a single Ukrainian drone which damaged a Tu-22M3 and destroyed a fuel truck. Three people were killed and five injured according to Russian state media. On 14 December 2022, an Iranian-built Shahed-136 drone hit a Kyiv apartment building. It had written on it "For Ryazan!!!."[14] Most likely,

---

13   "Ukraine's Operation Spiderweb: Security Service chief reveals details," *RBC-Ukraine*, 12 August 2025. Again, this timeline is from an interview on 12 August 2025 by Lt. General Malyuk. One cannot rule out that it is deliberate mis-information.

14   Andrew Roth and Julian Borger, "Explosions rock two Russian airbases far from Ukraine frontline," *The Guardian*, 5 December 2022 at https://www.theguardian.com/world/2022/dec/05/explosions-russia-airbases-far-from-ukraine-frontline-bombers and Tom Balmforth and Pavel Polityuk, "Russia launches drone attack on Kyiv, Ukraine hails air defences," *Reuters*, 14 December 2022 at https://www.reuters.com/

the unmanned aerial vehicle (UAV) that attacked Ryazan was flown from inside of Russia, not from Ukraine, due to a lack of range. This was the first such drone attack on a Russian air base.

The attack there on 1 June 2025 was of limited effectiveness. The local Russian governor confirmed that the base was attacked but stated that there were no injuries and a fragment from a shot-down drone had damaged the roof of a residential building. At least seven explosions were reported. None of the Tu-95MS and Tu-22Ms bombers based there were hit. Only the grass near the airfield was burned.[15] It is not clear why this attack was not successful. It may have been because the drones were launched from the back of a moving truck, although it does appear that the truck that attacked Olenya was also moving at the time of the launches, although very slowly. Most likely it was because of electronic warfare defenses (jamming) activated by Russia, as it appears that this attack occurred later than the other attacks.

The Ivanovo Severny (Ivanovo North) air base is located four miles (six kilometers) north of the city of Ivanovo (pop. 361,644 in 2021). Its concrete runway is 2,300 meters (7,546 feet) long. Ivanovo's population was 408,330 in 2010 demonstrating an 11% decline over 11 years. This is not unusual in the former Soviet Union. This city is 158 miles (254 kilometers) northeast of Moscow. It is part of the "Golden Ring of Russia" having first been mentioned in the records 464 years ago in 1561. It is almost on the 57th latitude line, making it as far north as the southern parts of Alaska like at Kodiak Island, just south of Anchorage.

The runway was built in 1935 and was used during World War II. It served in late 1942 as the original base for the Normandie French

---

world/europe/two-kyiv-administration-buildings-damaged-drones-attack-city-says-2022-12-14/.

15 See "Ukraine Attacked Strategic Bomber Bases in the Murmansk and Irkutsk Regions with Drones Brought on Trucks," *The Moscow Times*, 01.06.2025 at https://www.moscowtimes.ru/2025/06/01/ukraina-atakovala-bazi-strategicheskih-bombardirovschikov-vmurmanskoi-irkutskoi-iryazanskoi-oblastyah-a164927 and "Ukraine carried out a series of attacks on airfields based on Russian strategic aviation," *Vazhnyie Istorii*, 1 June 2025 at https://istories.media/news/2025/06/01/ukraina-provela-seriyu-atak-na-aerodromi-v-rossii-glavnoe/ and James Marson, Jane Lytvynenko, Brenna T. Snith, Serhii Bosak, "Inside the Ukrainian Drone Operation That Devastated Russia's Bomber Fleet," *The Wall Street Journal*, 3 June 2025 at https://www.msn.com/en-us/news/world/inside-the-ukrainian-drone-operation-that-devastated-russia-s-bomber-fleet/ar-AA1G2Dc0.

fighter squadron that was raised to fight in Russia from Free French forces. The base was upgraded in 1965 and received the Soviet Union's first delivery of Il-76s in 1974. It is home to the 144th Airborne Early Warning Aviation Regiment, and the VTA Training Center, the 810th Center for Combat Use and Re-training of Military Transport Aviation Flight Personnel (known as the 810th CBP I PLS). This last unit uses the A-50 and A-50U airborne early warning and control aircraft (AEW&C). It is the primary base for A-50s and usually has 16 aircraft of various types there.[16]

The base had previously been struck by a Ukrainian drone on 23 May 2025 and one A-50 was likely damaged.[17] This was a part of a much large drone attack on Russia on that day.

This base was far from any international border. The 1 June attack there damaged the radar domes of two A-50s.[18] The attack was not reported by Russian media, but videos were provided by Ukraine showed that two A-50s were seriously damaged, with one looking like it was destroyed. Not sure if the other seriously damaged A-50 is repairable. The aircraft were protected by sandbags or tires placed across their wings. These are nominally to help break up or reduce their signature. The drones went after their domes. As Russia has only six or seven of these aircraft operational, the loss of these two aircraft is a significant degradation in capability. It is possible that these were not operational aircraft, as Russian does have a number of non-operational A-50s that are stored at this base.[19]

The Olenya air base is even further north, being located in the Kola Peninsula 57 miles (92 kilometers) south of Murmansk. Its concrete runway is 3,500 meters (11,483 feet) long. Murmansk (pop. 270,384

---

16 "Beriev delivers first upgraded A-50U Mainstay," *Air Force Monthly*, No. 286, January 2012, p. 28.

17 Dmitry Novikov, "Drone Attack on Russia: Air Defense in Moscow, Strikes on the Lipetsk Region and Ivanovo," *Nastoyashcheye Vremya*, 23 May 2025 at https://www.currenttime.tv/a/33422547.html.

18 Joe Barnes, James Rushton, "Ukraine strikes Putin's prized spy planes," *The Telegraph*, 3 June 2025 at https://www.telegraph.co.uk/world-news/2025/06/03/ukraine-strikes-putin-prized-spy-plane/.

19 See Thomas Newdick, "Confirmed Losses of Russian Aircraft Mount After Ukrainian Drone Assault," *The War Zone*, 4 June 2025 at https://www.twz.com/air/firm-evidence-of-russian-aircraft-losses-after-ukrainian-drones-trikes. Also see "Spiderweb update – Chinese Satellite Images Show Destroyed Russian A-50 AEW&C," *Kyiv Post*, 3 June 2025.

in 2021) was the most northern port in Russia and was the hub of transport in World War I and World War II. It is the world's largest city north of the Arctic Circle, being well above the 68th degree latitude line, putting it at the level of the northern part of Alaska, two-thirds the way between Fairbanks and Point Barrow. Its population has been in severe decline since the collapse of the Soviet Union, being 468,039 in 1989, 446,137 in 2002, 307,257 in 2010 and 270,384 in 2021. This is a 42% decline over 32 years. It was founded in 1916 during the First World War as an ice-free port at the end of a newly constructed rail line so as to receive supplies from their allies (the British and the French).[20]

The air base was built around 1957 or before. It is home to the 40th Composite Aviation Regiment and has always been a base for strategic bombers. It reports to the 22nd Guards Heavy Bomber Aviation Division. It was reported by Project AviVector that as of 26 May 2025 there were two Tu-95MSs, three Tu-160s and two Su-34s (fighters) based there.[21]

The attack was carried out from a truck at a gas station. There is a Russian video showing a truck driving into a gas station at Olenegorsk. As the truck is driving out of the frame of the camera a drone can be seen flying away from the gas station. It is uncertain if that drone came from the truck, but this is what the poster of the video assumed.[22] If it did come from that truck, then it took off out of the top of the truck as the truck was still moving.

There were at least ten explosions at the airfield. According to the UK company Janes, four Tu-95 and one An-12 transport plane were destroyed there based upon their analysis of the images.[23]

---

20 The author's British grandfather was there in 1919. See *Mystics & Statistics* blog post "Murmansk," 26 January 2016 at https://dupuyinstitute.org/2016/01/26/murmansk/. Also see "Munity in Murmansk," 6 June 2024 at https://dupuyinstitute.org/2024/06/06/mutiny-in-murmansk/ and "I was in Liverpool," 25 July 2024 at https://dupuyinstitute.org/2024/07/25/i-was-in-liverpool/. It was my grandfather's time in Murmansk that peaked my interest in Russian history.

21 See: https://www.agents.media/ukraina-za-odin-den-unichtozhila-i-povredila-ne-menee-6-rossijskih-strategicheskih-bombardirovshhikov/

22 Roman Petrenko, "Ukrainian drones launched from lorries target Russian airfields, reports claim – videos," *Ukrainska Pravda 25*, 1 June 2025.

23 Helena Skinner, Chris Looft and Kerem Inal, "Aftermath of Ukraine drone strike on Russian airfields show in satellite imagery," *ABC News*, 5

Belaya air base is located in the Usolsky District, Irkutsk Oblast. The concrete runway is 4,000 meters (13,123 feet) long. The air base is 11 miles (18 kilometers) north of the town of Osulye-Siberskoye and 53 miles (85 kilometers) northwest of Irkutsk. Irkutsk (pop. 617,264 in 2021) is 2,612 miles (4,204 kilometers) east of Moscow, on the trans-Siberian railway. Irkutsk is in the heart of Siberia and surprisingly still maintains its population.[24] It is near Lake Baikal and the Mongolian border.

The air base was built in 1946, right after World War II. The runway was unpaved initially. It has regularly been used at a long-range aviation base and has 38 bomber revetments. It is home to the 200th Guard Heavy Bomber Aviation Regiment with Tu-22M3s, the 444th Heavy Bomber Aviation Regiment also with Tu-22M3 and the 181st Independent Composite Aviation Squadron with An-12s and An-30s. It reports to the 326th Heavy Bomber Aviation Division.

The attack there was also launched from a flatbed truck. According to Project AviVector, it was a target rich environment, there being on the base the day before the attack 52 bombers (including 35 Tu-22M3s, 6 Tu-95MSs and 7 Tu-160s) along with 30 MiG-31 fighters and eight auxiliary and transport aircraft.[25] It would appear that at least seven aircraft were destroyed, including four Tu-22Ms and three Tu-95MS. At least one other Tu-95MS was damaged.[26]

June 2025 at https://abcnews.go.com/International/aftermath-ukraine-drone-strike-russian-airfields-shown-satellite/story?id=122514076.

The TWZ analysis shows three or four Tu-85MS and one AN-12 destroyed. See Thomas Newdick, "Confirmed Losses of Russian Aircraft Mount After Ukrainian Drone Assault," *The War Zone*, 4 June 2025 at https://www.twz.com/air/firm-evidence-of-russian-aircraft-losses-after-ukrainian-drone-strikes.

24   Population in 1989 was 626,135.

25   "Ukraine destroyed and damaged at least 6% of Russian strategic bombers in one day," *Agentstvo*, 1 June 2025 at https://www.agents.media/ukraina-za-odin-den-unichtozhila-i-povredila-ne-menee-6-rossijskih-strategicheskih-bombardirovshhikov/. The article says that there were 52 bombers there but then only lists 48 by type.

26   On 2 June one analysis conclude that three Tu-95s were destroyed and one damaged. They also had one Tu-22M3 destroyed and three others possibly destroyed. Another analysis by Telegram channel AviVector on 4 June concluded that four Tu-22M3s and three Tu-95MSs were destroyed and possibly one Tu-95MS was damaged. See https://www.kyivpost.com/post/53749 and https://www.thebarentsobserver.com/

The ironically named Ukrainka air base is located in Ukrainka, Amur Oblast. The concrete runway is 3,500 meters (11,483 feet) long. The town of Ukrainka (pop. 1,160 in 2018) is in the far eastern part of Siberia. The air base is only 58 miles (93 kilometers) from the Chinese border. The nearest major Russian city is Khabarovsk (pop. 627,441 in 2021), some 347 miles (559 kilometers away).

It was built in 1955. The base is home to the 79th Heavy Bomber Aviation Regiment and the 182nd Guards Heavy Bomber Aviation Regiment. It has nearly 40 revetments. It reports to the 326th Heavy Bomber Aviation Division.

The attack there failed. The truck carrying the drones caught fire and exploded. No drones ever took off.[27] There are videos of a flatbed truck pulled over on the shoulder of the road. It is transporting two containers similar to the truck near Belaya. The back container on the truck is smoking. People are walking around it and towards it. One person is entering the door at the back of the container. It then explodes (see photo section).[28] Apparently the truck driver was the person going into the truck's cargo container and was killed in the explosion.

One major Russian bomber base was not targeted, Engels in Saratov Oblast. It is home of the 121st Guards Heavy Bomber Aviation Regiment and the 184th Heavy Bomber Aviation Regiment. It reports to the 22nd Guards Heavy Bomber Aviation Division. It does maintain Tu-22M3s and Tu-95MSs. It is unknown why it was not targeted.

---

security/satellite-images-from-olenya-show-4-strategic-bombers-destroyed/431046 and https://www.twz.com/air/firm-evidence-of-russian-aircraft-losses-after-ukrainian-drone-strikes.

The analysis by TWZ shows three destroyed Tu-95MS and four destroyed Tu-22M3 bombers. See Thomas Newdick, "Confirmed Losses of Russian Aircraft Mount After Ukrainian Drone Assault," *The War Zone*, 4 June 2025 at https://www.twz.com/air/firm-evidence-of-russian-aircraft-losses-after-ukrainian-drone-strikes.

27 "Spiderweb- Russian Manhunt for 'Agent' Who Duped Truck Drivers into Delivering Attack Drones," *Kyiv Post*, 4 June 2025 at https://www.kyivpost.com/post/53935.

28 "Truck carrying Ukrainian Drones explodes June 1 in Russia's Maur Oblast; Person enters container before blast," *DeepNewZ*, 1 June 2025.

Map 1: The five Russian air bases attacked on 1 June 2025.

The 22nd Guards Heavy Bomber Aviation Division appears to consist of four regiments, the 121st, the 184th, the 52nd and the 40th located at Engels, Shaykovka, Soltsy and Olenya. The 326th Guards Heavy Bomber Aviation Division appears to consist of four regiments, the 200th, 444th, 79th and 182nd located at the Belaya, Ukrainka, Temp and Tiska air bases, along with the 181st Composite Aviation Squadron at Belaya.

It appears that five or possibly six flatbed or cargo trucks were used and four crates of drones were launched each at Dyagilevo, Ivanovo, Belaya, and Olenya airfields. The Ukrainka airfield was targeted but the cargo truck stopped along the side of the road on the way there, the driver went inside of it and then it immediately exploded. We have photos from this incident (see photo section). It is a flatbed truck with two large cargo containers on it. This is the same set-up as used for the Belaya attack (see photo section). The photo of the truck in the Olenya air base attack shows a more traditional cargo truck. Other reports specifically mention flatbed trucks being used. As an armed drone weighs 18.3 pounds (8.3 kilograms), then 27 of them would be a container of at least 494 pounds (224.1 kilograms). This container was either in the roof of the cargo container or set upon the floor. The videos of the burnt-out remains do not clearly show which is the case.

Each crate appeared to carry around 27 drones based upon the photo provided (see photo section). One or two trucks did not arrive at their destination. Four crates of 27 drones equals 108 drones. It is claimed by the President of Ukraine that 117 drones were flown, which is nine more than what would be in four crates of 27. Perhaps each of the crates contained 30 drones. It was later stated by Lt. General Vasyl Malyuk, the head of the SBU, that 150 drones were used.[29] This could be five crates of 30 drones each.

The person who is claimed to have been the SBU agent who organized one or more, and possibly all, of these operations was a 37-year-old Ukrainian, Artem Igorevich Timofeyev. He was a resident of Russia's Chelyabinsk region, down in the southeastern corner of European Russia and on the border with Kazakhstan. Chelyabinsk in the seventh largest city in Russia with a population over 1.1 million. The Chelyabinsk region is mostly on the eastern slope of the southern Ural mountains, making it more in Asia than in Europe. The city of Chelyabinsk is in Europe. They share a border with Kazakhstan. It is rumored, and highly likely, that Timofeyev escaped Russia through Kazakhstan.[30]

Russia issued photos and details of the suspect on the Chelyabinsk Telegram and VKontakte channels. It is said that Timofeyev was born in Ukraine's Zhytomyr, lived in Kyiv, but moved to Chelyabinsk region a few years ago. In October 2024, he registered as the owner of a cargo transportation company and purchased several trucks. Now it is clear that this was preparation for this operation. It is said that five or six drivers were hired by Timofeyev to deliver frame houses to a specific location near the target areas. During the trip, they were contacted by cell phone and told to pull into a parking lots or gas stations. These ended up being the launch sites close to the airfields.[31]

29　"Ukraine's Operation Spiderweb: Security Service chief reveals details," *RBC-Ukraine*, 12 August 2025. The actual statement was "First and foremost, it is logistics – that is, delivering the equipment itself into the enemy's rear, which in our case means 150 combat FPV drones."

30　https://t.me/dva_majors/72892. This post does note that Kazakhstan and the United Kingdom signed a military cooperation agreement on 6 June 2025, five days after the Operation Spider's Web attack. It was for peacekeeping, language training and education of the Kazakhstani military personnel at higher military educational institutes in the United Kingdom. Suspect these two events are unrelated, but people do speculate.

31　"Spiderweb- Russian Manhunt for 'Agent' Who Duped Truck Drivers into Delivering Attack Drones," *Kyiv Post*, 4 June 2025 at https://www.kyivpost.com/post/53935. One account states "Russian law enforcement searched a concrete warehouse Sunday in Chelyabinsk…" and "Russian state media named a Ukrainian deejay who had been living in Russia and recently relocated to the city last year as one of the people responsible for logistics behind the drone attack, purchasing the trucks

The Russian drivers used are listed in a *Kyiv Post* article and it is worth repeating here. They are:

- At Olenya: The 55-year-old "Aleksandr" or Aleksander Zaytsev, is a resident of Chelyabinsk.[32] He was hired by Artem to transport four modular houses from Chelyabinsk to the Kola district in the Murmansk region. He loaded up his cargo. He said that an unknown person contacted him by phone and told him to stop at a Rosneft gas station that was close to Olenya airfield. It may have been Rosneft AEC No. 17 that was 3.85 miles (6.20 kilometers) to the southwest of the airfield.[33]

- At Belaya: The 61-year-old "Andrey" or Andrey Merkuryev, was hired by Artem to transport a modular house to the Irkursk region.[34] En route, he was called and told to pull into a parking lot near the Teremok Café in Usoly-Sibrskoye. This is around "six miles (ten kilometers)" from Belaya airfield. He said that almost immediately drones began to take off from the back of his truck. This does lead one to suspect that someone in the area was operating the controls remotely.

The Russian fast-food Teremok Café is right on highway P255 and by our measurement is only 3.70 miles (5.95 kilometers) from the airfield.[35] Like in the case of the suspect launch site in the Kola peninsula against Olenya, it is a pretty open area from the launch site to the airfield. This was probably as planned.

There were pictures released by the Governor of Irkutsk Oblast that shows what he states is the truck in the parking lot and a second photo showing the truck is burning.[36] This leads one to suspect that the trucks were blown up by the Ukrainian operators or by automatic command after the drones flew. It was a flatbed truck with two containers riding in the bed (see photo section).

---

that would carry the drones and coordinating the drivers." See: James Marson, Jane Lytvynenko, Brenna T. Smith, Serhii Bosak, "Inside the Ukrainian Drone Operation that devastated Russia's bomber fleet," *The Wall Street Journal*, 3 June 2025. Also see: https://t.me/astrapress/82682.

32 Listed in https://t.me/astrapress/82682 as 56-year-old Aleksandr Zaytsev. Listed in the *Kyiv Post* article as 55-year old "Aleksandr."

33 There are three options in Olenegorsk. Most likely option is Rosneft AEC No. 17.

34 Listed in https://t.me/astrapress/82682 as 62-year old Andrey Merkuryev. Listed in the *Kyiv Post* article as 61-year-old "Andrey."

35 Measured on Google Earth to the edge of the air base.

36 Samya Kullab, "A surprise drone attack on airfields across Russia encapsulates Ukraine's wartime strategy," *AP*, 2 June 2025.

It was claimed on Russian social media that at least 20 drones were launched.[37] This matches with the crates having at least 27 drones in them.

- At Dyagilevo: The 46-year-old Sergei Kanurin said that he was transporting modular homes from Chelyabinsk but while driving close to Ryazan, the roof of his truck suddenly came off and drones began flying out. It is hard to say how they remotely knew when to fly the drones while he was driving down the road. The distance from Chelyabinsk to Ryazan is 861 miles (1386 kilometers) as the crow flies or 1,044 miles driving distance (1,680 kilometers). There is a major highway, E30/M5, just to the west of Ryazan that goes right by the Dyagilevo airfield, around 1.20 miles (1.93 kilometers) away from it. This leads me to suspect that there was a Ukrainian SBU agent in the area monitoring this road who then activated the drones. This was the one attack that did not do significant damage to any planes.
- At Ivanovo Severny: A fourth driver, named in one source as 56-year-old Mikhail Ryummin, loaded his truck in Chelyabinsk and was used to launch drones at the Ivanovo Severny air base. The distance from Chelybinsk to Ivanovo is 795 miles (1,279 kilometers) as the crow flies.[38]
- At Ukrainka: The fifth truck caught fire near the village of Seryshevo en route to Ukrainka airfield. Seryshevo is a little over five miles (eight kilometers) from Ukrainka airfield. The driver was apparently killed after he entered the trailer that then exploded. There is a video of this (see photo section). Not sure why the cargo containers caught fire. As the explosion clearly occurred just as the driver entered the container through the door, the explosion was most likely initiated because of his entry. This could have been trip-wired or initiated by observers. The fact that the truck that attacked Belaya also blew up indicates that they were rigged to explode after launching so as to destroy the evidence.

There was perhaps a sixth truck. A driver was reported found strangled by a plastic cord. They did not provide a location of where this incident occurred, but a gruesome picture was posted to social media of the strangled driver.[39] One does wonder if a sixth airfield was targeted. One wonders if it was Engels. A strangled driver indicates that SBU agents were operating in the area.

The count of drones argues against this. If Ukraine indeed shipped 150 drones for this operation, as Lt. General Vasyl Malyuk states in his

---

37   Roman Petrenko, "Ukrainian drones launched from lorries target Russian airfields, reports claim – videos," *Ukrainska Pravda 25*, 1 June 2025.

38   See https://t.me/astrapress/82682.

39   See the gruesome image on Telegram from Supernova+: https://t.me/supernova_plus/39637.

interview of 12 August 2025, and there are at least 27 drones per crate (see photo section), then there are not enough drones for a sixth truck. Also, Lt. General Malyuk stated in a recent interview that five suitable vehicles were purchased.[40]

In an interview given by Lt. General Vasyl Malyuk on 12 August 2025 he stated that before they sent the trucks out with the drones, one of the Ukrainian agents accidently pressed a button and opened the roof of the truck, which allowed one of the truck drivers to see the drones sitting in their crates. The Ukrainian agent invented a fictional explanation that the drones were needed to track the animal population, because the houses were supposed to be hunting houses. As Malyuk stated "The driver who saw this was 63 years old. Well, that is, he is of age and is essentially on 'you' with gadgets. That's why he ate our story."[41] This was probably the 61-year-old driver at Belaya referred to as "Andrey."

President Zelenskyy stated on Sunday evening that all those involved in Spider's Web has been safely evacuated back to Ukraine. We have not been able to confirm this, but Russia has not reported having caught any of the perpetrators. Most likely there were Ukrainian SBU teams at each of the destinations who activated the drones. The fact that one crate was activated as the truck was driving down the road, and another driver may have been strangled reinforces that view of the operation. It is possible that all SBU agents got out of Russia by Sunday, 1 June, but not likely for those operating near Ryazan and Ivanovo. They are not near any international borders.

The timing of the attacks
The attacks should have started around 10:30 Moscow time. The attacks were planned to be simultaneous, but issues arose with the ground control stations, which were not on the trucks (also implying SBU agents were near each air base). This caused delays that ultimately allowed the Russians at some air bases to activate electronic warfare and other air defense measures.[42]

---

40   "Ukraine's Operation Spiderweb: Security Service chief reveals details," *RBC-Ukraine*, 12 August 2025.

41   "Operation 'Web' was supposed to take place before 9 May, but it had to be postponed because Russian truck drivers 'got drunk.' SBU Chief Malyuk spoke about the details of the operation.," *Dev.UA*, 13 August 2025 at https://dev.ua/en/news/operation-web-was-supposed-to-take-place-before May-9-but-it-had-to-be-postponed-because-russian-truck-drivers-got-drunk-sbu-chief-malyuk-spoke-about-the-details-of-the-operation.

42   According to an exchange with an anonymous source. One of the earliest reports of the attack was from the Telegram channel

Now 10:30 is an interesting time for the attack. The advantage of this time is that most of the bombers are back at their bases after doing their strikes at night. The disadvantage of this time, is if the alarm is raised, then all people are in place at the bases and they can quickly stand up their defenses. As the plan was to use innocent Russia truck drivers to drive the drones to their destination, then they kind of needed to launch during the day. The other option would have been to fly them into the attack at night after the driver had parked the truck at a hotel or their destination. These locales may not have been close enough the airfields.

Was the attack delayed for a month?

In an interview with the head of the Ukrainian SBU, Lt. General Vasyl Malyuk, he stated that Operation Spider's Web started one month late because the recruited Russian divers got drunk during Easter, May holidays, and 9 May.[43] It is distinctly possible that the operation was scheduled for early May and had to be delayed due to driver unavailability. I gather from the interview that Ukraine was planning to conduct this operation in early May, vice on 9 May. May 9th is "Victory Day" in the Soviet Union and is still officially celebrated in Russia. This day marks the end of the "Great Patriotic War" and the Soviet victory over Nazi Germany. It is no longer formally celebrated in Ukraine starting in 2014 (the year Russia took Sevastopol and Crimea and the troubles in the Donbas started). This story, of course, does fit a stereotype and could simply be propaganda (now called information warfare).

---

supernova+, which at 12.34 CET was posting videos from locals showing very tall columns of smoke at Olenya. See: https://t.me/supernova_plus/39611. It is an hour later in Russia and it does take time to identify and report events, which does argue for the attack occurring on or before 13:30 Russian time.

43   A one-minute video clip of the interview by program "We-Ukraine" with Malyuk in Ukrainian is provided by Tymofiy Mylovanov @Mylovanov on X at https://x.com/Mylovanov/status/1955691926151209173. Also see: "'Russians have gone on a bender': Malyuk revealed new details of Operation Spider's Web," *Khartyiya '97%*, 14 August 2025 and "Operation 'Web' was supposed to take place before 9 May, but it had to be postponed because Russian truck drivers 'got drunk.' SBU Chief Malyuk spoke about the details of the operation.," *Dev.UA*, 13 August 2025 at https://dev.ua/en/news/operation-web-was-supposed-to-take-place-before May-9-but-it-had-to-be-postponed-because-russian-truck-drivers-got-drunk-sbu-chief-malyuk-spoke-about-the-details-of-the-operation and "Ukraine's Operation Spiderweb: Security Service chief reveals details," *RBC-Ukraine*, 12 August 2025.

Electronic Warfare as drone defense

One of the significant defensive capabilities in drone defense is electronic warfare. Probably a quarter or more of the drone attacks against Ukraine are deflected or defeated by these means. In the case of Dyagilevo air base, it was probably why most of the drones failed to even hit the air base. They were launched from the back of the moving truck, but it appears to have otherwise been ineffective. We suspect that this was because this attack occurred after the other three attacks and the base defenses had been fully alerted. They then jammed the drone navigation, with some drones hitting the fields outside of the airport and setting the grass on fire.

The Soviet Union has always had strong electronic warfare capabilities. It was a potential disabling surprise if the Cold War ever turned into a hot war. Russian still has those capabilities.[44] Russian electronic warfare capabilities include: 1) degrading radar, 2) degrading communications (jamming) of cell phones, satellites, etc., 3) degrading navigation and guidance systems (i.e. shutting down GPS) 4) GPS spoofing (transmitting a false GPS signal to deceive a GPS receiver), 5) directly affecting weapons systems (for example getting a drone or smart bomb to detonate prematurely), 6) jamming other communications with drones (i.e. intercept and block video signals), 7) electronic deceptions means, 8) tapping into cellular networks, 9) electromagnetic reconnaissance (monitoring electronic emissions), and 10) use of lasers to interfere (electro-optics).

The Russia electronic warfare units often work by scrambling the systems used to navigate drones to their targets. This would certainly include GPS (Global Positioning System) which is used in many commercial navigation systems, including on iPhones. In the case of the Pantsir-S air defense systems, it not only has a dozen surface-to-air

---

44   Rajesh Uppal, "Russia's Electronic Warfare Dominance: A Comprehensive Overview," *IDST*, 6 August 2024 at https://idstch.com/geopolitics/ russias-electronic-warfare-dominance-a-comprehensive-overview/. A somewhat alternate view is provided by "The Invisible Russia-Ukraine Battlefield," *WIRED*, 23 December 2024 which says in part "It wasn't until Russia's full-scale invasion of Ukraine in February 2022 that the world got to see the extend of Russia's EW prowess. And it was a dud." "Russian EW was a no-show" wrote Bryan Clark, director of the Center for Defense Concepts and Technology at the Hudson Institute, in a July 2022 analysis for IEEE Spectrum. And "Russia's systems were 'not very mobile, not very distributed,'" Clark tells WIRED. Their relatively small number of big systems, Clark says, "weren't really relevant in the fight.'"

missiles and two 30mm autocannons to help defend again drones, but also has electronic jamming to degrade or confuse drones that is part of the system or often operates with it.

The use of AI

The drones can connect to the cellular networks to be controlled. Russia would be expected to shut these down if an attack was expected. They apparently also were set up to fly themselves to the target if they lost communication with its controller.

It was stated by the SBU that "During the operation, modern UAV control technology was used, which combined autonomous artificial intelligence algorithms and manual operator intervention. In particular, some UAVs, due to signal loss, switched to performing the mission using artificial intelligence along a pre-planned route. After approaching and contacting a specifically designated target, the warhead was automatically triggered."[45]

This also supports the assumption that they were SBU teams at each location with their reference for "manual operator intervention." They fact that they could switch to artificial intelligence "due to signal loss" indicates the sophistication of these small drones.

It also appears that AI was used to optimize the target locations of the targeted planes, specifically targeting the areas of the planes where maximum damage could be caused, weapons pylons carrying missiles and over the wing fuel tanks. They trained the AI using the collection of strategic bombers at the Ukrainian-based Poltava Museum of Long-Range and Strategic Aviation. The museum had a Tu-22M3, a Tu-160 and a Tu-95MS.[46]

The drone videos

The videos from the drones were sent back to Ukraine the same day. This could have been done using regular cell tower lines. They could have also been collected by SBU agents in the area, and at that time or later forwarded back to Ukraine.

---

45   Thomas Newdick, "Confirmed Losses of Russian Aircraft Mount After Ukrainian Drone Assault," *The War Zone*, 4 June 2025 at https://www.twz.com/air/firm-evidence-of-russian-aircraft-losses-after-ukrainian-drone-strikes.

46   Steve Brown, "Ukraine Trained AI for its 'Spiderweb' Airfield Drones Attacks at Aviation Museum," *Kyiv Post*, 2 June 2025.

Targeting

It is clear from some of the videos that the drones flew to specific locations on the planes before they exploded. In the case of the A-50s, they appear to have gone for the radar domes at the top of the aircraft. For the bombers, it appears they went for the area where the main wing was connected to the body.

Damage done

The count, done by various people analyzing the photos are that the total Russian losses were:

> Dyagilevo: No planes were hit
> Ivanovo: One A-50 looks like it was destroyed and another one was seriously damaged.
> Olenya: Four Tu-95MSs and one An-12 transport plane were destroyed.
> Belaya: Four Tu-22M3s and three Tu-95MSs were destroyed. At least one other Tu-95MS was damaged.
> Ukrainka: Never attacked

This is a total of at least one A-50 destroyed, seven Tu-95s and four Tu-22M3s and an An-12 destroyed for a total of 13 aircraft. At least one A-50 and one Tu-95MS were seriously damaged. Losses may have been higher but there is no clear evidence for this.

Other estimates put the count at 10–11 Tu-95s and Tu-22M3s.[47] That observer notes that some of the bombers were armed with Kh-101 cruise missiles, meaning they were preparing for strikes on Ukraine later that day. The U.S. DOD estimate was 20 aircraft were hit of which ten were destroyed.[48]

The Ukrainian estimate (SBU) was 13 destroyed out of a total of 41 hit.[49] The Ukrainians claimed that the attack resulted in the destruction and damage of 41 aircraft, including Tu-95MS and Tu-22M3 strategic bombers, as well as at least one A-50 AEW&C aircraft. President Zelenskyy said on Wednesday (4 June 2025) that half of the 41 Russian

---

47   Thomas Newdick, "Confirmed Losses of Russian Aircraft Mount After Ukrainian Drone Assault," *The War Zone*, 4 June 4 2025 at https://www.twz.com/air/firm-evidence-of-russian-aircraft-losses-after-ukrainian-drone-strikes.

48   Phil Stewart and Idrees Ali, "Exclusive: Ukraine hit fewer Russian planes that is estimated, US. officials say," *Reuters*, 4 June 2025.

49   Phil Stewart and Idrees Ali, "Exclusive: Ukraine hit fewer Russian planes that is estimated, US. officials say," *Reuters*, 4 June 2025.

aircraft struck were too damaged to be repaired. The damage was valued by Ukraine at an approximate $7 billion, with many of the aircraft destroyed not in production.[50]

Now the Osa drones cost only $2,000 each, but it is not a simple matter of comparing the cost of 117 drones to the cost of a dozen bombers. This was a complex extended operation that required setting up a false-front business operation for an extended period, employed multiple agents, purchased trucks, and had to develop and test the cargo systems and drones. Still, it was a relatively inexpensive operation that netted a big result.

Needless to say, the loss of seven of Russia's 55 or 58 Tu-95s was a significant degradation of their strategic bomber force.

---

50 Thomas Newdick, "Confirmed Losses of Russian Aircraft Mount After Ukrainian Drone Assault," *The War Zone*, 4 June 2025 at https://www. twz.com/air/firm-evidence-of-russian-aircraft-losses-after-ukrainian-drone-strikes and Phil Stewart and Idrees Ali, "Exclusive: Ukraine hit fewer Russian planes that is estimated, US. officials say," *Reuters*, 4 Jun 2025 and Chris York, "'Russian bombers are burning en masse' – Ukraine's SBU drones hit 'more than 40; aircraft in mass attack, source says," *The Kyiv Independent*, 1 June 2025 at https://kyivindependent. com/enemy-bombers-are-burning-en-masse-ukraines-sbu-drones-hit-more-than-40-russian-aircraft/ and Vlad Litnarovych, "Russian Key Strategic Airbases Under Massive Attacks, Here's What We Know," *United24Media*, 1 June 2025 at https://united24media.com/latest-news/ russian-key-strategic-airbases-under-massive-attacks-heres-what-we-know-8797.

Another source gives the amount as $2 billion, vice $7 billion: "SBU drones hit over 40 Russian bombers, including A-50, Tu-95, in special operation," *The New Voice of Ukraine*, 1 June 2025 at https://english. nv.ua/nation/sbu-targets-over-40-russian-aircraft-including-at-belaya-airfield-video-shows-50518605.html.

Also see Kateryna Mykhailova, "Russia Lost over $10B from Ukrainians Drones Strikes This Year, Commander Says", *Kyiv Post*, 24 June, 2025. This article states that Ukraine drone strikes inflicted over $10 billion in damage to Russia between January to May 2025. This apparently does not include the 1 June strike. They calculate it to be $1.3 billion in direct damages including the destruction of old refining, energy, logistics and transport facilities. They add at least another $9.5 billion in indirect losses resulting from halted industrial operations, disrupted transportation and blocked logistics chains. These figures are probably hard to independently confirm.

Chapter 2

THE WAR TO DATE

"The fight is here; I need ammunition, not a ride."

President Volodymyr Zelenskyy
25 February 2022[1]

On Thursday, 24 February 2022 Russia invaded Ukraine. This dramatic attack threatened Kyiv and Kharkiv, surrounded Sumy and Chernihiv, and took Kherson. By around the middle of March, the Russian advances appeared to have stalled out. At the end of March Russia began withdrawing from large parts of northeast Ukraine, including from around Kyiv, Chernihiv and Sumy. By the first week of April, these areas had all been reclaimed by Ukraine. This ended the first phase of this war.

This war is now heading into its fourth year, making it the largest and bloodiest war in Europe since World War II, over 80 years ago. We currently break this war into nine phases:[2]

1. The six-week war and the Battle for Kyiv: 24 February–4 April 2022. This first phase was a dynamic war of maneuver where Russia ambitiously attempted to take multiple major cities, including Kyiv, with insufficient forces. At the end of this period, Russian withdrew from northeast Ukraine and focused on more limited and restricted operations. Russia held onto the cities of Kherson, Melitopol and Berdiansk, and had Mariupol surrounded.

---

1   Glenn Kessler, *Washington Post*, 6 March 2022, "Zelensky's famous quote of 'need ammo, not a ride' not easily confirmed" at Zelensky's famous quote of "need ammo, not a ride" not easily confirmed (msn.com).

2   And for practical purposes, each phase is the subject of a book or projected book by us.

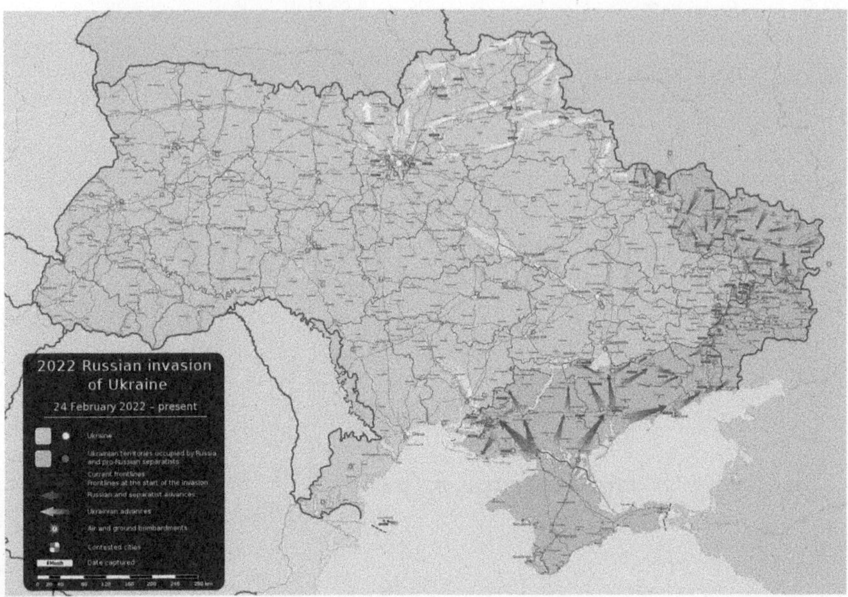

Map 2: Positions as of 7 April 2022.

2. The Siege of Mariupol: 25 February–20 May 2022
Mariupol was the largest city taken by Russia during this war.
3. The Battle of the Donbas: 18 April–7 August 2022
Starting with attacks on Izium in March 2022, Russia attempted to wrest the remaining elements of Lugansk and Donets provinces from Ukraine. They targeted four cities, and took two, Severodonetsk and Lysychansk. These would be last two cities (out of six) taken by the Russian army in this war.
4. Ukraine counteroffensive: 29 August–11 November 2022
This was Ukraine's counteroffensive to re-take Kherson and its offensive at Balakliya. The offensive reestablished Ukrainian control of significant parts of Kherson Province and Kharkiv Province and reclaimed one of the six cities taken by Russia in this war. By the end of this offensive, the front line traces of the two armies settled and there has not been a significant shift in the front line since November 2022, although there has certainly been a lot of fighting. For all practical purposes, this war has been stalemated for the last three years.
5. The Battle of Bakhmut: 7 October 2022–20 May 2023
This was the extended fight for control of the town of Bakhmut. It was a town of limited economic and military value that became the focus of repeated offensives over several months. It was also the introduction of the Wagner Group as a major combat faction in this war.

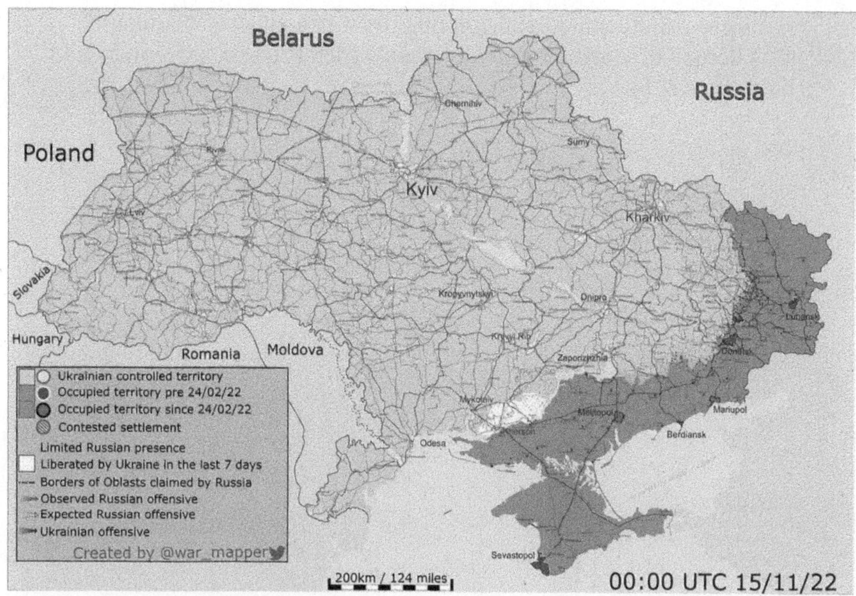

Map 3: Positions as of 15 November 2022.

6. Ukrainian Spring Offensive: June 2023
   This was the Ukrainian Spring Offensive that fizzled out after one
   week. With the Ukrainians building up for more than six months, the
   offensive quickly established that the Ukrainian Army was not yet
   ready for the offense and the Russian Army was more than capable of
   defending itself.

7. Battle of Avdiivka: 10 October 2023–17 February 2024
   This was to date the largest of a number of Russian limited offensives.
   It took the town of Avdiivka, which was only nine miles (15 kilometers)
   from Donetsk, which Russian separatists had held since 2014.

8. Ukraine's Kursk Offensive: 6 August 2024–April 2025.
   This latest dramatic change in the front lines came about when Ukraine
   advanced into the Russian province of Kursk in the area north of Sumy.
   This expanded the front and created additional complications for
   Russia. Still it was not an earthshaking advance, having taken in the
   first week only 390 square miles (1,000 square kilometers) of territory.
   Ukraine was effectively driven out of the province by April 2025.

9. Battle for Pokrovsk – 18 July 2024–1 December 2025.[3]
   This was largest of a number of Russian limited offensives. This offensive started on 18 July 2024 and as of September 2025, more than a year
   later, was still continuing. They had not yet taken Pokrovsk, although it
   is clearly in danger. As Pokrovsk is just a town in Donetsk Oblast, it is

---

3   Russia claimed full control over the town of Pokrovsk on 1 December.
    Not sure it that is the end of the battle.

not a geographically significant objective. Pokrovsk is 43 miles (70 kilometers) northwest of Donetsk, which Russian separatists had held since 2014.

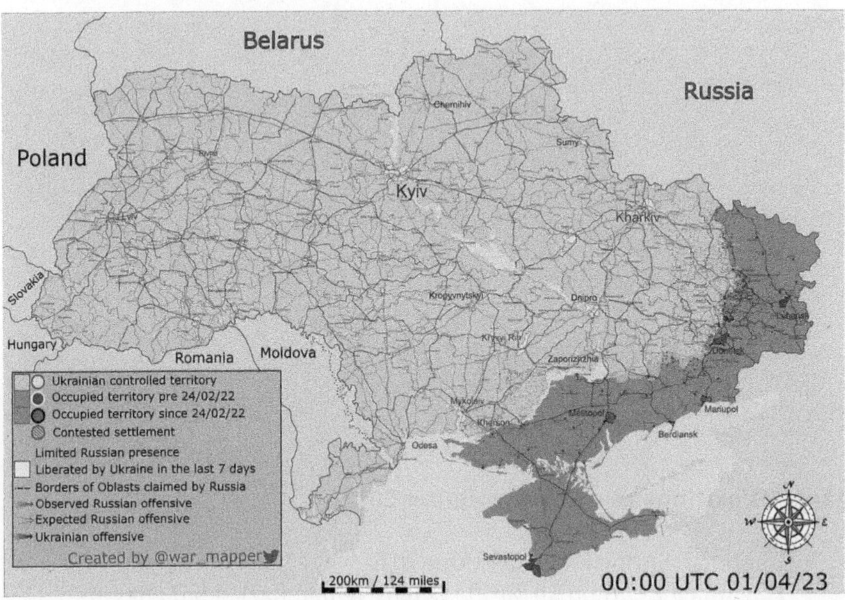

Map 4: Positions as of 1 April 2023.

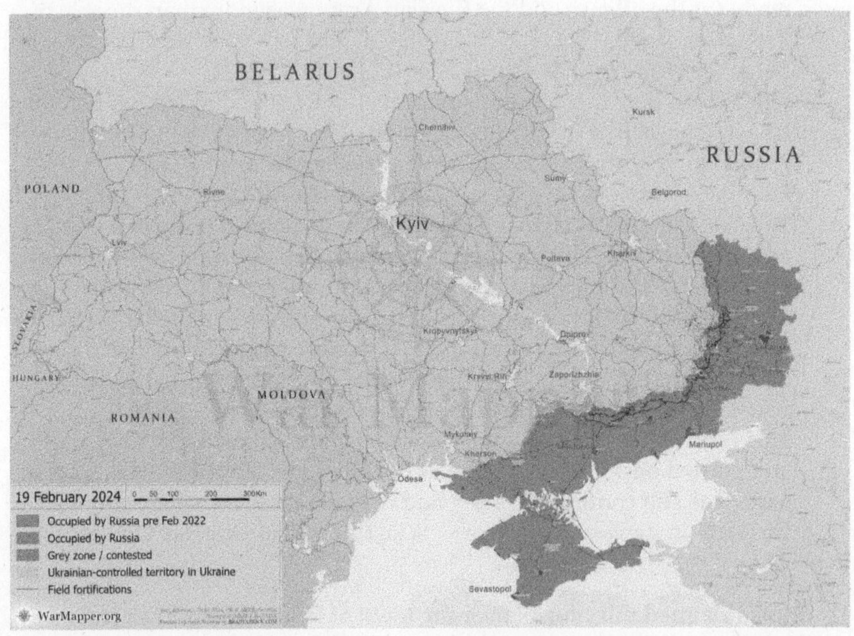

Map 5: Positions as of 19 February 2024.

Map 6: Positions as of 9 April 2025.[4]

At the start of the war, the areas of Sevastopol, Crimea and separatist-controlled areas of Lugansk and Donetsk consisted 7.05% of Ukraine. Their offensive in February and March of 2022 took another 18.81%. At its peak Russia had control of over a quarter of Ukraine.

After the Russian withdrawal in early April they ended up with 20.28% of Ukraine under their control as of the end of April 2022. After the August to November 2022 offensive this dropped to less than a fifth of Ukraine (17.61% as of the end of November). It has remained less than a fifth since then.

As of April 2025 Russian controlled all of Sevastopol and Crimea, 99.18% of Luhansk, only 69.20% of Donetsk, 72.42% of Zaporizhzhia Oblast but not the capital, 63.89% of Kherson Oblast but also not the capitol, and only 3.35% of Kharkiv Oblast.

As of late September 2023 Russia took from Ukraine only 188 square miles (487 square kilometers) of territory.[5] In 2024 they took around

---

4   War Mapper's excellent maps have not been updated past April 2025.

5   More specially Russia took 331 square miles of territory in 2023 and Ukraine was able to reclaim 143 square miles back. See: Josh Holder, "Who's gaining ground in Ukraine? This year, no one," *New York Times*,

1,236 square miles (3,200 square kilometers) of territory. This is an additional 0.54% of Ukraine's territory taken over the course of a year. This is not much. Fairfax County VA., right outside of Washington D.C, is 406 square miles (1,050 square kilometers). As of March 2025 Russia held 18.30% of Ukraine.[6]

In the first five months of the war, Russian took a total of only six cities from Ukraine (Kherson, Melitopol, Berdiansk, Mariupol, Severodonetsk and Lysychansk). Four months later Ukraine reclaimed one city (Kherson). In the ensuring three years of warfare, no other cities have changed hands. Many towns have, and there have been multiple offensives by both sides. Russia has slowly advanced across Ukraine and Ukraine has counterattacked back, but for all practical purposes the war has been stalemated for three years. As the front lines have failed to move, the air campaign has increased, starting in earnest on 10 October 2022 and continuing unabated to the present day.

Map 7: Map of Ukraine and its major cities.

---

28 September 2023. There was little action in the last three months of the year.

6   All these stats are taken from War Mapper.

The Bombing Campaigns

A major part of this war over the last three years has been the bombardment of Ukrainian cities by Russia. While aerial attacks against cities have been a part of this war since the beginning, it was the fall and winter of 2022–2023 when there was a serious Russian strategic air campaign to try to collapse the Ukrainian electrical grid. This effort failed, but at a cost to Ukraine of lives and material.

This effort to shut down the Ukrainian power infrastructure started in earnest on 10 October 2022.[7] It was at a time when the Ukrainian Army was on the offensive at towards Kherson and had already had a successful offensive in September that broke through at Balakliya and then reclaimed most of Kharkiv province and parts of Lugansk and Donetsk provinces. This was the single most effective Ukrainian ground offensive of the war.

On 10 October, Russia initiated this air campaign with an attack of 84 cruise missiles and 24 drones. Ukraine claimed that 54 or 56 were shot down.[8] This air campaign started two days after the first and most successful Ukrainian attack on the Kerch Strait Bridge (see Chapter 9). According to Ukrainian reporting, at least 14 people were killed and nearly a hundred were wounded in those air strikes. The strikes plunged Ukraine into blackouts, with hundreds of thousands of people left without power. Ukraine reported that 70 infrastructure sites were damaged. Russian President Vladimir Putin said that his forces used "precision weapons" to target key energy and military command facilities. He also stated that the air attacks were in retaliation for Ukraine's "terrorist act" of attacking the bridge. At least ten cities were hit, including Kyiv, Kharkiv and Lviv.[9]

It was followed up by major strikes on 11, 22, and 31 October and the following month on 15, 17 and 23 November (see Appendix I). It

---

7   There were previous strikes on power facilities, including a strike on Kharkiv TEC-5 on 11 September with Kalibr cruise missiles. Russia also hit the Karachun dam upstream from the city Kryvyi Rih with maybe eight cruise missiles on 14 September. This second strike clearly appears to be a revenge strike not based upon any military necessity.
The Kharkiv TEC-5 was seriously attacked again on 22 March 2024.

8   We record 54 shot down this day based upon the Ukrainian Air Command reported. The CBS News article cited below reports the figure of 56.

9   "Russia rains missiles down on Ukraine's capital and other cities in retaliation for Crimea bridge blast," *CBS News*, 10 October 2022.

was not the systematic daily bombardment that we saw later, but was much more scattered, with many days of relative quiet in between the busy days. Between 10 October and 19 November, after 41 days of airstrikes, Ukraine recorded 556 drones and missiles had been shot down or otherwise intercepted, including 277 Shahed drones, 252 cruise missiles, and 18 ballistic missiles. While the drones were an issue, it was the cruise missiles and ballistic missiles that carried a larger punch and were harder to shoot down (especially the ballistic missiles). We don't have a count of how many were fired as neither Ukraine or Russia were systematically publishing this data at this time but clearly based upon the counts of what was shot down, maybe more than 700 drones and missiles had been fired at Ukraine.[10]

On 19 November the Ukrainian's Prime Minister and President said that nearly half of the country's power grid was shut down and ten million Ukrainians were without electricity.[11] According to the United Nations, as of 25 November 77 people had been killed and 272 wounded in these strikes.[12]

The attacks continued into 2023. Russia did a large strike on 9 March against "critical infrastructure" but did not do any other major strikes against Ukraine until late April. The 9 March strike was 89 drones and missiles including an impressive 66 cruise missiles. They then did not do any strikes of greater than 21 drones and no more than two cruise missiles until 28 April. That day they fired off 25 drones and missiles at Ukraine including 21 cruise missiles. This was a full seven-week break which certainly gave Ukraine the chance to rebuild its power grid and infrastructure. It was the breathing space that Ukraine needed. The strikes in April were not focused on the power grid.

The first air campaign against the Ukrainian power grid ran from 10 October 2022 to 9 March 2023, and then Russia gave up. Russia may have run down their cruise missile and ballistic missile inventory and

---

10   Ukrainian Interior Minister Denys Monstyrskyi stated the Russian had launched nearly 600 missile attacks on Ukraine between 10 October and 23 November. This figure seems low as it would indicate that less than 60 drones and missiles hit Ukraine during that time, while it appears that 39 missile and 15 drones got through on 10 October alone. See: "UN: Russian attacks on Ukraine's energy system have killed 77 civilians since Oct. 10," *The Kyiv Independent*, 25 November 2022.

11   George Wright, "Ukraine war: Almost half Ukraine's energy system disabled, PM says," BBC, 19 November 2022.

12   "UN: Russian attacks on Ukraine's energy system have killed 77 civilians since Oct. 10," *The Kyiv Independent*, 25 November 2022.

so had to take a break. It was reported by a private Ukrainian company that between October 2022 and April 2023 Russia launched 1,200 attacks on Ukraine's energy system, in which every thermal power and hydro-electric plan in the country sustaining some damage.[13] In late April it appeared that Russians had shifted away from targeting Ukraine' power network and was back to focusing on military targets and logistical hubs.[14]

The first Russia air campaign against the infrastructure was a failure. It was very effective, reducing the Ukrainian power grid by almost half, but it simply lacked the weight to do more than that. Russia would then take a six-month break and only start their new air campaign against the power grid on 21 September 2023. This campaign would be much heavier and as a result was more effective. They were both air campaigns conducted primarily by drones and missiles, with very few aircraft involved in these attacks.

Then starting late May and early June of 2023 Russian began to regularly bomb Kyiv in what can only be consider a terror bombing campaign.[15] While there were clearly military and industrial targets among their bombing targets, a significant number of targets appeared to be civilian residences, apartments, and such. It appeared that a strategic bombing campaign had now mutated into a terror bombing campaign. On 28 May Russia launched more than 40 drones over Kyiv. The Ukrainian Air Force Command counted 54 Shahed drones, which

---

13 Victoria Butenko, "'We are totally ready': Ukraine prepares for fresh Russian attacks on energy as winter nears," *CNN World*, 10 November 2023. This claim is according to DTEK, the country's largest energy company.

14 "UK Intelligence assesses Russia's latest missile strikes on Ukraine," *Ukrainska Pravda* 25, 3 May 2023.

15 There were multiple attacks on Kyiv before then, but what stands out is the daily bombing of Kyiv in the first couple of days of June that clearly indicate a change in the nature of the aerial bombardment campaign. See Appendix I. The attacks on 1 and 2 June were directed at Kyiv.
      The targeting of Kyiv did start before June. On 20 May Russian fired 18 Shahed-136 drones at the Kyiv region and they fired on 28 May a record number of 54 Shahed drones, most of which were focused on the Kyiv region. On 29 May they fired 11 Iskander-K cruise missiles and Iskander-M ballistic missiles at Kyiv. On 30 May they launched 31 Shahed drones, of which 29 were shot down over Kyiv.

was a new record. Ukraine claimed it shot down 52. One person was killed in Kyiv by falling debris.

This new "terror bombing campaign" was occurring just as Ukraine was getting ready to unleash its much heralded spring offensive. It does appear like Russia deliberately targeted Kyiv, as opposed to targets closer to the front, for the sake of trying to degrade Ukraine's will to prosecute this war. They were no longer targeting just infrastructure or military targets. It was noted by one writer that the May missile offensive may have cost Russia $1.7 billion in drones and missiles (mostly from the expensive cruise and ballistic missiles). Of those maybe 600 drones and missiles, more than 90% failed to reach their target.[16]

Russia had tried to collapse the Ukrainian government with the initial six-week ground campaign. That failed. They then entered into negotiations with the Ukrainians in Turkey in May 2022. That failed. Russian then started a strategic air campaign against the Ukrainian power grid in October 2022. That had clearly failed by March 2023. Russia still had considerable aircraft, drones and missiles so they kept bombing. But at this point, around late May and early June 2023, the target list has shifted to include a lot of marginally military targets and clearly some civilian targets. At this point, the bombing campaign had mutated into the terror bombing campaign to force Ukraine to once again negotiate. These negotiations finally started again in Turkey in May of 2025. They also failed. In the meantime Ukraine struck back at the Russian bomber force on 1 June 2025.

---

16   Pete Shmigel, "Russia's month of missile madness: 90% of projectiles failed, $1.7 billion spent," *Kyiv Post*, 31 May 2023. He does not note how much it cost Ukraine to defend against these attacks.

The article notes that Russia fired at least 563 drones and missiles during May and 533 were destroyed (95%). The article stated this included 401 Shahed-136 of which 362 were destroyed by Ukrainian air defenses (90%), 114 Kh-101 cruise missiles of which 106 were destroyed (93%), 29 Kalibr cruise missiles of which 29 were destroyed (100%), 7 Kinzhal missiles of which 7 were destroyed (100%), and 16 Iskander (they don't give the type) or which 16 were destroyed (100%), 5 Kh-22 cruise missiles of which 5 were destroyed (100%), 12 S-300 surface-to-air missiles missile of which 5 were destroyed (42%) and 7 other unnamed missiles of which 7 were destroyed (100%). It also listed the number of missiles by type fired and destroyed each day.

Our counts (see Appendix I) are at least 614 fired and 576 did not reach their intended targets (94%).

A major part of the Russian bombing campaign was conducted by the inexpensive Iranian-built Shahed drones. In fact, it is part of what made it possible. While the ballistic missiles like the Xh-47 and Iksander-M carried a much larger payload, it was the inexpensive Iranian-built Shahd drones which became the workhorse of this effort and still are today. The ballistic missiles like the Iskander-M have a warhead from 1,060 to 1,540 pounds (480 to 700 kilograms). Also commonly used was the Kh-47M2 air-launched ballistic missile which was fired from Tu-22M3 bombers.

Some of the cruise missiles they regularly used also carried a hefty payload. The Kh-59 was a stealth air-launched cruise missile with a warhead of 661 pounds (300 kilograms). The Ukrainians called it a "controlled aviation missile" in their reports, but it still looks a lot like a cruise missile and we count it as such. The Kh-101 is another air-launched cruise missile with a warhead of 881 pounds (400 kilograms). It is fired from Tu-95MS and Tu-160s. The Kalibr cruise missile had a warhead of 882 to 1,102 pounds (400 to 500 kilograms). The Iksander-K, fired from the same launcher as an Iskander-M, had a warhead that weighed 1,060 pounds (480 kilograms). The Shahed drone only had a warhead of 66 to 110 pounds (30 to 50 kilograms).

So while the Shahed drone did not carry near as much punch, it carried enough of a punch to be deadly at times. It was also slower and easier to intercept than the cruise missiles and certainly the ballistic missiles. Less than 10% of these drones would get through each night. The rest would get shot down, directed off course or lose their way. Still, it was cheap, and Russia was regularly firing over 100 Shaheds a month by May 2023. This was the problem as invariably five or ten drones would find a target each night, resulting in damage and casualties no matter what the Ukrainians did. Added to that, the drone costs less than most air defense measures, especially missiles, making it an advantageous weapon in a zero-sum cost game. The estimate of the air campaign costing Russia $1.7 billion in missiles does not calculate the cost of Ukrainian air defense missiles. It was possibly higher. Therefore, the Shahed drone became one of the mainstays of what had become a daily Russian terror bombing campaign.

The Shahed drone was first observed in combat in Ukraine on 13 September 2022.[17] It was spotted in the Kupyansk region. The town

---

17   "Iranian Shahed-136 Kamikaze Drones Already Used by Russia (First Photos and Specs)," *Defence Express*, 13 September 2022 at https://en.defenceua.com/weapon_and_tech/iranian_shahed_136_kamikaze_drones_already_used_by_russia_first_photos_and_specs-4207.html.

of Kupyansk (pop. 26,627 in 2022 estimate) is around 60 miles (97 kilometers) east of Kharkiv. It is only 23 miles (37 kilometers) from the Russian border. The drone was clearly was being used operationally at that point, vice being used to shell cities.

The Ukrainian Air Force Command on their Facebook page noted the first Shahed drone on 20 September 2022. They stated that at about 16:00 hours in the Mykolaiv region Ukrainian anti-aircraft units shot down a Russian kamikaze drone Shahed-136. The stated that it was of Iranian production and that the Russians had marked it as a "Geran-2." They stated that it weighed 200 kilograms and had a wingspan of 2.5 meters.

For the month of September 2022, there was no systematic bombardment of cities. See table overleaf Ukrainian shoot-down claims for September.

This is a total of 22 Shahed drones shot down. They do not report yet as to the number observed, but one gathers that the number shot down in close to the number observed flown (within 90%). Just for the record, 57 other drones were also shot down. Most of the other drones were Orlon-10s. There were also 35 cruise missiles and "controlled aviation missiles" (Kh-59s) shot down and no ballistic missiles shot down. This was still an air bombardment campaign by Russia primarily focused on military targets.

The Air Force Command Staff was not yet providing counts of what they were observing. They were providing claims of what they shot down, which is what was listed above. How many of these claims were actually shot down, as opposed to just observed and shot at, is hard to say. Traditionally, over half the claims made in an air battle are false.[18] But regardless of the actual success rate in shoot downs, the list does serve as a decent indication of the level of activity, as it does appear that for September of 2022, Russia was only firing around four drones and missiles a day at Ukraine.

The number of missiles and drones fired at Ukraine was reported on 4 September and a few times after that in September. On 4 September it was at least ten missiles, of where at least three were Iskander Cruise missiles or Kh-59 "controlled aviation" missiles and there was at least

---

18   Specifically, see my book *Kursk: The Battle of Prokhorovka* (Aberdeen Books, Sheridan, CO, 2015), pages 839–41, 872–9, and 1326 where I compared kill claims to actual losses reported by the opposing side. The same with *Aces at Kursk: The Battle for Aerial Supremacy on the Eastern Front, 1943* (Air World, Barnsley, UK, 2024); pages 274–5 among others.

	Total	Shahed Drone	Mohajer-6 Orlan-10 Forpost Kartograf Drone	Kh-101 Xh-59 Iskander-K Kalibr Cruise Missile	Mi-8 Ka-52 Helicopters	Su-24 Su-25 Jet
1 September	No report					
2 September	1		1			
3 September	10		5	5		
3 Sep (10:30)	2		1		1	
4 Sep (09:00)	2			2		
4 Sep (23:00)	3		2	1		
5 Sep (15:00)	3		3			
5 Sep (19:00)	2			2		
6 September	6			5 (of 6)	1	
7 Sep (10:00)	3		2		1	
8 September	7		6		1	
9 September	No report					
10 September	4		3	1		

11 September	9			9 (out of 12)		
12 September	No report					
13 Sep (17:00)	3		1			2
14 September	5		1			4
15 September	2		1		1	
16 Sep (08:30)	1					1
16 Sep (14:30)	4		1	3		
17 September	6		5		1	
18 September	No report					
19 September	7		5	1		1
20 Sep (18:00)	2	1 *				1
21 September	5		4	1		
22 September	7	4 *	3			
23 September	9	6 *	1		1 Mi-8	1
24 September	No report					
25 Sep (18:00)	4	2 *			1 Mi-8	1
26 September	4	4 *				
27 September	4		3			1
27 Sep (15:00)	4		3			1

28 Sep (22:00)	4			4 (of 5)		
29 Sep (17:00)	5		3			2
29 Sep (24:00)	5	5 (of 7) *				
30 September	4		3		1	
Total	137	22	57	34	9	15
					7 were Ka-52s	

*First report by Air Force Command of a Shahed-136 was on 20 September. From their report, one can conclude that they thought this was a big deal. All but two of the drones they previously reported on in September were Orlan-10s or unidentified.

The following day the drones shot down were not identified. On the 22nd it stated that it shot down four Shahed-136 drones with two medium-range anti-aircraft missiles. The drones were marked "Geran-2." The other three drones were not identified, but we assume because of the nature of the reporting that they were not Shahed-136s. The graphics now show a different symbol for the Shahed drone versus other drones.

For the 23rd all six drones shot down were identified as Shahed-136s. Shaheds were shot down on the 25th, 26th and 29th of September.

one S-300 surface-to-air missile. This was the one of the few days in September that Ukraine provided a daily missile count. They were still not systematically reporting this but that would change over time. Traditionally counts over overflying planes tend to be accurate to plus or minus 50%[19] With modern radar systems, this may even be more accurate.

		Kh-59	
		Kh-101	
		Iskander-K	S-300
	Shahed-type	**Cruise Missiles**	**Other**
4 September	+8	+7	+1
6 September	+1	+1	
11 September	+3	+3	
28 September	+1	+1	
29 September	+2		
Additional	+15	+12	+1

On the night of 11 September, the Ukrainian Air Force Command reported at 20:30 that they were attacked by 12 missiles, six winged Kalibr missiles from ships in the Black Sea and six winged Kh-101 missiles launched from aircraft from the area of the Caspian Sea. They reported that they shot down nine of the 12 missiles using anti-aircraft units.[20] So for the month of September Ukraine claimed to have shot down or deflected 137 drones and missiles and there were at least an additional 15 that were fired at them and not shot down. This is a total of at least 152 drones and missiles fired at them or over five a day.

For the first nine days of October the air continued at the same low rate as in September with around an average of four drones or missiles a day being fired.

---

19   Again see *Kursk: The Battle of Prokhorovka* or *Aces at Kursk*, page 176. For 5 through 11 July 1943, Soviet estimates of German sorties was within 14% of the German sortie count.

20   See their Facebook page for 11 September 2022 at https://www.facebook.com/kpszsu.

| | | | | Mohajer-6 | | Ka-52 | |
| | | | | Orlan-10 | Kh-59 | Mi-8 | Su-25 |
	Total	Shahed Type	Other Drones	Cruise Missiles	Helicopters	Jets
1 October	No report					
2 Oct (02:00)	5	5 (of 7)				
3 Oct (12:00)	1					1
4 October	3	1			1	1
5 Oct (02:00)	7	6	1			
6 Oct (02:00)	9	9				
6 Oct (11:00)	3	2	1			
6 Oct (20:00)	5	3	2			
7 Oct (08:00)	1				1	
7 Oct (21:30)	3	3				
8–9 October (11:30)*	5	1	2	1		1
Total	**42**	**30**	**6**	**1**	**2**	**3**

*This was an active night, with six Tu-22Ms and seven Su-35s reported firing four Kh-22s and two Kh-59s and 16 S-300s.

Again, this was a similar level of activity compared to before. Ukraine over the first nine days of October claimed to have shot down 42 aerial vehicles, including 30 Shahed drones and at least two others were fired that were not intercepted or deflected for a total of 44.

The night of 10 October 2022 was the first night of the new air war. Between 06:00 and 11:40 Ukraine reported that more than 80 missiles were fired across Ukraine. They noted that Kh-101s and Kh-555s were launched from the Caspian region by 11 Tu-96s and Tu-160s strategic bombs. Kalibr cruise missiles were launched from ships in the Black Sea. Iksander ground-based missiles were launched from various directions. Ukrainian defender claimed that 45 missiles were shot down as were 9 out of 12 Shahed-136s.

These official communiques tended to be colorful, with the headline for this day being "Air defense shuts down more than half of Racists' rockets." "Racists" being a Ukrainian contraction for "Russian fascists." The communique opens with the sentence "On October 10 at 6:00 AM the infected dictator gave the command to attack peaceful cities of Ukraine . . ." "The infected dictator" obviously refers to Russian President Vladimir Putin. Regardless, this was a big air attack, the biggest since early in the war. It clearly targeted cities and targets in cities vice military targets in the countryside.

On 11 October, from 03:30 to 05:30, the Ukrainian Air Command reported eight more Shahed-136 drones striking in the south of Ukraine in the Odesa region. Five were claimed to be shot down. At 09:00 four Kh-101 cruise missiles fired by Tu-95s and Tu-160s, again operating from Caspian Sea area, were claimed destroyed. These are incomplete snapshots from Ukrainian reporting. It probably does not give the complete picture but certainly gives a valid partial view of that picture. Between 09:30 and 13:00 they report another 14 Kalibr cruise missiles shot down. It is not reported how many were spotted or how many got through. As of 13:30 Ukraine reported two mass missile strikes on cities and critical infrastructure in different parts of Ukraine using Kh-101s fired from Tu-95MSs, naval Kalibr cruise missiles and Shahed-136 drones. They reported a total of 28 cruise missiles, 16 Kh-101s and 12 Kalibrs. Ukraine reported shooting down 33 vehicles, 20 cruise missiles and 13 Shahed drones. So at least eight cruise missiles got through.

This air campaign continued for the rest of the month and for subsequent months. It is certainly a story deserving its own book, but is not the subject of this book. Therefore, we will just report the shoot down stats for the rest of the month. The record for the rest of the month of October shows:

	Total	Shahed Type	Other Drones	Zala Lancet / Kalibr / Kh-101 / Cruise Missiles	Ka-52s	Su-25 Jets
10 Oct (11:30)	54	9		45		
10 Oct (14:30)	1					1
10 Oct (18:30)	13	13				
11 Oct (05:30)	5	5				
11 Oct (09:00)	4			4		
11 Oct (13:00)	14			14		
11 Oct (13:30)	33	13		20		
12 Oct (08:00)	*12*	*12*				
12 Oct (08:58)	*4*				*4*	
12 October	24	17		2	5	
13 Oct (06:00)	6	6				
13 Oct (17:00)	5			5		
14 Oct (08:00)	8	8				
15 Oct (00:30)	7	6			1	
16 Oct (22:30)	11	11				
17 Oct (07:00)	18	15		3		
17 Oct (10:00)	11	11				
17 Oct (22:00)	10	8		2		
18 Oct (10:00)	12	6		5		1
19 Oct (08:00)	13	13				
19 Oct (10:30)	1				1	
19 Oct (15:30)	14	10		4		
20 Oct (02:00)	14	14				
21 Oct (16:00)	1					1
22 Oct (02:00)	10	10				
22 Oct (11:00)	18			18		
22 Oct (12:00)	1				1	
22 Oct (16:00)	1				1	

23 Oct (02:00)	16	16				
24 Oct (13:30)	2				2	
24 Oct (21:30)	1				1	
25 Oct (21:00)	2	2				
25 Oct (21:30)	1	1				
26 October	No report (actually reported as no report)					
26 Oct (17:00)	1				1	
26 Oct (24:00)	20	19		1		
27 Oct (08:40)	2				1	1
28 October	No report					
29 October	No report					
30 Oct (08:00)	1					1
30 Oct (16:00)	1				1	
31 Oct (08:20)	1				1	
31 Oct (09:00)	44			44		
31 Oct (18:45)	2				2	
Total (10–31)	**403**	**213**		**167**	**18**	**5**
Average per day	18	10		8	1	0

Note: Numbers in italics are not included in these totals.

Most of the Shahed drones were being shot down over the Odesa and Mykolaiv regions, meaning they were primarily operating against local tactical targets. This was also the case for most Kalibr cruise missiles.

Ukraine did provide the estimate that from 13 September to 19 October, 223 Shahed-136 drones had been shot down. This report was filed on their Facebook before their 10:30 report on 19 October. So we assume that it includes the drones reported shot down at 08:00 19 October but not the drones reported shot down at 15:30 on 19 October. The ten drones launched at 15:30 on 19 October were reported to have come from Belarus, north of Kyiv.

The daily reports above add up to 136 Shahed drones reported shot down (22 in September, 30 from 1–9 October, and 84 from 10–19 October). It is not certain when and where the other 87 drones were lost. Added to that, certainly other drones lost their way and did not hit targets. Not sure how Ukraine was counting this. It is not reported how many of those drones did hit their targets, but this was a considerable barrage, especially considering that they had only first seen this drone on 13 September. A month later, hundreds were flying at Ukraine.

The report of 22 October for 1100 stated that ten Tu-95s and Tu-160s flying in the Volgodonsk district of the Rostov region fired 17 Kh-101 cruise missiles. There were also 16 Kalibr cruise missiles launched from the Black Sea area. There were 13 Kh-101 claimed shot down (76% shot down) as were five Kalibr missiles (31% shot down). It is not known how many of the cruise missiles hit their target.

The month ended, after a seven-day quiet period, with a massive Halloween attack on the last day. They reported more than 50 Kh-101s, again fired from the Volgodonsk district of the Rostov region and certainly fired from bombers. Ukraine claimed 44 shot down (up to 86% shot down).

So ended October 2022. The Russians had introduced the Iranian-built Shahed-136 to the battlefield on 13 September. Starting 10 October, the Russians unleashed a war against Ukraine's power infrastructure. While this was a much heavier bombardment than Ukraine had undergone in September, it was still relatively light. From 10 October to 31 October they averaged at least 8 cruise missiles and 10 Shahed-136 drones a day. This is based upon Ukrainians reports of interception. The actual numbers fired were 10 to 50% higher.

This was a major effort. In the previous 40 days (1 September – 9 October) a total of 173 planes, helicopters, cruise missiles and drones had been used. In the last 20 days, it was 403. While this was a significant bombardment, it was far from overwhelming. The Ukrainian power grid continued to operate but with repeated interruptions.

For November, the campaign against infrastructure continued with major strikes reported on 15, 17 and 23 November. For 15 November it was at least 96 drones and missiles fired. Ukrainian Air Force Command reported that 14 Tu-95 missile carriers were involved along with Black Sea Fleet ships and Shahed-136 drones. In two slightly contradictory reports it was said that 96 drones and missiles were launched. Their early report said it was about 70 Kh-101 cruise missiles, 20 Kalibr cruise missiles fired from a naval base, and 10 Shahed drones, which is 100 drones and missiles. They claimed to have shot down 77 of the cruise missiles (92%), all ten Shahed drones and one Orion drone and one Orlan-10 drone. This was the largest attack since 10 October.

For the 17th, it was a much smaller strike with 18 Xh-101 cruise missiles from nine Tu-95s. Only four were intercepted (22%), as were two Kh-59 cruise missiles and five Shahed drones. Total strike size was at least 25 drones and missiles.

The strike on the 23rd was larger, at least 75 drones and missiles. This included Kh-101 cruise missiles launched from 10 Tu-95s. It was a total of 70 Kh-101 and Kalibr cruise missiles and five Lantset drones. There were 51 reported intercepted out of the 70, or 73%.

For December major strikes were made on 5, 16, 29 and 31 December. The 5 December strike consisted of more than 70 missiles. This included 38 Kh-101 cruise missiles caried on 8 Tu-95s. It also included 22 Kalibr cruise missiles fired from ships of the Black Sea fleet. Finally Tu-22M3 bombers fired three Kh-22 cruise missiles, and Su-35 fighters fired six Kh-59 "guided aviation" missiles and one Kh-31P. Ukraine claimed to shot down 60 of the missiles, or 86%.

A similar-size strike was conducted on the 16th consisting of 76 cruise missiles. They also fired 27 S-300 air-to-air missiles at the cities. Ukraine claimed to have shot down 60 of the cruise missiles or 79%.

Russia ended the year with two big strikes. On the 29th it was another 70 cruise missiles of which 58 were claimed destroyed (83%). Ukraine also took down four Orlan-10 and other reconnaissance drones and 11 Shahed drones. It was at least 87 drones and missiles for this day. They followed this up with 16 Shahed drone strikes on the 30th and then on the 31st struck with 20 cruise missiles. Twelve Kh-101s were shot down along with an Orlan-10 drone.

For 2022, the single biggest strike may have been on 16 December when they sent at least 103 drones and missiles towards Ukraine. This included at least 76 cruise missiles. This may have been bigger than the strike on 10 October, where Ukraine reported 108 drones and missiles were sent to attack them. These were the only two Russian strikes in 2022 to be in excess of a hundred drones and missiles. This would become a common occurrence by late May 2023.

As a result of this extending bombing campaign, the International Criminal Court (ICC) indicted four Russian officials for war crimes. The indicted officials included the Russian Defense Minister Sergei Shoigu, the Chief of the General Staff Valery Gerasimov, the Commander of Long Range Aviation Sergey Kobylash, and the Commander of the Black Sea Fleet Viktor Sokolov. An arrest warrant was issued in March 2024 and an indictment was issued in June 2024. Shoigu is now Secretary of the Security Council while Gerasimov had continued as Chief of the General Staff (Commander of the Russian Armed Forces). Sergey Kobylash is now the Commander of the Russian Air Force since July 2024. Victor Sokolov was reported killed on 22 September 2023 by a Storm Shadow cruise missile as part of Ukraine's Operation Crab Trap.

The ICC had already indicted Vladimir Putin on 17 March 2023. This was significant as it was the first indictment by the ICC of a head of a major state. They had previously indicted four other heads of states, but they were from Cote d'Ivoire, Kenya, Libya and the Philippines.

The effects of these indictments are limited as long as these officials do not travel. Russia is not a party to the ICC so its officials are protected as long as they do not travel outside of Russia or to a country that is a member of the ICC. Countries that are not members of the ICC include Russia, China, India, North Korea and Turkey. Almost all other countries in Europe are a member of the ICC except for Belarus and Vatican City. Canada and Mexico are members, but the United States is not. Therefore, it is not safe for Putin or any other indicted official to travel to or over these countries. The countries are obligated by treaty to arrest him and turn him over to the ICC.

The Russian missiles used

Shahed and variants: The Shahed-136 an inexpensive originally Iranian-built drone, or loitering munition. It has a delta-wing shape with an explosive in the tip. The drone itself weighs 441 pounds (200 kilograms), and is 11½ feet (3.5 meters) in length with a wingspan of over eight feet (2.5 meters). This is not a small drone, standing larger than a man.[21]

The warhead is estimated to weigh a rather hefty 66–110 pounds (30 to 50 kilograms). Its maximum speed is only about 115 mph (185 km/h) although its operational range is an impressive 1,600 miles (2,500 kilometers). It can loiter for up to 12 hours.

Its real virtue as a weapons systems is its cost. Its manufacturing cost is estimated to be between $10,000 and $50,000 and its export cost is reported to be as high as $193,000 and its cost for production in Russia is $165,500 per drone.[22] Iran produces thousands each year. Russia has now set up its own factories and is making them also, called the Geran-2. This has created the means to send 100 to 400 munitions

---

21   See "The rise of Shahed drones: Russia deploys Iran's cost-effective weapon in Ukraine conflict; here's all about the drone," *The Economic Times*, 2 August 2023.

22   Andrew Buncombe, "Russia paid Iran 'in gold bullion' for drones used in attacks on Ukraine," *The Telegraph*, 7 February 2024 at https://www.telegraph.co.uk/world-news/2024/02/07/russia-paid-billions-gold-bullion-shahed-drones-ukraine-war/. As the subtitle of the article notes "Leak reveals minister's claim that $1.75 billion contract was signed for 6,000 Shaheds and Kremlin 'paid in literal gold'."

a night at Ukraine. They were first observed in combat in Ukraine on 13 September 2022.[23]

Kh-22 Byrya or Storm is an older long-range anti-ship cruise missile. It has a 2,205-pound (1,000-kilogram) warhead. It can be launched from the Tu-22M, Tu-22K and Tu-96K22.

Kh-31 is an air-to-surface missile carried by MiG-29s, Su-35s and Su-57s. The Kh-31A is an anti-ship missile and the Kh-31P is an anti-radiation missile. It has a 207-pound (94-kilogram) warhead for the A version and a 192-pound (87-kilogram) warhead for the P version.

Kh-35 is a fast anti-ship cruise missile. It can be fired from a variety of air, naval and land platforms. The warhead is 320 pounds (145 kilograms).

Kh-47M2 Kinzhal is an air-launched ballistic missile. It can be launched by Tu-22M3 bombers, MiG-31K interceptors, or Su-34 fighter-bombers. The warhead is large but its size is not stated.

Kh-59/69 is a stealth air-launched cruise missile. It can be fired from a variety of airplanes. The warhead is 661 pounds (300 kilograms).

Kh-101 is an air-launched cruise missile. It is fired from Tu-95MS and Tu-160s. The warhead is 881 pounds (400 kilograms).

Kalibr is a cruise missile that can be launched from a variety of air, land or sea platforms. It has a warhead of 882 to 1,102 pounds (400 to 500 kilograms).

Iskander-K is a 9K720 Iskander firing a 9M728 cruise missile. The warhead weighs 1,060 pounds (480 kilograms).

Iskander-M or 9K720 Iskander or the SS-26 is a mobile short-range ballistic missile. It is launched from the back of a 16-wheel transporter. The warhead weighs from 1,060 to 1,540 pounds (480 to 700 kilograms).

---

23 "Iranian Shahed-136 Kamikaze Drones Already Used by Russia (First Photos and Specs)," *Defence Express*, 13 September 2022 at https://en.defenceua.com/weapon_and_tech/iranian_shahed_136_kamikaze_drones_already_used_by_russia_first_photos_and_specs-4207.html.

It is the replacement for the SCUD missile that were used by Iraq in the 1991 Gulf War.

The Shahed drones cost tens of thousands of dollars. So a launch of 100 of these in a night may cost Russia less than $20 million. The cruise missiles tend to cost a half-million to a million dollars each. So a launch of 10 of these in a night, it would cost Russia $5–10 million or more.

Nuclear capability
The following planes were capable of carrying nuclear bombs, and up until 2022, this was their primary mission: Tu-22M2, Tu-95MS and Tu-160s.

Chapter 3

THE RUSSIAN STRATEGIC BOMBER FORCE

"We're satisfied to be able to finish off the United States first time round. Once is quite enough. What good does it do to annihilate a country twice? We're not a bloodthirsty people."

Nikita Khruschchev
@ 1970[1]

The Russian "Long-Range Aviation" was a command created by the Soviet Union in 1936. By 1938 they had formed up three air armies, evolving by 1939 so that each army consisted of two air brigades with a total of four air regiments. This was reorganized after the war with Finland in 1940 into a single command under the General Staff (Stavka) and consisting of five air corps, three separate air divisions and one separate air regiment. This organization was revised during

---

1   From the book *Khruschev Remembers: The Last Testament* (Little, Brown and Company, New York, 1974), page 530. The entire quote is "I remember President Kennedy once stated . . . that the United States had the nuclear missile capacity to wipe out the Soviet Union two times over, while the Soviet Union had enough atomic weapons to wipe out the United States only once . . . When journalists asked me to comment . . . I said jokingly, 'Yes, I know what Kennedy claims, and he's quite right. But I'm not complaining . . . .We're satisfied to be able to finish off the United States first time round. Once is quite enough. What good does it do to annihilate a country twice? We're not a bloodthirsty people.'"

    The quote attributed to Khrushchev that "The survivors [of a nuclear war] would envy the dead" cannot be confirmed. See: https://www.bartleby.com/lit-hub/respectfully-quoted/nikita-sergeyevich-khrushchev-18941971-3/.

World War II but in 1944 still consisted of five air corps and a number of separate divisions and regiments.

They served throughout World War II. In 1941 it consisted of over 1,300 TB-2, TB-7 and IL-4 bombers. In February 1942 General Aleksandr Golobanov took command. In August 1943 he was promoted to Marshal of Aviation at the age of 38 and the following year as Chief Marshal of Aviation. As the war progressed, the Long-Range Aviation (ADD) force was nearly 3,000 aircraft of which 1,800 were combat aircraft.

On 6 December 1944 the ADD was disbanded as an autonomous force and became the 18th Air Army in the Red Army (Soviet) Air Force. It was regrouped back into the Long-Range Aviation Force in April 1946 and back into three air armies. It was a branch of the Soviet Armed Forces and after the dissolution of the Soviet Union, continued as a branch of the Russian Air Force and the Ukrainian Air Force. The branches were tasked with the long-range bombardment of strategic targets and after World War II, this meant nuclear weapons. It was the equivalent of the U.S. Air Force Strategic Air Command (SAC).

The Russian Long-Range Aviation Force was disbanded in 1998 and became the 37th Air Army. In 2009 the 37th Air Army was disbanded and reformed as the Long Range Aviation Command. It consists of two divisions, the 22nd Guards Heavy Aviation Division and the 326th Heavy Bomber Aviation Division.

The commander of the Russian Long-Range Aviation Command from 2016–2024 was Lt. General Sergey Kobylash, born 1965 in Odessa. In 2024 a warrant for his arrest was issued by the International Criminal Court. The current commander is Sergey Kuvaldin.

With the fall of the Soviet Union in 1991, the newly stood-up Ukrainian Long-Range Aviation Group had 1,100 combat aircraft in three air armies. This group was disbanded in 2007 and all their Tu-95s and Tu-22Ms were either handed back to Russia or scrapped.

The Aircraft

The Russian Long-Range Aviation Command consists of three main heavy bombers and two major support aircraft. Their three main bombers are the Tu-95MS, the Tu-22M and the Tu-160. Support is provided by the A-50 and the Il-78 transport and aerial refueling aircraft.

The Tupolev Tu-95 "Bear" is Russia's old standby strategic bomber, as old as the American B-52 and still propellor driven. It is the only mass-produced swept wing aircraft power by propellors. It was first flown in 1952 and introduced into service in 1956. Its first combat use was in late 2015 during the Syrian Civil War. It is currently expected to continue serving until 2040. The Tu-95 was earlier designated as the Tu-20.

It is powered by four Kuznetsov NK-12 turboprop engines with a pair of contra-rotating propellers. The tips of the propeller blades move faster than the speed of sound, making it very loud. The wings are swept back at a 35-degree angle. Each engine produces 14,795 horsepower and were designed with the help of imprisoned German engineers from Nazi Germany.[2]

The plane is manned by a crew of six or seven, with a maximum speed of 575 mph (925 km/h), a range of 9,300 miles (15,000 kilometers) and a service ceiling of 45,000 feet (13,716 meters).

Production of the plane ceased in 1993 with over 500 built. The plane did undergo a modernization program in recent times. There are no manufacturing facilities set up to replace them.

The Tupolev Tu-95MS is an upgraded Tu-95 with enhancement made to the navigation systems, electronics weapons and targeting systems. It also includes four external hardpoints to allow the aircraft to carry eight Kh-101/102 cruise missiles. Only airplanes built from 1986 and after were modernized, about 30 to 35 aircraft. The first modernized plane was completed in early 2015. As of 2020, Russia still had 55 Tu-95MSs still in service.

A second modernization effort, the Tu-95MSM, included upgraded radars, navigation system and airborne defense, and engines. The tail turret was also removed. The first Tu-95MSM flew in 2020.

The Tupolev Tu-22 "Blinder" is Russia's supersonic medium bomber. Its first flight was in 1959, started building in 1960 and introduced into service in 1962. Somewhat of a disappointment due to a myriad of problems, many were built as reconnaissance aircraft vice strategic bombers. It did have operational use by Libya in Tanzania, Chad, Sudan in 1979–87 and two were shot down. It was successfully used by Iraq in the Iran-Iraq War from 1980–8 with seven lost during the war. All remaining Iraqi T-22s were destroyed by the United States during

---

2   The lead German engineer was Austrian-born Ferdinand Brandner
     (1903–86). He was an SS Standartenführer (Colonel) in Nazi Germany and
     worked at Junkers. He was captured by the Soviet Union in the spring
     of 1945. He was released from the Soviet Union in 1953 and returned to
     Austria and later worked for Egypt (1959 to 1962 or later) and the People's
     Republic of China (1972–3). He passed away in Salzburg.

the 1991 Gulf War. The only Soviet use of the Tu-22 occurred in 1988 during their withdrawal from Afghanistan.

It is powered by two turbojet engines. The wings are swept back at a 55-degree angle. Because of its high landing speeds, it needs to operate from airfields with at least a 3,000-meter runway.

The plane is manned by a crew of three, with a maximum speed of 940 mph (1,510 km/h) or Mach 1.42, a range of 3,000 miles (4,900 kilometers) and a service ceiling of 43,600 feet (13,300 meters).

Production of the plane ceased in 1969 with 311 built. At the time of the dissolution of the Soviet Union, 154 remained in service. Leading up to the war with Ukraine, only about ten were still available held in reserve.

The Tupolev Tu-22 M "Backfire" is Russia's variable-wing missile-carrying strategic bomber. It was developed from the Tu-22 to correct its inadequacies. The upgrade was massive, it was effectively a new plane and the two planes do not look similar. It was first manufactured in 1967, the first flight was in 1969 and it was introduced into service in 1972. It was used by Russia in Chechnya in 1995 and in the war with Georgia in 2008. One was shot down by a Georgian-operated but Soviet-built BUK-M1 (SA-17 "Grizzly") surface-to-air missile in 2008. This was probably the same surface-to-air missile system used to shoot down Malaysia Airlines Flight 17 in July 2014 and a Ukrainian MiG-29 in August 2014 over Ukraine. Tu-22Ms were used in the Syrian Civil War starting from 2016 to at least 2021.

It is powered by two powerful Kuznetsov NK-25 afterburning turbofan engines.

The plane is manned by a crew of four, with a maximum speed of 1,241 mph (1,997 km/h) at 30,000 feet (9,140 meters) or a speed of Mach 1.88, a range of 4,200 miles (6,800 kilometers), and a service ceiling of 43,600 feet (13,300 meters).

Production of the plane ceased in 1993 with 487 built. At the time of the dissolution of the Soviet Union, 370 remained in service in the Commonwealth of Independent States (CIS), which included 60 with Ukraine. According the IISS in 2024 Rusia had 57 Tu-22Ms in service. However, Ukrainian intelligence estimated in 2023 that only 27 were in operational condition. The plane did undergo a modernization program in recent times. No replacement was ever built for the Tu-22 series. The United States' B-1 Bomber is a more modern comparative aircraft.

The Tupolev Tu-160 "Blackjack" was the last strategic bomber developed by the Soviet Union (none have been developed by Russia). It is a variable-sweep wing supersonic strategic heavy bomber that is larger than a B-52. Its first flight was in 1981, it started being built in 1984 and its introduction was in 1987. Its first combat use was in late 2015 during the Syrian Civil War.

It is powered by four powerful Kuznetsov NK-32 afterburning turbofan engines. This is the most powerful engine ever fitted to a combat aircraft. This engine, when overhauled and upgraded, is referred to as the NK-32M. Only a few of these have been delivered.

The plane is manned by a crew of four, with a maximum speed of 1,380 mph (2,220 km/h) at 40,000 feet (12,200 meters) or a speed of Mach 2.05, a range of 7,600 miles (12,300 kilometers), and a service ceiling of 52,000 feet (16,000 meters).

Production of the plane first ceased in 1992. To date, only 41 (9 test and 32 for service) had been built. At the time of the collapse of the Soviet Union (1991) Russian had 13 of these bombers and Ukraine ended up with 19. Eight of the Ukrainian bombers were purchased by Russia, along with 3 Tu-95MS bombers, and 11 Tu-160s were scrapped. As of 2022, Russian had 17 Tu-160s in service. The production line was reopened to modernize the aircraft, with the modernized version re-labeled as Tu-160Ms. This is the one bomber that Russian can continue to produce and the production line was reopened around 2019, with the intention of increasing active inventory to 30 or more active by 2025–2030. The current models has been upgraded and it is intended to build 50 new Tu-160Ms. Only two were delivered in 2022 and production has remained slow and only four aircraft were delivered in 2024. It is claimed that their current inventory (as of 2025) is 19 Tu-160s of which five are in repair and modernization. Two others are under construction.[3]

This aircraft was originally built in response to the United States' B-1 Bomber program. It is not a stealth aircraft though.

The Tupolev PAK DA is the next-generation stealth strategic bomber intended to complement and eventually replace the antique Tu-95. According to a report by *Izvestiya* in 2023, three prototypes were expected to ready for preliminary testing in 2023 with state test to begin in 2026. They were expected to enter production in 2027. As of June 2025, there are no reports of a prototype being completed. Therefore it appears that production is delayed at least until 2029.

---

3   James Thomson, "Drone Swarms Shift Strategy: Russia's Tu-160s now test Alaskan airspace," *MSN*, 29 July 2025 reported that only 16 are operational, only three new Tu-160Ms have been produced since 2022 and each aircraft costs more than $500 million.

The Beriev A-50 "Mainstay" is an AEW&C plane based on the Il-76 transport plane. It first flew in 1978 and entered service in 1985. Around 42 were built by 1992. It is powered by four Soloviev D-30KP turbofan engines.

The plane is manned by a large 15-person crew, including 10 mission operators. It has a maximum speed of 530 mph (850 km/h), a range of 4,700 miles (7,500 kilometers) and a service ceiling of 50,900 feet (15,500 meters). The aircraft can be refueled in flight.

On top of the plane is a rotodome holding the antenna for the Liana surveillance radar. The dome is 30 feet (9 meters) in diameter. The detection range of the radar is 400 miles (650 kilometers) for air targets and 190 miles (200 kilometers) for ground targets. The A-50 can control up to ten aircraft for either air-to-air or air-to ground missions.

Production of the plane ceased in 1992. A modernization program began in 2003 as the A-50U, with the first upgraded plane delivered in 2011. As of September 2023 there were eight A-50U aircraft. Ukraine's Defense Intelligence stated that as of 25 February 2025 Russian had only six operational A-50s (assumed A-50Us). The A-50s primarily operate out of Ivanovo Severny air base.

Production of the plane has been resumed by Rostec as of 2024 but it is likely to be years before we see any new aircraft.

The Beriev A-100 is the replacement for the A-50. It is built on an Il-76MD-90A transport plane. It is similar to the A50U but used the new Vega Premier Active Phased Array Radar.

It is powered by four Aviadvigatel PS 90-76 turbofan engines. It has a maximum speed of 560 mph (900 km/h). The detection range of the radar is 370 miles (600 kilometers) for air targets and 250 miles (400 kilometers) for ships.

A development contract was signed in 2006. A flying laboratory flew in 2017. In 2022 the A-100 made its first flight with radar turned on. It was expected that the first planes were to be delivered in 2024, but sanctions may have delayed that. According to one source they have built as of 2025 an A-100LL and an A-100. The IISS *The Military Balance 2025* book does not show any in service.

The Il-78 is an aerial refueling pane based upon the Il-76 transport plane. It first flew in 1983, began manufacturing in 1984 and entered service in 1984. An upgrade version, the Il-78M with higher fuel capacity was first flew in 1987. Between 1984 and 1993 32 Il-78s, 13 Il-78MS and an Il-78E export version for Libya were built. The production line is still open. A total of 53 have been built.

It is powered by four Aviadvigatel D-30 KP turbofan engines.

The plane is manned by six crew. It has a maximum speed of 530 mph (850 km/h), a range of 4,500 miles (7,400 kilometers), and a service ceiling of 39,000 feet (12,000 meters).

The Il-78 can transfer a maximum of 57.7 tonnes of fuel with internal tanks only or 85.7 tonnes of fuel with removeable additional tanks. The Il-78M can transfer 105.7 tonnes of fuel.

As of 2019, Russian has 19 Il-78s and Il-78MS in service.

Production has continued. The latest export version is Il-78MK-90A. Six export versions, the Il-78MKI, were order by India in 2002. Ukraine inherited 20 Il-78s with the collapse of the Soviet Union. It has sold six to the Algerian Air Force in 1998, one to Angola in 2001, one to the United States in 2005, four to the Pakistan Air Force in 2006, and three to the Chinese Air Force in 2011. India does not always have the best relations with Pakistan and China and it is clear that Ukraine is their supplier while Russia supplies India.

The Bomber Force

The current Russian strategic bomber force consists of:

Plane	Number Operational	IISS (2025)[4] Strategic	Aerospace
Tu-95	0		
Tu-95MS	55	58	31
Tu-95MS mod			27
Tu-22	10 in reserve		
Tu-22M	57 (27 operational?)		55
Tu-22M3			1 (in overhaul)
Tu-22MR			
Tu-160	19 (14 operational)	13 + (3 in test)	6
Tu-160 mod			7 + (3 in test)
Total bombers	96 operational ?	71	IISS is double counting

It is clear that IISS is double counting here between the Strategic and Aerospace forces. There are 58 Tu-95s total and 13 operational Tu-160s giving them 71 nuclear-capable strategic bombers.

---

4   *The Military Balance 2025* (Routledge, UK, February 2025).

Plane	Number Operational	IISS (2025)[5] Aerospace
A-50	0	0
A-50U	6	7
A-100	2?	0
Il-78	19	5
Il-78M		10

The International Institute of Strategic Studies (IISS) in London specifically lists the Russians having in 2025:

    71 BBR (Long-Range Aviation Command)
- 6 Tu-160 "Blackjack" with Kh-55SM (RS-AS-15B "Kent") nuclear LACM
- 7 Tu-160 mod "Blackjack" with Kh-55SM (RS-AS-15B "Kent")/Kh-120 (RS-AS-23B "Kodiak") nuclear LACM
- 31 Tu-95MS "Bear H" with Kh-5SM (RS-AS-15B "Kent") nuclear LACM
- 27 Tu-95MS mod "Bear H" with Kh-55SM (RS-AS-15B "Kent")/Kh-102 (RS-AS-34B "Kodiak") nuclear LACM
- 3 Tu-160M in test.

Note that the Su-22Ms are not part of the Long-Range Aviation Command. The Su-22Ms are listed under the Aerospace Forces (as are the Tu-95s and Tu-160s a second time).

The Russian strategic nuclear force

The American strategic nuclear force doctrine is dominated by the idea of Triad, three roughly equal nuclear Forces – missiles, submarine-launched missiles and bombers – able to deliver destructive force with each of these three branches. The Russians have the same three branches but more oriented towards their strategic rocket forces. They have 324 ICBMs (compared to 400 Minutemen III for the United States), 12 SSBN-armed submarines with 192 SLBMs (compared to 14 SSBNs armed with up to 280 SLBMs for the United States) and 71 strategic bombers (compared to 66 for the United States, 46 B-52Hs and 20 B-2As).

Therefore, even though the Russian strategic aircraft were being used to attack Ukraine with conventional weapons, this attack did degrade Russia's strategic nuclear capability.

---

5   *The Military Balance 2025* (Routledge, UK, February 2025).

Chapter 4

UKRAINIAN COVERT OPERATIONS

"Red wine with fish. Well, that should have told me something."
Fictional character James Bond
From the film *From Russia with Love* (1963)

The Security Service of Ukraine (SBU)

Operation Spider's Web was put together by the Security Service of Ukraine (SBU) headed by Lt. General Vasyl Malyuk. It is the main internal security agency for Ukraine and reports directly to President of Ukraine, Volodymyr Zelenskyy. Its duties include counter-intelligence and combating organized crime. It also had its own special forces (Spetsnaz) unit, the Alpha Group.

Vasyl Malyuk is only 42 years old. He has a law degree. He has been the head of the SBU since 7 February 2023 and was acting head from 18 July 2022. He has headed the SBU for most of this war. In 2014 he became involved in operations in Donbas. He was involved in the Battle of Hostomel in early 2022. He was still a Colonel at that point but was quickly promoted thereafter. He first came to work for state security agencies in 2001.

The SBU was created in September 1991 after Ukraine had declared its independence from the Soviet Union the previous month. After the "Revolution of Dignity" in 2014, which threw out the Russian-leaning government of Victor Yanokovich, the SBU went through an extensive restructuring to try to reduce corruption and the infiltration of the SBU by Russian intelligence agencies.

The war started on 24 February 2022. Soon after, in July 2022, the head of the SBU, Ukrainian politician Ivan Bakanov, was dismissed

54

because of concerns over the failure to halt the collaboration of SBU agents with Russia. He was a childhood friend of President Zelenskyy. He was replaced by 39-year old Brigadier General (now Lt. General) Vasyl Malyuk, who was a professional SBU officer as opposed to a political appointee.

The SBU then conducted a series of operations in support of the war effort. This included in October of using a truck loaded with explosives to seriously damage the 12-mile (19-kilometer) long bridge to Crimea that lies across the Kerch Strait. They also carried out multiple attacks using sea drones against Russian navy ships in the Black Sea in 2023. Its efforts also included at least five assassinations inside of Russia.[1] These operations clearly showed that Ukraine had an extensive network of agents inside of Russia, and as important, that Russia was no longer getting warning of Ukrainians operations from agents inside of the SBU. Still, things were far from perfect inside of the SBU, for as recently as February 2025 the SBU arrested its chief of counter-terrorism on suspicion of working for Russia since 2018. In this case, the colonel had been recruited in Vienna in 2018 and "mothballed" for several years. Russia resumed contact with him in December 2024 and he transmitted information to Russia at least 14 times after that.[2] Russia's use of long-term sleeper agents is a particularly effective tactic, and they have clearly done the same several times in the United States.[3]

It is not surprising that Ukraine has an extensive network of agents inside Russia. According to the Russian census of 2021, there were 884,007 Ukrainians in Russia. They made up 0.68% of all the people

---

1   Among then was a killing of senior Russian naval officer in a car in Crimea in 2022, the killing of a high-ranking officer in the GRU (military intelligence) outside of his house in a village in the Moscow region also in 2022, the killing of Darya Dugina in 2023, the daughter of Russian ideologue Alesander Dugin, by using a car bomb to smash into her Toyota Land Cruiser, the killing of Russian missile scientist Mikhail Shatsky in 2024, and the killing of the head of the Russian Army Chemical Weapons Division, Igor Kirillov, by an explosive device in December 2024.

2   This was Colonel Dmytro Kozyura. See Robert Greenall, "Senior Ukraine official accused of being Russian 'rat'," *BBC News*, 12 February 2025.

3   Most notable was the arrest of ten Russian sleeper agents in June 2010 in New Jersey, New York, Massachusetts and Virginia. Later an eleventh agent was arrested in Cyprus, and a twelfth agent was arrested in Washington state. The 2013 television series *The Americans* was inspired by the Soviet deep-cover agent program.

who declared their ethnicity and this does not include all of the people who parents were of Ukrainian descent. One of the last leaders of the Soviet Union was born in Ukraine, as was the commander at the start of the war of the Russian Long-Range Aviation Command. Many Russians have relatives in Ukraine and many Ukrainians have relatives in Russia. It is a fertile ground for special operations.

The Alpha Group is the SBU's special operation (Spetsnaz) unit. The Soviet Spetsnaz were first deployed during the Battle of Kursk in July 1943. In July 1974 the Alpha Group was created by the KGB Chairman, Yuri Andropov (later head of the Soviet Union). A Ukrainian territorial detachment was created in Kyiv in 1990. The Kyiv territorial Group A was converted into Service C of the SBU in 1992 and re-labeled as the Alpha Group in 1994. Russia still mains its own Alpha group. In 2014, the Ukrainian Alpha Group was purged and reorganized. It is alleged that Alpha group snipers had fired on protesters during the "Revolution of Dignity." The Vostok Battalion, a unit fighting for the separatist Donetsk People's Republic, was founded by an SBU Alpha group defector and several of his men.

The next big operation by the SBU was Operation Spider's Web on 1 June 2025.

Planning for the Attack

It is claimed that this drone attack came about as a result of a request made in late fall 2023 by President Volodymyr Zelenskyy to the head of the SBU. At that time, the Russian air force was pummeling the Ukrainian cities and its power grid. This was a large effort, often more than a hundred cruise missiles and drones a day. Invariably some were getting through the Ukrainian air defenses. Zelenskyy wanted to know how can Ukraine fight back.

In October 2024 Ukraine had set up a business in Chelyabinsk. This was the cover operation headed by a 37-year-old Ukrainian, Artem Timofeyev. He obviously had one or more assistants working with him. They then registered the firm as a house construction business, selling pre-fabricated hunting lodges. That they were pre-fabricated hunting lodges means that they came with electronics, solar panels, EcoFlow batteries and all the material that was needed for a modern house, or to operate drones. The drones in storage were able to be kept continuously powered, which was needed for operating in colder climates. It also provided a useful cover story, for when one truck driver spotted the drones, they were able to convince the driver that these drones were to be used for spotting game, a completely believable excuse for a hunting lodge.

An office was set up and rented, warehouse space was rented and the five trucks were purchased by its agents in Chelyabinsk. There may have been more than one warehouse.[4] The five truck drivers used were hired by them under well-paying contracts. They had them do a number of other deliveries for them so that this would all seem like normal business. They were just Russian truck drivers. They had no idea of the role they were about to play. One would end up dying in the operation.

The drones were smuggled into Russia almost certainly via nearby Kazakhstan. Chelyabinsk was only 74 miles (119 kilometers) from the border. Border guards could be bribed and the drones hidden in pre-fabricated housing crates that could be shipped across the Russian-Kazakhstan border to Chelyabinsk. As the head of the SBU said in an interview "Speaking of logistics, I should note that we drew on our experience in fighting transnational crime, when we studied in detail how international drug cartels secretly deliver various prohibited substances to different corners of the world without detection by customs or border authorities." As he further elaborated "If you read between the lines and look at it professionally, I think many have noticed certain parallels between the first strike on the Crimea bridge." So, Ukraine smuggled material into Russia to bomb the Crimea bridge in 2022 and used their developed skills to do the same for Operation Spider's Web. He also said in both cases, that Ukraine didn't employ smugglers, but relied on customs officials in Russia. As Malyuk says "Who are, by their nature, very corrupt. At a certain stage, they actually played to our advantage in delivering the cabins I mentioned."[5]

The cargo trucks were in at least two cases flatbed trucks with two containers carried on them. The roof was rigged on the containers to open on command and the drones could then be ordered to fly out.

With drones armed, placed in pre-fabricated containers, the rigged roofs on trucks, and five hired truck drivers, everything was set up so that the trucks could drive out of Chelyabinsk on Thursday, 29 May 2025. Artem Timofeyev and his two or more assistants then went "on

---

4   In the interview, Malyuk says that one of these warehouses was even
     in the same city block as Russia's FSB headquarters for the Chelyabinsk
     region, which implies more than one warehouse. See: Matthew Loh,
     "Ukraine studies drug cartels to learn how to sneak drones into Russia
     for its 'Operation Spiderweb' attack," *Business Insider*, 13 August 2025.

5   Matthew Loh, "Ukraine studies drug cartels to learn how to sneak
     drones into Russia for its 'Operation Spiderweb' attack," *Business Insider*,
     13 August 2025.

vacation," leaving the country to what we assume is an unsuspicious destination and then from there returning to Kyiv. They were back in Ukraine by Sunday, 1 June, the day of the operation.

The drivers were then sent to each to a specific location, and told that the customer would arrive, pay for them and pick up the houses. Therefore, when they were called and told to pulled over at a given locale, it seems like part of the planned transaction.

The one complicating factor was that all five trucks were supposed to arrive outside their respective air bases at about the same time, 10:30 in the morning according to one anonymous source. This apparently did not happen. It is hard to imagine how with trucks driving from Chelyabinsk to Murmansk, or from Chelyabinsk to Irkutsk, or from Chelyabinsk to Amur Oblast near the Chinese border, how these trucks were going to be coordinated to arrive at the same time. They apparently did not.

The one unknown aspect of the operation was whether there were SBU agents in the areas of each of the air bases to launch the drones. It is possible that everything could be automatically activated from Kyiv, the roofs come off and then the drones fly off. More likely, there were a small teams of agents at each of the five sites who then sent the signal to open the top of the container and for the drones to fly. In two of the cases, the drones started flying as soon as the truck pulled into the gas station or parking lot that they were told to. This would be hard to pre-program. It may have been possible to call truck drivers from Kyiv and order them to go to those areas. It may have been possible to then initiate the attack from Kyiv. The suspicion is that there were people in the area who initiated the launch.

The two operations that were not successful reinforce this narrative. One truck started launching drones while it was driving down the highway near the base. We suspect this truck was arriving later than the rest and therefore they needed to get the attack launched before the Russians could be warned and prepare to defend the air base. So instead of taking the time to have the truck stop somewhere, they initiated the launch while it was still on the nearby highway. This was the attack that failed and some of the drones crashed into the grass near the airfield but none of them hit planes. We suspect this was because electronic interference (jamming) had already been initiated by the base defenders and therefore none of the drones were able to successfully fly to the airfield. Suspect this means that this attack happened a half-hour or later then the first three (successful) attacks. It is assumed that an SBU agent in the area was observing the truck and initiated the launch, although this also could have been done remotely from Kyiv.

In the other failed attack, the truck was pulled to the side of the road in an unpopulated area in Amur Oblast and several people were gathered around it. The truck was already smoking, so one wonders if something had gone wrong inside the cargo compartment, which caused the driver to pull over. Then someone, probably the truck driver, chose to enter the door at the back of the rear container. The truck immediately exploded. This could have been done automatically, but there was a slight delay (see video). Suspect that a nearby observer initiated the explosion, as opposed to having all the five trucks boobytrapped just in case. This signal probably had to initiated locally as opposed to all the way from Kyiv to Ukrainka, which was across almost all of Russia to the Chinese border. The truck that attacked Belaya in Irkutsk Oblast also exploded, but after it had already launched all its drones. This again argues for a local observer who initiated it as opposed to it doing so automatically.

This means that five teams of at least two agents were located outside each of these bases. If so, these people had to slink away after the attack in mid-morning and make their way to safe houses or out of the country. Needless to say, none of this has been discussed by Ukrainian sources.

The request from Volodymir Zelenskyy to do something came in the fall of 2023. The cover business was set up in October 2024. This implies a year for planning, organizing and setting up the operation. The primary Ukrainian agent may have already been in Chelyabinsk. The operation was initiated at the beginning of May, but was delayed a month to the lack of availability of some of the drivers. So from the time of setting up the business until they were ready to attack was at most seven months. If it could only take seven months to actually conduct such an operation, then more operations like this could be forthcoming.

The drones used

The drones used were developed by the Ukrainian company First Contact. This company has been making drones since 2014.[6] They make a number of different small drones includes the Osa, the Vidsich, and the Val-1 submarine drone.

---

6   "Ukraine launches mass production of First Contact Vidsich UAV," *Army Recognition Group*, 24 October 2023 at https://www. armyrecognition.com/archives/archives-land-defense/land-defense-2023/ukraine-launches-mass-production-of-vidsich-unmanned-aerial-vehicle.

The Osa drones, according to First Contact, have a top speed of around 93 mph (150 km/h), can carry a payload of 7.3 pounds (3.3 kilograms) and can remain airborne for 15 minutes. This implies that its operational range is effectively no more than 23 miles (37.5 kilometers).

First Contact is owned by the non-profit company Alliance "New Energy of Ukraine." The Chairman of the board and CEO since 2012 is Valerii Borovyk. He also serves in the special forces as part of the National Guard of Ukraine.[7]

The shipping container used appears to carry at least 27 drones (see photo section). This could mean four shipping containers for the four bases that were attacked or 108 drones plus nine other drones.

The advantage of the Osa drones is that they employ a sealed construction, making them more suitable for long-distance transport inside trucks and resilient enough to use in varied weather conditions. These particular models had two skids integrated into the bottom frame of the drone, which served to carry the shaped-charge warheads (see photo section).[8]

It is claimed that they cost $2,000 each.[9]

Subsequent attacks

On 3 June, the SBU carried out an attack on the Crimean Bridge, detonating underwater explosives damaging the bridge support structure. This is discussed in depth in Chapter 9.

---

7   His Linkedin account is here: https://ua.linkedin.com/in/valeriy-borovyk-92584847. He has been CEO of Alliance since January 2012. He is the author of two books *It's Time to Win* and *New Energy of Life*. His hometown is Chernihiv. See: https://www.aljazeera.com/news/2022/9/9/in-ukraine-humanitarian-drones-can-save-lives.

He also funds a number of efforts included a school for female drone pilots. See https://www.northcountrypublicradio.org/news/npr/1135633681/ukrainian-women-have-started-learning-a-crucial-war-skill-how-to-fly-a-drone.

8   https://euromaidanpress.com/2025/06/03/meet-first-contacts-osa-the-ukraine-fpv-drone-used-to-strike-russian-bombers-in-spiderweb-operation/.

9   James Marson, Jane Lytvynenko, Brenna T. Smith, Serhii Bosak, "Inside the Ukrainian Drone Operation that devastated Russia's bomber fleet," *The Wall Street Journal*, 3 June 2025.

Russia's Revenge Attacks

Russia carried out multiple revenge attacks against Ukraine using drones and missiles. This was after the 1 June attack and the 3 June attack. More and larger attacks were conducted as we moved into July. These are discussed in the following chapters. In the meantime, the Ukrainian and Russian secret services continued fighting their own covert war, which had been going on since before the start of this war.

On Thursday 10 July, shortly after 09:00, an SBU officer, Colonel Ivan Voronych, was gunned down in a parking lot outside the entrance of his apartment building in Kyiv's Holosiivskyi district. An assailant approached him on foot and shot him five times with a pistol. He then fled on foot from the parking lot.[10]

Two FSB agents, a man and a woman, had been dispatched to Ukraine in the last two months. They had trailed their target to establish his daily routine. They were then directed to a safe house where they were able to pick up a pistol with a silencer. This was the weapon the man used for the assassination.

On 13 July Ukraine was able to track down and "neutralize" the two FSB agents, including the assassin, at a safe house in a village near Kyiv. SBU said they resisted arrest, there was an exchange of fire and the two people were "eliminated."[11]

Colonel Ivan Voronych was a SBU Special Operations Center (Alpha Group) officer and had certainly been involved in covert operations, probably including assassinations inside of Russa.[12] It is not known if he was directly involved in the drone attack.

---

10   Aleks Phillips, "Ukrainian intelligence officer shot dead in Kyiv," *BBC*, 10 July 2025.

11   The actual quote from Lt. General Vasyl Malyuk (SBU) was "During the arrest, they resisted, and there was a firefight, so the scum were eliminated." See: "Ukrainian intel eliminates Russian agents who murdered top Security Service officer in Kyiv," *RBC-Ukraine*, 13 July 2025.

12   See Kateryna Tyshchenko, "Ukrainian Security service colonel shot dead in Kyiv reported to have planned 2015 killing of Russian militant Mozgovoi," *Ukrainska Pravda*, 19 July 2025.

Chapter 5

PEACE TALKS

"If I'm president, I'll have that war settled in one day, 24 hours.
I'll meet with Putin, meet with Zelensky . . . and within 24 hours, that war will
be settled."

Donald J. Trump
10 May 2023[1]

The first peace talks between Ukraine and Russia occurred shortly after the war began. There were almost from the beginning attempts to achieve a ceasefire and reach a peace. There was certainly some precedent for this. Russian had been amenable in 2008 to a negotiated solution two weeks (actually 16 days) into the offensive into Georgia. This solution was to replace the existing government in exchange for the Russian Army withdrawing. The Russian Army was on the outskirts of the capital and there were insufficient regular Georgian forces in front of it. They did negotiate a settlement to remove the current government of Georgia which had foolishly initiated the war with an attack on separatists in Ossetia. Russia then withdrew.

But the situation in Georgia only remained quiet for a while. There were strong anti-government protests in March 2023 and again in April–June 2024. Then extensive anti-government protests in Georgia started on 28 October 2024, but they have yet to remove the current Russian-leaning government. The EU does not recognize the results of the election and the United States and many European nations have protested the recent parliamentary and president elections and sanctioned the leaders of the ruling Georgia Dream Party. Georgian

---

1   Interview with CNN on 10 May, 2023 at https://www.wsj.com/video/watch-trump-says-as-president-hed-settle-ukraine-war-within-24-hours/0BCA9F18-D3BF-43DA-9220-C13587EAEDF2.

democracy protests continue as of August 2025 against a backdrop of repression. This is still an unresolved conflict.

Russia had also resolved the Chechen crisis by a negotiated settlement, after two bitter wars. This settlement put a Chechen warlord, Akhmat Kadyrov, in charge of Chechnya and kept it as part of the Russian Federation. Kadyrov had been one of the Chechen warlords that was fighting Russia. He has since been a Russian, or at least, a Putin loyalist. His son is now head of Chechnya and is providing troops for the war in Ukraine.

Russia also did a carefully controlled seizure of Sevastopol and Crimea, threatening the Ukrainian army and naval forces there with overwhelming force, but then allowing them to disarm, withdraw and return to Ukraine. These two areas were seized with very limited casualties, a total of five people killed.[2]

They also negotiated a settlement to suspend the fighting in Ukraine in February 2015. This was the Minsk Accords, which did not end all fighting, but did in fact hold the front lines in place and end most of the fighting, at least until 24 February 2022.

So there was a history and precedent of Russian negotiating during the midst of these contests and ending them quickly. The First Chechen War was the longest of these conflicts. It lasted the better part of two years (one year, eight months, two weeks and six days). The Second Chechen War was shorter, almost nine months (eight months and 24 days). It was then followed by an extended insurgency that lasted almost nine years (eight years, 11 months and 15 days assuming an end date of 16 April 2009).[3] The war in Abkhazia in 1992–3, which established a quasi-independent region in the western part of Georgia, lasted a little over a year (one year, one month and 16 days). The Transnistria War in 1992 lasted for almost five months (four months, two weeks and five days). This ended up establishing an independent

---

2   One Crimean SDF trooper and two Ukrainian servicemen were killed in military operations from 27 February to 26 March 2014. See: https://www.reuters.com/article/us-ukraine-crisis-military-idUSBREA360GB20140407/. Crimea was annexed by Russia on 18 March 2014. There were also two civilian deaths during the protests on 26 February 2014. See: https://archive.kyivpost.com/article/content/euromaidan/two-die-in-rallies-outside-crimean-parliament-says-ex-head-of-mejlis-337708.html.

3   The end date of 16 April 2009 is from when Russia ended its "counter-terrorism operation." See: http://news.bbc.co.uk/2/hi/europe/8001495.stm.

Russian-speaking region in Moldova that still exists today and is protected by Russian peacekeeping forces. The war in Georgia lasted a little over two weeks. The seizure of Sevastopol and Crimea was over in a month (with Russian annexing them). The first war in the Donbas lasted 13 months. So, there was some precedent and wars tended to be limited in scope and duration.

This current war started on 24 February 2022. On 28 February, talks with Russia were conducted near the town of Lyakhavichy, inside southwestern Brest region of Belarus and about 30 miles from the Belarusian-Ukrainian border. This came about through the mediation of the President of Belarus, Alexander Lukashenko. The talks were initially held in person at one of his official countryside residences. This was going on while Russia, marching out of Belarus, was trying to take the capital Kyiv and sending assassination teams to kill the Ukrainian president. This was the first of several meetings over the course of a week. The lead negotiator for the Russia was Vladimir Medinsky, a senior advisor to President Putin. The Ukrainian Defense Minister Oleksii Reznikov also attended. On 3 March 2022 Medinsky spoke to the press about the negotiations, saying "Negotiations with the Ukrainian side have just ended, during which we discussed all three blocks of issues, military issues and humanitarian issues, and the issue of the future political resolution of the conflict."[4] No agreement was reached but "the key issue we've resolved today is the issue of saving people, saving the civilians who found themselves in a combat zone." Later in March there were free-passage corridors set up to allow civilians in Mariupol to escape.

This does open up the question, was Russia already aware as of 28 February, after the fourth day of their campaign, that their initial offensive was going to fail, and now was the time to talk? This was supposed to be a 72-hour blitzkrieg that would end the current Ukrainian government. Now, on day five of the war, they were meeting in a country residence to talk about a ceasefire and peace.

Still, at the start of these negotiations, Russian pressed for Ukraine to capitulate and agree to their long list of demands. It appears to be that Russia was attempting to accomplish at the negotiating table what it was not achieving on the battlefield. As the battle continued, it became clear that Russia's military situation was not a strong as it initially

---

4   https://www.nprillinois.org/2024-05-06/the-story-behind-2022s-secret-ukraine-russia-peace-negotiations. Also see: https://www.foreignaffairs.com/ukraine/talks-could-have-ended-war-ukraine.

looked, and that Ukraine was more than able to resist them in combat on the ground as well as at the negotiating table. "War is politics by another means,"[5] and in this case the shifting fortunes on the field of battle were driving the changing stature of the peace negotiations. The two were intricately linked.

Further meetings were held in Belarus on 3 March and 7 March, the talks continued afterwards online.[6] On 10 March, the foreign minister of Russia, Sergey Lavrov, and the foreign minister of Ukraine, Dmytro Kuleba, met in Ankara in Turkey.[7]

They then met again on 28 March in Istanbul. While the Russians had taken two cities (Melitopol and Kherson) in the first week of the war, they had taken no cities since then. In fact, they were contemplating (or planning) to withdraw from the areas around Kyiv and large parts of northeastern Ukraine. They met for one day on 28 March and on 29 March Medinsky stated: "Yesterday, the Kyiv authorities, for the first time in all of the previous years, declared their readiness to reach agreements with Russia. They gave us the written principles of a possible future agreement." These principles, according to Medinsky, included Ukraine not joining NATO, a renunciation of nuclear weapons (which they had already done with the Budapest Accords in 1994), a renunciation of other weapons of mass destruction (i.e. chemical and biological), and not holding military drills with foreign participation (i.e. the partnership for peace program) without the agreement of the Russian Federation. The Ukrainians did not provide details of the negotiations, but the same day, the lead negotiator for the Ukraine side, David Arakhamia, said that a final agreement could be near. He said "We think that we have worked through enough

---

5   This rather significant quite by Clausewitz is often misunderstood by many Americans. They tend to consider war and politics to be two distinctly separate subjects, and diplomacy starts as war ends. Nothing could be further from reality.

6   Ivan Grek in his article gives the location of these two meetings as Brest. He does state that the 28 February meeting was at Gomel, which contradicts other sources. See: https://www.russiapost.info/politics/ agreements#:~:text=The%20Istanbul%20communique%20likely%20 included%20nonaligned%20status%20for.

7   https://www.swp-berlin.org/publications/products/ comments/2022C65_PeaceTalksRussia_Ukraine.pdf

material so that a meeting between the presidents of Ukraine and the Russian Federations can be made possible."[8]

What they did not state was how the agreement addressed the separatist movements in Luhansk and Donetsk or the Russian annexation of Crimea and Sevastopol. It is assumed at this stage that Luhansk and Donetsk would remain independent and Crimea and Sevastopol would remain part of the Russian Federation.

What was different from the talks that started on 28 March compared to talks that started on 28 February was that it was now clear that Ukraine had successfully held back the Russian onslaught and was going to survive as a nation.[9] Its government was not going to be replaced and its president had not been assassinated. This meant that the relationship and status between the two warring parties was different than it was a month earlier. Putin's goals themselves may have changed, going from to replacing the government of Ukraine and indirectly ruling over more than half of Ukraine, to trying to find a favorable permanent position in the Donbas. It appears that the revised Russian political aims, and therefore the revised war aims, were now to complete the occupation of the Donas, which to date, Ukraine had successfully resisted.

On 29 March the Turkish Foreign Ministry stated that the talks were concluded. They had lasted one day.[10] The Ukrainian ten-point plan, also known as the Istanbul communique, was published on 29 March by a young Russian journalist.[11] The plan was stated to be 1) Ukraine declares itself a neutral state and receives international security guarantees, 2) the international security guarantees would not extend

---

8   https://www.nprillinois.org/2024-05-06/the-story-behind-2022s-secret-ukraine-russia-peace-negotiations

9   For example, *The Dupuy Institute* made a blog post on 13 April that stated "At this point, it looks like Ukraine had been saved." See: https://dupuyinstitute.org/2022/04/13/at-this-point-it-looks-like-ukraine-has-been-saved/.

10   https://www.reuters.com/world/middle-east/turkey-says-ukraine-russia-talks-istanbul-concluded-2022-03-29/#:~:text=Peace%20talks%20between%20Russian%20and%20Ukrainian%20negotiating%20teams,

11   https://meduza.io/en/slides/ukraine-s-10-point-plan#:~:text=Journalist%20Farida%20Rustamova%20obtained%20a%20list%20of%20the. Text is repeated in this article: https://michael-von-der-schulenburg.com/how-the-chance-was-lost-for-a-peace-settlement-of-the-ukraine-war/#:~:text=The%20text%20of%20the%20Istanbul%20Communiqu%C3%A9%20of%20March.

to Crimea, Sevastopol or certain areas of the Donbas, 3) Ukraine vows not to join any military coalitions or host any foreign military bases or troop contingents and the guarantors of the treaty would confirm their intention to promote Ukraine's membership in the European Union, 4) guarantor-states will provide assistant if Ukraine is attacked, 5) any such armed attacks will be reported to the UN Security Council, 6) there will be consultation with the guarantor-states about implementing protections against possible provocations, 7) the treaty enters into force after a) Ukraine's neutral status is approved by a nationwide referendum, b) the introduction of appropriate amendments to the Ukraine constitution, and c) ratification of the parliaments of Ukraine and the guarantor-states, 8) bilateral negotiations will be conducted for 15 years to resolve issues related to Crimea and Sevastopol, 9) they will continue consultations to prepare and agree on the provisions of the treaty, and 10) they will consider if possible to hold a meeting between the presidents of Ukraine and Russia. Basically, Ukraine 1) declares itself neutral, 2) its security is guaranteed by the U.S. and NATO, and 3) Russian keeps Crimea and Sevastopol and the LPR and DPR continue to exist where their borders stand (Russian officially recognized them on 21 February 2022).

It did seem that as of 29 March that a peace agreement was near. It never happened. In April Alexander Chaly, a Ukrainian negotiator and former First Deputy Minister of Foreign Affairs, said they were close to a finalized peaceful settlement in the middle of April to the end April. But, for some reason it was postponed. This postponement was permanent as of the time of writing and the war has continued for two and half years now. It looks to continue into 2025. In the meantime, by early April, the Russian Army had completely withdrawn from around Kyiv and northeastern Ukraine. Was this withdrawal a part of the peace negotiation process or was it strictly for military reasons?

How close were they to reaching peace may in fact be overstated by the participants. The following day, the Kremlin rejected talks on Crimea and Putin clearly stated that the time was not yet ripe for a ceasefire or a meeting with Zelenskyy.[12] Clearly Russia was not willing to consider any discussion of Crimea and Sevastopol, as they had annexed them and now considered them part of the Russian Federation.

---

12   https://www.swp-berlin.org/publications/products/
comments/2022C65_PeaceTalksRussia_Ukraine.pdf#:~:text=ruary%20
2022.%20The%20Istanbul%20Communiqu%C3%A9%20laid%20out%20
Ukraine%E2%80%99s

Work on a draft treaty continued online through the first half of April in spite of over a thousand murdered Ukrainian civilians being unearthed near Bucha.[13] The final draft of the agreement was prepared on 15 April, but these two sides were still far apart on many issues. One of the two main unresolved issues was security guarantees where Ukraine wanted the U.S. and NATO to guarantee their security (effectively like being a member of NATO) while Russian wanted it under the United Nations Security Council, where Russia held a veto. In effect, Russia's position did not guarantee Ukraine's security, especially as they had previously guaranteed under the UN in the Budapest Memorandum in 1994, which they violated, and Russia could veto any UN action. The other unresolved issues were the status of Crimea, Sevastopol and the Donbas. Whereas Ukraine appears to have recommended kicking the can down the road, it refused to accept Russian annexation of Crimea and Sevastopol or its recognition of the LPR and DPR. Russia considered Crimea and Sevastopol already theirs, and they had built an expensive bridge across the Kerch Strait to connect it to Russia. They clearly were also considering annexing Luhansk and Donetsk (which they later did).

Amid the murdered civilians being unearthed around Bucha and the stories of the brutal fighting and civilian casualties at Mariupol and the lack of any actual progress, the talks were finally broken off on 17 May, first by Ukraine and then Russia officially withdrew the same day. This was the day after the Azovstal steel works in Mariupol was taken by the Russians, effectively ending resistance in Mariupol.

One does wonder if this discussion would become the basis for a future peace agreement in 2025 or 2026? Would Ukraine or Russia have been better served by this peace agreement in April 2022 than by what they may end up with in 2025 or 2026 or later?

The second round of peace negotiations came about directly at the initiative of U.S. President Donald Trump. He was elected to the presidency for a second time on 5 November 2024 and took office as the president on 20 January 2025.

President-elect Trump immediately began conversations directly with Vladimir Putin and Volodymyr Zelensky in early November 2024. Donald Trump and Vladimir Putin were reported to have talked

---

13   The Bucha massacres were first uncovered on 2 April 2022. By July 2022 Kyiv police had exhumed 1,346 bodies.

on 7 November.[14] Trump had spoken to Putin multiple times during his campaign.[15] The President of Ukraine had spoken to Trump back in September and then talked to him the day after the election, on 6 November, in a call that included businessman Elon Musk.[16]

The first substantive progress towards peace talks did not come until May 2025, when a Russian delegation finally agreed to meet with a Ukrainian delegation in Turkey. This was effectively round two of the previous failed talks. The calls made and hoops people had to go through to reach this point are a little exhausting to recount and we will not detail it here. Some of it is controversial and political with lots of statements issued by various parties that did not always reflect well on them. These phone calls and discussions dragged on for months. It even included a ceasefire against energy infrastructure deal effective 19 March and an abortive "Black Sea deal" almost made on 25 March but never implemented. The ceasefire devolved into accusations from both sides of violations and both efforts quickly fell apart. The ceasefire officially ended on 18 April.

Both parties appeared to be reluctant participants, primarily because it was clear that Russian wanted to hold onto Crimea, Sevastopol, and the four provinces they had annexed, while it is clear that Ukraine wanted them all back. There was not a lot of middle ground here, especially as Russia was demanding all of Zaporizhzhia and Kherson

---

14   See "Trump talked to Putin, told Russia leader not to Escalate in Ukraine," *Washington Post*, 10 November 2024 at https://www.washingtonpost.com/national-security/2024/11/10/trump-putin-phone-call-ukraine/ and Alexander, Dubowy, "The Kremlin Said Trump-Putin Phone Call Never Happened. Why?," *The Moscow Times*, 12 November 2024 at https://www.themoscowtimes.com/2024/11/12/the-kremlin-said-trump-putin-phone-call-never-happened-why-a86990.

15   "Trump had as many as 7 private calls with Putin since leaving office, Bob Woodward writes in new book," *PBS News*, 8 October 2024 at https://www.pbs.org/newshour/politics/trump-had-as-many-as-7-private-calls-with-putin-since-leaving-office-bob-woodward-writes-in-new-book.

16   Hanna Ziady "Zelensky wants to "work directly' with Trump on ending Ukraine's war with Russia," *CNN*, 30 November 2024 at https://edition.cnn.com/2024/11/30/europe/zelensky-trump-ukraine-russia-war-intl/index.html and Tara John, Victoria Butenko, Nic Robertson and Kristen Holmes, "Elon Musk joined Trump—Zelensky call amid concerns for the future of Ukraine War," *CNN*, 8 November 2024 at https://www.cnn.com/2024/11/08/europe/ukraine-trump-elon-musk-zelensky-intl-latam.

provinces, which they had formally annexed, even though they did not control all of the land and did not control the majority of the people, nor did they control the capital city of either province. Ukraine and Russia also held completely opposing positions on joining NATO and other security guarantees.

The two delegations met in Turkey on 15 May for the first time since April 2022. Vladimir Medinsky, an aide to President Putin, led the Russian delegation. He had led the previous rounds of unsuccessful talks in 2022. The Ukrainian delegation was led by Defense Minister Rustem Umerov. Umerov was of Crimean Tatar descent and had been born in Uzbekistan in 1982 back when it was part of the Soviet Union. His family had been deported from Crimea in 1944 and had returned there in 1989. He was part of the Ukrainian peace delegation in the spring of 2022 and had been involved in negotiating prisoner exchanges. Rustem Umerov is Muslim.

President Zelenskyy of Ukraine was in Turkey that same day but in Ankara not Istanbul where the talks were being held. This was not the meeting between Putin and Zelenskyy that some people were envisioning. President Trump was in the Middle East at this time. So it does appear that people were in position for a high-level summit in Istanbul if such an effort was desired.

The talks started poorly as their positions were not only far apart but diametrically opposed on many issues. The only areas they could productively discuss was exchange of prisoners and repatriating the bodies of dead troops. This effort was successful with them agreeing to a prisoner exchange of 1,000 people that successfully occurred on 23 to 25 May.

Both sides had also agreed to hand over as many as 6,000 dead bodies as well as sick and seriously wounded prisoners of war, and those prisoners under the age of 25.[17] This exchange got delayed due to disagreements but eventually started on 11 June with an exchange of over a thousand bodies, and continued on through 16 June.

Otherwise the talks stalled from the beginning and no real progress was made. No attempt to bridge the gap occurred.

On 1 June Ukraine attacked Russia's strategic bomber bases. Talks continued at the Ciragan Palace, now a five-star hotel in Istanbul, at 13:00. On 2 June the talks in Turkey ended, although not officially

---

17   Paul Adams, Tiffany Wertheimer, "Ukraine collects 1,212 bodies in latest swap with Russia," *BBC News*, 11 June 2025.

in response to the drone attacks. It was clear that they had already reached the limit of what they could accomplish, so it was probably as good a time as any to end them.

For the rest of the month of June nothing really significant further happened with the peace talks. The United States Senate began discussing further sanctions against Russia, but there clearly were no further plans for peace discussions. Further U.S. military aid to Ukraine was still uncertain.

The three positive developments that came out of the talks were a prisoner exchange of 1,000 prisoners on each side that occurred in May, the exchange of bodies that occurred in June, and the exchange of severely wounded that also occurred in June.

There was a "third round" of negotiations at the Ciragan Palace in the evening of 23 July between the Ukraine and Russia delegations. This meeting ended after less than hour. The delegation leaders were again Rustem Umarov and Vladimir Medinsky. They ended up announcing another prisoner exchange of more than 1,200 prisoners on each side.

Otherwise, the war continued. It was clear that the two parties were further apart in June 2025 than they were in April 2022. This was after three years of war.

Chapter 6

THE PRISONER EXCHANGES

Suddenly, a Chinese soldier stuck his head over the rim of the foxhole.

They saw him, yelled "There is one" and immediately leaped for him.

The poor Chinese soldier took off running. They ran for a mile or two through the "no man's land" between the lines (which would became the DMZ) and eventually the two larger Americans were able to run him down and capture him.

Now, they were in the middle of the (soon be called) DMZ, in the middle of the night, dragging along a captured Chinese soldier, and not quite sure where their foxhole was. Furthermore, in their haste to get him, they forgot to grab their guns. For the two unarmed Americans dragging a Chinese prisoner through the dark, it was a very long and tense walk back to their foxhole.

They did get their three-day pass to Japan.

From a story by William A. Lawrence (Col. USA) from Korea in 1953.[1]

Ukraine and Russia had been exchanging prisoners since almost the start of this war. The first prisoner exchange occurred on 1 March 2022 before the Ukrainians and Russians had even sat down in Istanbul for the first round of peace talks. It continued until June when prisoner exchanges then halted for the two months of July and August for reasons not yet known. They then began again in September and continued for a year through August 2023. From September through December 2023 there were no exchanges, but they were then reinitiated in January 2024. That effort was tragically interrupted on 24 January 2024 when a Russian Il-76 transport plane went down near Belgorod that Russia reported was carrying 65 Ukrainian prisoners of war, along

---

1   From the blog post "Korean War Story," *Mystics & Statistics*, 14 November 2017.

with six Russian crew and three escorts. It crashed near the village of Yablonov, 44 miles (70 kilometers) to northeast of Belgorod at 11:00. Russan claimed that the plane was shot down using a U.S.-supplied Patriot missile system. Belgorod is only 25 miles (40 kilometers) from the Ukrainian border.

Even after that tragedy, the two nations were still able to continue prisoner exchanges, with the next one being on 31 January 2024 with 207 Ukrainian soldiers, national guard, border guards and a police officer were exchanged for 195 Russian soldiers. Between 1 March 2022 and 6 May 2025 the count of prisoners exchanged were at least 4,631 Ukrainian soldiers and volunteers and 170 civilians conducted in at least 64 trades.[2] There was a similar number of Russians prisoners in these exchanges. On 6 May 2025 the two countries exchanged 205 Russian soldiers for 205 Ukrainian prisoners. This was the fifth swap for 2025 and by some counts the 64th prisoner exchange of the war.[3]

Finally, on 16 May 2025 a thousand-person prisoner exchange was agreed to as a byproduct of the Turkish Peace Talks. The two delegations met for the first time on Friday, 16 May and after less than two hours of discussion agreed to a large prisoner swap. They agreed to nothing else over the next two weeks of talks. We do not know how involved the U.S. President was in these negotiations, but he was the first to announce the exchange, doing so a week later on Friday morning, 23 May, on his social media account with *Truth Social*.

This was the largest single prisoner swap of the war. It was conducted over three days from 23 to 25 of May, with 390 exchanged on 23 May (270 Ukrainian military and 120 Ukrainian civilians), 307 exchanged on 24 May and 303 exchanged on Sunday, 25 May. The Ukrainian prisoners released included people from the armed forces, national guard, State Border Guard Service and State Special

---

2   The number of the trade is in accordance with the Ukrainian Coordination Center for Treatment of Prisoners of War. The Wikipedia article on casualties during the war lists another 13 prisoner releases in 2022 and 2023 exchanges that are not numbered.

3   Ivana Kottasova, Victoria Butenko, Slitland Vlasova and Eve Brennan, "Ukraine and Russia exchange hundreds of prisoners, part of the biggest swap of the war," *CNN World*, 23 May 2025. The count is from the Ukrainian Coordination Center for Treatment of Prisoners of War. They do make the statement in the article that "The department said at the time that 4,757 Ukrainian citizens have been released since March 2022." The count we have is 4,631 soldiers and volunteers and 170 civilians totaling 4,801.

Transport Service. Seventy of the prisoners were survivors of the siege of Mariupol from February to May 2022.

While these exchanges were occurring, Russia was still sending waves of drones and missiles at Ukraine, 176 on the 23rd, 264 on the 24th and 367 on the 25th. The Sunday bombardment killed at least 12 people and wounded dozens of others. That Sunday attack of 367 drones and missiles was the largest single aerial attack to date in the war.

This large attack by Russia in the middle of peace negotiations, in the middle of a prisoner exchange, was a very poor public relations move. U.S. President Donald Trump, who seemed vested in achieving peace in Eastern Europe and had been considered by many to be too favorable to Russia, ended up commenting to reporters on that Sunday:

I'm not happy with what Putin is doing. He's killing a lot of people, and I don't know what the hell happened to Putin. I've known him a long time. Always gotten along with him, but he's sending rockets into cities and killing people, and I don't like it at all. Okay, we're in the middle of talking, and he's shooting rockets into Kyiv and other cities. I don't like it at all. I'm surprised. I'm very surprised.[4]

Later that evening Trump wrote on his *Truth Social* account that:

I've always had a very good relationship with Vladimir Putin of Russia, but something has happened to him. He has gone absolutely CRAZY!" He is needlessly killing a lot of people, and I'm not talking about soldiers. Missiles and drones are being shot into Cities in Ukraine, for no reason whatsoever. I've always said that he wants ALL of Ukraine, not just a piece of it, and maybe that's proving to be right, but if he does, it will lead to the downfall of Russia![5]

Needless to say, these comments were different in tone and substance to previous comments made by Donald Trump about Vladimir Putin. He did continue writing on *Truth Social* as part of the same long paragraph that:

---

4   Quotes from "Russia and Ukraine complete 1,000 prisoner swap; Moscow launches large drone and missile attack," CBS NEWS, 25 May 2025.

5   Maureen Chowdhury, Matt Meyer and Isabelle D'Antonio, "May 25, 2025: Trump presidency news," CNN Politics, May 25, 2025.

Likewise, President Zelenskyy is doing his Country no favors by talking the way he does. Everything out of his mouth causes problems, I don't like it, and it better stop. This is a War that would never have started if I were President. This is Zelenskyy's, Putin's, and Biden's War, not "Trump's," I am only helping to put out the big and ugly fires, that have been started through Gross Incompetence and Hatred.[6]

This appears to have been the point when President Trump moved away from his hard-to-understand close relationship with Putin. He did mention on the Sunday that he was considering further sanctions against Russia. He also began to move towards providing more direct support to Ukraine, which came about in July of 2025 in the form of more Patriot missiles. Needless to say, Donald Trump's relationship with Zelenskyy has always been troubled.

Just to make the sure the point was not missed, Russian fired another 364 drones and missiles at Ukraine on 26 May. The rest of May was quieter, but the political damage had been done.

The prisoner exchanges continued with another exchange of unstated numbers occurring on 4 July.[7] Then another large exchange occurred on 23 July with the release of 1,200 Russian soldiers and two civilians for at least 1,100 Ukrainian soldiers and civilians. This was part of a deal discussed in the brief meeting in Istanbul on 23 July.[8] On 28 July, Zelensky stated that Ukraine had brought home 5,857 people from captivity, with an additional 555 released outside of formal exchanges.[9] There was another smaller exchange on 14 August for 84 Russian soldiers for 33 Ukrainian soldiers and 51 civilians.

These prisoner exchanges are part of the landscape and appears to be something that Ukraine and Russia will continue to do regardless of the state of peace negotiations. Russia holds thousands of more prisoners than Ukraine.

---

6   https://truthsocial.com/@realDonaldTrump/
     posts/114571369956761390.

7   "Russia carries out 8th prisoner exchange with Ukraine since Istanbul talks," *The Moscow Times*, 4 July 2025.

8   "The Ministry of Defense announced the completion of a large exchange of prisoners with Ukraine," *Interfaks*, 23 July 2025 at https://www.interfax.ru/russia/1037749 and "Over 1,000 Prisoners exchanged in the latest Russia-Ukraine swap under Istanbul agreement," *Caspian News*, 29 July 2025.

9   "Over 5,800 Ukrainians returned from Russian captivity since full-scale invasion – Zelensky," *The New Voice of Ukraine*, 28 July 2025.

Both sides had also agreed at Istanbul to hand over as many as 6,000 dead bodies as well as sick and seriously wounded prisoners of war, and those prisoners under the age of 25. The actually agreement, according to a post made on Facebook by Rustem Umerov on 2 June was:

It seems the Russians are once again stalling for time, trying to create a "diplomatic show" for the U.S. without taking real action.

The only actual progress — the release of our people from captivity.

We have reached agreements on:
– exchange of all severely wounded and critically ill soldiers — "all for all"
– exchange of all soldiers aged 18–25 — "all for all"
– return of the fallen — 6,000 for 6,000

We also handed over a fully verified list of abducted Ukrainian children. The return of even part of them would be a humanitarian act — if Russia truly wants to move toward peace.

We also proposed a meeting at the leadership level by the end of June. Because only those who actually make decisions can bring about real decisions.

And if this is just another attempt to buy time, then there should be one response: tougher international sanctions.

Ukraine remains committed to strength, principle, and common sense.

We want peace. But not at any cost — and not on the aggressor's terms.

After some inexplicable delays, the first exchange of over a thousand bodies occurred on 11 June as part of this deal. On that day, Russian handed over to Ukraine 1,212 bodies of Ukrainian soldiers in exchange for 27 Russian bodies. This was not the first such exchange of this war, as thousands of bodies had already been exchanged in this war in 70 different exchanges.[10] On 16 June Ukraine received the remains of 1,245

---

10   "Russia and Ukraine exchange more bodies of war dead, Kremlin aide says," *Reuters*, 17 July 2025. Some of the larger exchanges in recent times have included 1) on 14 February 2025 an exchange of the remains of 757 Ukrainian soldiers for the remains of 45 Russian soldiers ("Russia and Ukraine exchange more than 800 soldier's bodies," *The Moscow Times*, 14 February 2025); 2) on 28 March of 9,090 bodies of Ukrainians

Ukrainian soldiers and citizens in exchange for the bodies of 78 Russian servicemen. This was the final repatriation under the peace accords. It resulted in a total of 6,057 Ukrainian dead being returned in June.[11]

The exchange of prisoners under the age of 26 begin on 9 June with the first soldiers being exchanged. There was no count provided on the number of prisoners exchanged, but there were videos showing the exchange that clearly show more than a dozen Ukrainians being freed. The exchange continued for several more days and including severely wounded soldiers, the critically ill and men under the age of 26. On 10 June they exchange the severely injured and ill. These were the people with amputated limbs, infections, chronic diseases. Some of

for 43 Russian bodies ("Ukraine and Russia exchange nearly 1K bodies of fallen soldiers," *The Moscow Times*, 28 March 2025), 3) on 18 April of 909 bodies of Ukrainians for 41 Russian bodies ("The number of bodies of dead soldiers of the Armed Forces of Ukraine during the exchange with Russia had increased dramatically – 'Country'," *EADaily*, 19 April 2025); 4) on 16 May 2025, just as the Istanbul talked started, of 909 bodies of Ukrainians for 34 Russian bodies ("34 vs 909: Ukraine and Russia exchanged the bodies of the dead," *EADaily*, 16 May 2025).

The second article include the following graph:

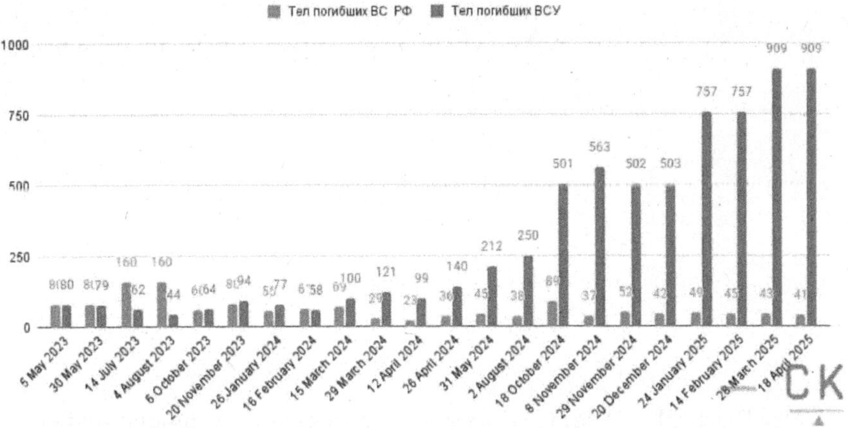

11   Tim Zadorozhnyy, "Ukraine receives 1,245 bodies of fallen soldiers and citizen, concluding Istanbul repatriation deal," *The Kyiv Independent*, 16 June 2025.

the liberated soldiers were diagnosed with hepatitis and tuberculosis.[12] The next exchange was on 12 June. Again no count was provided, but some of those released were enlisted soldiers, including sergeants, from the siege of Mariupol in February–May 2022. Some of those released this day were some previously considered missing in action.[13] Again a perusal of the videos show more than a dozen.

It is felt by some that these prisoner exchanges are a positive part of the peace process. They probably are, but the number of negative events, especially the attempted bombardment of Ukrainian cities on many days by hundreds of drones and missiles, does not strongly support the narrative that these two nations are moving towards peace. In fact, it does appear that no peace is under consideration for the duration of the 2025 military campaign season. This campaign season is expected to continue until November 2025, when the weather brings fighting to a temporary halt. So, after another six months of fighting and perhaps more taking of territory, then maybe the two parties will be ready to discuss some mutual agreeable compromise. Otherwise this war will continue into 2026.

12   Elza Diachenko, "Ukraine exchanges part of severely wounded soldiers from Russian captivity," *Gwara Media*, 10 June 2025.

13   "Another Ukraine-Russia prisoner swap: wounded missing now home (photos, video)," *RBC-Ukraine*, 12 June 2025.

Chapter 7

THE ATTACK ON THE RUSSIAN AIR FORCE

"You're right now not in a very good position… You're not in a good position. You don't have the cards right now…"

U.S. President Donald Trump to
Ukraine President Volodymyr Zelenskyy
28 February 2025[1]

The attack on the Russian air bases has been described in detail in the opening chapter of this book. Ukraine's SBU claimed that 13 airplanes were destroyed and a total of 41 were hit. The specifics of these losses is also discussed in the opening chapter of this book.

Let us look for a moment at the three of the five targeted bases that were actually hit. At Ivanovo photos clearly show two A-50s hit, of which one appears to show a seriously damaged fuselage. This is shown in the first two images of the "planes damaged or destroyed" part of the photo section. We have adjudicated that one A-50 was destroyed and other was seriously damaged. What we do not know is if either of those planes were operational before the attack.

At Olenya air base up near Murmansk it appears that four Tu-95s and one An-12 transport plane were destroyed. One can see in the photo section the photo analysis dated 3 June 2025 that was done by the telegram site "AviVector."

At Belaya out in Siberia four Tu-22Ms and three Tu-95MSs were destroyed. At least one other Tu-95MS was damaged. One can see

---

1   Sarah D. Wire, "Watch the video: Trump and Zelenskyy argue in the Oval Office," *USA Today*, 1 March 2025.

seven destroyed planes in the photo taken on 4 June and included in the photo section of this book. We have included multiple photos of this attack, as it was the most successful of the three attacks that damaged or destroyed airplanes.

By our counting, there were at least one A-50, seven Tu-95s, four Tu-22M3s and an An-12 destroyed for a total of 13 aircraft. At least one A-50 and one Tu-95MS were seriously damaged. Losses may have been higher but there is no clear evidence for this.

The photographic evidence, from multiple sources, is available to review. There is not much to dispute here. So it is provided in the photo section.

Needless to say, the attack on the Russian airfield generated a response from Russia. This is discussed in Chapters 8 and 11.

The political aspects of this operation may have been more important than the military aspects. The U.S. role in this war is significant. The Ukrainian defensive budget for this war has been about one-third from Ukrainian resources, about one-third from European NATO countries and about one-third from the U.S. With their own resources, the resources of the other NATO countries, and the resources of the United States, they have effectively been able to fight Russia to a standstill for the last three years. But, the scenario changed on 5 November 2024 when Donald Trump was elected President of the United States.

He was not committed to continuing support for Ukraine, wanting better relations with Russia and for the two parties to negotiate a peace agreement immediately. Six months into his administration (the U.S. President does not take office until 20 January), it appears that the attempts at a peace agreement failed, with the negotiations making no progress in May and the delegations withdrawing from Turkey on 2 June. It also appeared that Trump now understood that Russia was going to continue the war, if that is how one reads his comments on 25 May. The Ukrainians then tweaked the bear (Russia) on 1 June with their drone attack.

The drone attack looked devastating. It was clever and inspiring. It was not as significant as people made it out to be in the week after it occurred, but it still was a nice hit on Russian strategic bomber forces. Its political impact was that it clearly showed that Ukraine was still in the fight and was more that capable of fighting back. They still had cards to play.

These events, coupled together, have now led to a shift in United States' policy back to further sanctions against Russia and providing aid to Ukraine. Whether that will be at the level of $60 billion a year in military aid that the Biden administration was providing is yet to seen, but it probably will not be. Still, with the rest of Europe expanding their defense industry, the means for Ukraine to continue the war is still there. Therefore, the real value of this strike is more than the estimated $7 billion in losses they cost Russia. Its real value may well be in the tens of billions of aid that other countries are inspired to provide.

Operation Spider's Web certainly provided that inspiration.

Chapter 8

THE RUSSIAN AIR ATTACKS

"The more bombers, the less room for doves of peace."

Nikita Khrushchev
14 March 1958[1]

The Russians were not exactly sitting peaceful and quiet before the Ukrainian attack of 1 June 2025. From 22 through 26 May Russian had fired over 100 drones and missiles each night at Ukraine, culminating in an attack of 367 drones and missiles on 25 May followed by 364 drones and missiles the next night. On 25 May this included 60 cruise missiles and nine ballistic missiles. The following night it was another nine cruise missiles. The rest of the attacks were done by Shahed-type drones, some 653 of them over the two days.

The peace talks started on 15 May, and on that night before they met in Turkey, Russia fired 110 Shahed drones at Ukraine. The following night they fired another 112. Russia continued firing drones and missiles at Ukraine throughout the peace talks, peaking at 273 fired on the night of 18 May and then again rising to four days of heavy bombardment on 23 through 26 May (176, 264, 367 and 364 fired respectively). On the night of 31 May they unleashed an attack consisting of 114 drones and missiles. This was the attack the day before Ukraine struck back.

At no time during the peace process did the incessant bombardment of Ukraine stop. From 15 May through 2 June, which is when the talks ended, Russia had fired around 2,902 drones and missiles at Ukraine, including 78 cruise missiles with warheads of 661 to 1,102 pounds (300 to 500 kilograms) and 38 hard-to-intercept ballistic missiles with

---

1   A speech on Moscow radio, Tim Collie, "Living in Doomsday's Shadow," *Tampa Tribune*, 6 August 1995.

warheads of 1,060 to 1,540 pounds (480 to 700 kilograms). Russia was not a country ready to make peace.

It is clear that Russia was not going to relax or relent on its bombardment of Ukraine. The Ukrainian attack on Russia of 117 drones on 1 June was significant. According to Ukrainian reports, in the month of May Ukraine was attacked by 4,005 drones, 73 cruise missiles and 47 ballistic missiles.[2] This is an average of 142 drones and missiles a day. This is not an even exchange.

The Russians did strike Ukraine on the night of 31 May to 1 June with 472 Shahed-type drones, four cruise missiles and three ballistic missiles. Part (most?) of this strike occurred before the Ukrainian attacks on the air bases on that Sunday morning (1 June). This strike, recorded by Ukraine between 19:30 on 31 May and 13:30 on 1 June, was the largest strike ever made on Ukraine. The previous largest strike had been 367 drones and missiles on 25 May. Not sure how much of this attack on 1 June was done in response to Ukraine's attack, if at all. Not sure how much this strike was degraded by Ukraine's strike. Some of the attacked bombers were loaded with missiles when they were hit at around 10:30 in the morning.

Ukraine reported that of the 479 drones and missiles that attacked on 1 June, 213 were shot down, including 210 Shaheds and three Kh-101 and Iskander-K cruise missiles; and that 172 were suppressed or lost. This would imply that 94 drones and missiles got through.

Among all their actions on 1 June, Russia launched missiles at the location of one of Ukrainian training battalions located in the Dnipropetrovsk region, in the southeast area of the country. These strikes killed 12 soldiers and wounded 60.[3] In response to this strike, the same day, Major General Mykhailo Drapatyi, age 42, resigned. He was the Commander of Ground Forces of the Armed Forces of Ukraine.[4] This was the overall commander of the Ukrainian Army.

In a war that has resulted in thousands of deaths, this one attack on the training facility resulted in the resignation of Drapatyi. As he stated "As commander, I failed to ensure full execution of my orders. I didn't push hard enough, didn't convince, didn't change attitudes. That's my

---

2   Our count in Appendix I is higher because of two S-300s.

3   Telegram channel for UA Land Forces, 1 June 2025, 05:29. It stated that those were losses as of 12:50.

4   Telegram channel for Mikhailo Drapatii, 1 June 2025, 09:08. He also confirmed the figure of 12 dead.

responsibility."[5] Apparently the troops were no longer supposed to be training in a manner that made them vulnerable to such strikes.

He was reassigned on 3 June to Commander of the Joint Forces Command of the Armed Forces of Ukraine, a division of the General Staff of the Armed Forces of Ukraine. On 19 June Brigadier General Hennadii Shapovalov, age 46 or 47, took over as Commander of the Ground Forces. He had previously been commander of Operational Command South, one of the four operational commands of the Ukrainian Ground Forces.

Back on 1 March a similar strike had resulted in "several dozen dead and up to a hundred wounded" according to Ukrainian sources, and up to 150 soldiers killed including up to 30 foreign instructors according to Russian sources.[6] These deadly strikes were something had happened before and it was not supposed to happen again. At that time the Commander-in-chief of the Armed Forces of Ukraine, General Oleksander Syrsky, age 59, temporarily suspended the head of that attacked training center and the commander of the unit attacked. These training battalions are a legitimate target of war.

Then on 3 June Ukraine hit the bridge to Crimea with two underwater drones. They damaged the bridge but did not shut it down. This did not have a big impact on the ability of Russia to supply or support Crimea, which had been an issue for a while, but it did produce another "revenge strike" (my choice of words) by Russian on 6 June of 452 drones and missiles. This was only the second 400+ drone and missile strike since the start of this war. They then did it again on 9 June with 499 such weapons and another 322 the following night. It is clear that Russia was embarrassed and angered by these Ukrainian attacks and was taking this anger out on the Ukrainian population with repeated drone and missile strikes.

In Ukraine, the air defense was struggling to halt every drone and missile. On the night of 1 June, they claimed to have shot down 213 drones and missiles and 172 drones and missiles did not locate their targets. This was still 94 drones and missiles that hit targets in Ukraine.

---

5   Yuri Zoria, "Russia launches largest nighttime drone strike of the war, targets Dnipro with missiles," *Euromaidan Press*, 1 June 2025.

6   "Russia hit the location of the training unit of the Ground Forces of the Armed Forces of Ukraine. 12 people were killed," *The Moscow Times*, 1 June 2025.

Ukraine recorded impacts in 18 places.[7] That night's record-breaking attack of 479 drones and missiles, including 472 Shahed drones, ended up only injuring four Ukrainian civilians. On the other hand one Russian Iskander missile hit an undisclosed training facility in Ukraine that same night killing 12 soldiers and wounding at least 60.[8] The Russian attack the night before (31 May) using 114 drones and missiles was deadly, killing ten and wounding or injuring 33.[9]

Meanwhile, also during the night of 1 June, even before the Ukrainian drone attacks in Russia, a train with 388 passengers derailed in Russia's western Bryansk province. There was an explosion on the route which collapsed a railway bridge. The passenger train, which was traveling from Belgorod province to Moscow, derailed at the bridge. The resulting crash killed seven and injured another 66, of which 47 were hospitalized.[10] While this was not one of the deadliest Ukrainian attacks on Russia, it was significant.

A second railway bridge also collapsed that night in the Kursk region, derailing a freight train. At least one worker was injured.[11] It was a busy night for the Ukrainian secret service. On the night of 31 May, Ukraine also attacked a railway in southern Ukraine, which derailed a freight train that was heading towards Crimea. The train was carrying fuel tanks. Ukraine has attacked Russian rail and rail bridges before, although really only started their attacks in November 2023 with an explosion on the 11th derailing a freight train in Ryazan province using an Improvised Explosive Device (IED), and two attacks on the 30th, one by sabotage of the railway near Moscow and one being a series of four explosions in the world's longest rail tunnel, the 15-kilometer long

---

7   David Brennan, "Ukraine targets Russian airfields in major drone attack," *ABC News*, 1 June 2025.

8   Yuri Zoria, "Russia launches largest nighttime drone strike of the war, targets Dnipro with missiles," *Euromaidan Press*, 1 June 2025.

9   Oleksiy Pshemyskiy, Morgan Winsor and Jon Haworth, "At least 10 killed, 33 injured in Russian attacks across Ukraine overnight, officials say," *ABC News*, 21 May 2025.

10   David Brennan, "Ukraine targets Russian airfields in major drone attack," *ABC News*, 1 June 2025.

11   David Brennan, "Ukraine targets Russian airfields in major drone attack," *ABC News*, 1 June 2025.

Severomuysky Tunnel in the far eastern Siberian Republic of Buryatia that unsuccessfully targeted a freight train.[12]

The deadliest attack against Russia occurred on 30 December 2023 when Ukraine "shelled" the city of Belgorod. The attacking weapons were reported to be "Czech-made" Vampire rockets and Ukrainian-built Vilkha (Olkha) missiles fitted with cluster-munition warheads.[13] According to Russia it resulted in the death of at least 25 people and the wounding of 108.[14] Belgorod (pop. 339,978 in 2021 census) is only 25 miles (40 kilometers) north of the border with Ukraine. It is 49 miles (79 kilometers) north of Kharkiv, Ukraine's second largest city.

This was not unprecedented for the day before, on 29 December 2023, Russia had fired 122 cruise and ballistic missiles and 36 drones on

---

12   "Media: SBU set off explosion in railway tunnel in Russia's Far East," *The Kyiv Independent*, 30 November 2023.

13   "Shelling kills 21 in Russian city of Belgorod following Moscow's aerial attacks across Ukraine," *AP*, 30 December 2023. This has not been verified. The Vampire missile referred is certainly the L3Harris Vampire. It was ordered by the U.S. DOD in January 2023 to be shipped to Ukraine. See "L3Harris VAMPIRE Multi-purpose Weapon System, USA," *Army Technology*, 9 February 2023. Not sure why Russian press refers to it as "Czech-made" as L3 Harris is a U.S. company located in Florida and its purchases and deployment to Ukraine was funded by the U.S. This was a system first developed in 2021, and advanced prototype was submitted to the DOD and April 2022, and was included in the U.S. $3 billion security assistance packed in August 2022. The contract for $40 million was to deliver 14 Vampire systems. Four systems were delivered by mid-2023 and the other ten planned to be delivered by the end of the year.
      The Vilkha has a maximum range of 70 kilometers and a warhead weight of 250 kilograms. The Vilkha-M has a maximum range of 130 kilometers and warhead weight of 170 kilograms. Its 300mm launchers are mounted 12 to a vehicle. The Vilkha entered service in 2018 and the Vilkha-M was first used in combat in May 2022. See: Howard Altman, "Ukraine is using guided rockets with more range than HIMARS-launched ones," *TWZ*, 1 March 2023.

14   Radina Gigova, Darya Tarasova, Mariya Knight, Maria Konstenko. Tim Lister and Xiaofei Xu, "Russia says toll from Ukrainian shelling on border city has risen to 24 as it vows to retaliate," *CNN World*, 21 December 2023. They give a total of 24 killed and 108 wounded. Victoria Safronova, "Ukraine war: Russians find no shelter in border city of Belgorod," *BBC News Russian*, 4 January 2024 says it was 25 killed. Wikipedia (30 December 2023 Belgorod Shelling) says it was 25 killed and 108 wounded.

Dyagilevo air base (NASA FIRM 2024-10-19, the terrain imagery is older and undated).

Dyagilevo air base with planes, including A-50s, Tu-22Ms and Tu-95s. 12 September 2013 (photo by Aleksandr Beltyukov).

Ivanovo Severny air base (NASA FIRM 2024-11-03, the terrain imagery is older and undated).

Ivanovo Severny air base with A-50s (from "Mechnikef," undated but on or before 17 February 2011).

Olenya air base (NASA FIRM 2024-10-17, the terrain imagery is older and undated).

The British battleship HMS *Glory* in Murmansk (1918 or 1919).

Belaya air base (NASA FIRM 2024-10-18, the terrain imagery is older and undated).

Tupolev Tu–22M0, one of ten pre-production aircraft at Belaya air base, 10 August 2005 (photo by Gleb Osokin of the Russian AviaPhoto Team).

Ukrainka air base (NASA FIRM 2024-11-03, the terrain imagery is older and undated).

A Tupolev Tu-95 taking off from the Ukrainka air base in April 2006 (photo by Dmitriy Pichugin at https://russianplanes.net/id45088).

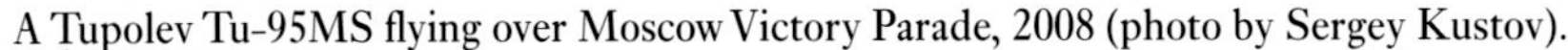

A Tupolev Tu-95, 15 May 1974 (source DOD).

A Tupolev Tu-95MS flying over Moscow Victory Parade, 2008 (photo by Sergey Kustov).

A Tupolev Tu–22, 1 August 1982 (source DOD).

A Tupolev Tu–22M3M Gefest, 2 July 2015 (photo by Dmitry Terekhov).

A Tupolev Tu-160 flying over Moscow, Victory Day Parade 2015 (photo by Aleksandr Beltyukov).

A Beriev A-50U, 10 March 2017 (photo by Sergey Lutsenko and Timofey Nikishin).

An Ilyushin Il-78M, 2013 (photo by Konstantine Tyurpeko).

The Osa Drones

The Osa FPV drone (First Contact).[1] It is a quadripod takeoff platform and lacks a battery and munition.

---

1   From "Ukraine's First Contact Company is Developing A.I.-powered Aerial Attack Drones," *Defense Express*, 6 January 2024 at https://en.defence-ua.com/weapon_and_tech/ukraines_first_contact_company_is_developing_ai_powered_aerial_attack_drones-9093.html.

The Osa FPV drone (First Contact). Still appears to lack a munition.

The Osa drone with its integrated skids. These carried the shaped–charge explosives (Tsenzor.net).[2]

---

2 https://euromaidanpress.com/2025/06/03/meet–first–contacts–osa–the–ukraine–fpv–
   drone–used–to–strike–russian–bombers–in–spiderweb–operation/.

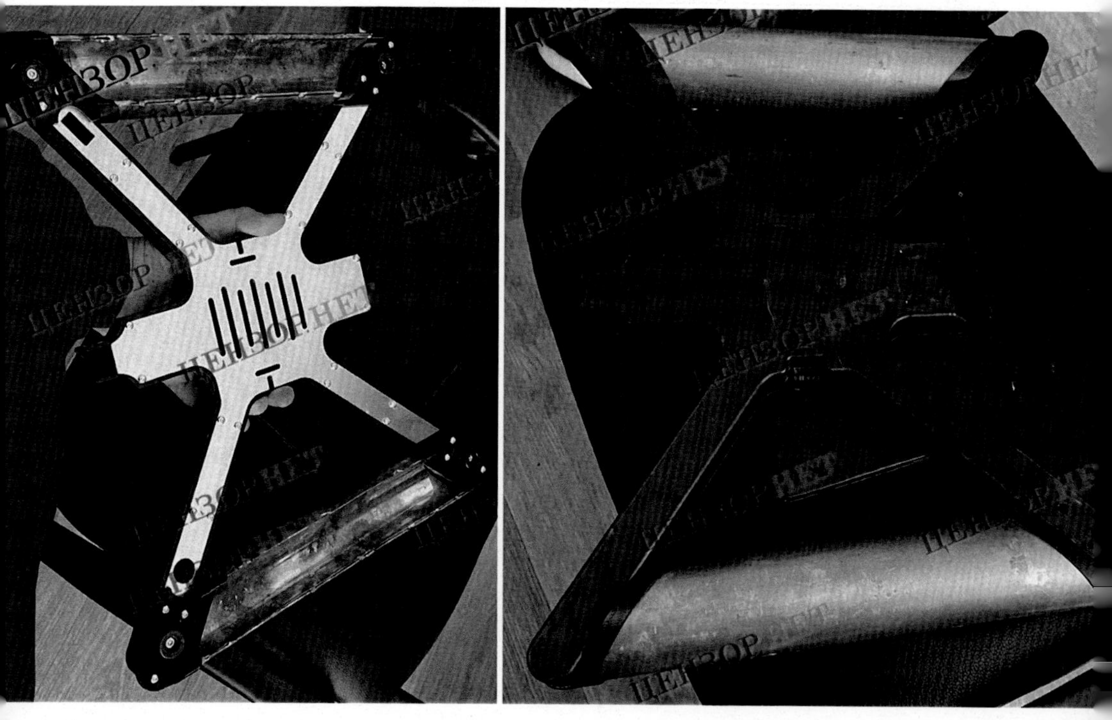

The Osa drones is what appears to be their shipping containers (SBU).[3] There appear to be 27 drones in this container.

---

3   James Marson, Jane Lytvynenko, Brenna T. Smith, Serhii Bosak, "Inside the Ukrainian Drone Operation That Devastated Russia's Bomber Fleet," *The Wall Street Journal*, 3 June 2025.

Picture of truck driving into a petrol station at Olenegorsk, Murmansk Oblast.[4]

---

4   Roman Petrenko, "Ukrainian drones launched from lorries target Russian airfields, reports claim – videos," *Ukrainska Pravda 25*, 1 June 2025. It is not certain if this is the truck. The video this picture is taken from shows the truck drive into the station and past the camera. Then a drone is seen flying in the sky.

Picture of truck used to release the drones that attacked Belaya air base. Photo released by the Governor of Irkutsk Oblast on Sunday, 1 June 2025.[5]

---

5   Samya Kullab, "A surprise drone attack on airfields across Russia encapsulates Ukraine's wartime strategy," *AP*, 2 June 2025.

Same truck, now on fire.

A similar truck exploding near Ukrainka, Amur Oblast, 1 June 2025.[6]

---

6   "Truck carrying Ukrainian Drones explodes June 1 in Russia's Amur Oblast;
     Person enters container before blast," *DeepNewZ*, 1 June 2025.

Chart from Ukraine Air Force Command Facebook page posted on 3 June 2023 showing activity for May 2023.

Chart from Ukraine Air Force Command Facebook page posted on 9 July 2025. This is the biggest attack of the war.

The Shahed drone, as deployed by the Houthis in Yemen (Dan Zeevi).[7]

———————————

7   Photo taken from article by Dan Zeevi, "Yemeni Houthis Display Iranian Drones and Loitering Missiles," *Defense Updated*, 27 September 2022.

A Russian Olan-10 reconnaissance drone being carried by a soldier. It is not armed. It has been in use since the war in Donbas in 2014. The photo is dated 27 August 2020 (Ministry of Defense of the Russian Federation).

Planes Damaged or Destroyed

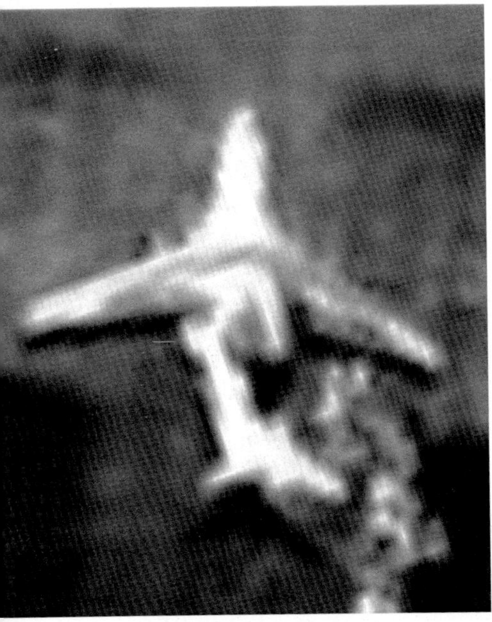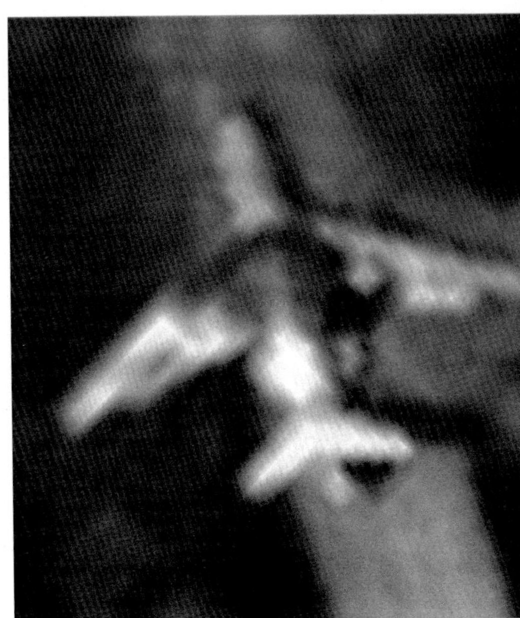

Blurred image of the two Beriev A-50s hit at Ivanovo Severy air base. The one on the left looks like it has been destroyed (from @TallbarFIN, 3 June 2025). Some of the dark areas across the wings are where tired were stacked.

Photo analysis done by the Telegram site "AviVector" on 3 June 2025 of Olenya air base. It shows what they are counting as four Tu-95MS destroyed and an An-12 destroyed. The other four images in this series shows each of the destroyed planes in more detail.

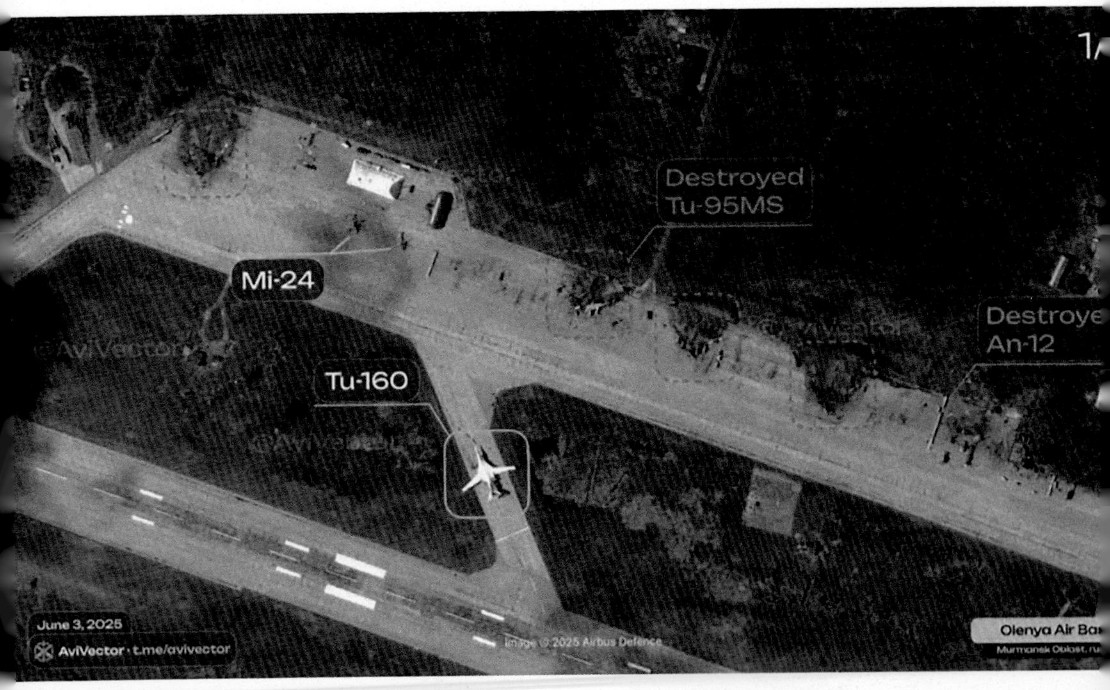

Ukraine in the largest and deadliest strike of the war to date. Ukraine claimed to have intercepted 87 of the missiles (71%) and 27 of the drones (75%). These strikes killed at least 55 Ukrainians and wounded more than 160.[15] It is estimated that eighteen Tu-95 strategic bombers were used, launching at least 90 Kh-101 missiles by about 06:00.[16] This included nine Tu-95MS from Olenya air base near Murmansk.[17]

Russia then followed-up on 2 January 2024 with 134 drones and missiles, staring the 35 Shahed drones early in the morning followed by at least 99 missiles (70 Kh-101, 12 Iskander-M, 10 Kh-47, and 4 Kh-31P, 2 S-300 and at least one North Korean Hwasong-11A (KN-23) missile). Ukraine claimed to have intercepted all 35 drones (100%) and 72 out of 99 missiles (73%). Both S-300s targeted on Kharkiv got through and did 11 of the Kh-101 targeted at Kharkov and Kyiv. Have not been able to confirm the status of the North Korea missile but it was claimed in a White House briefing by National Security Communications Advisor Rear Admiral John Kirby.[18] Ukraine State Emergency Service reported five people were killed and 130 were wounded in Kyiv and Kharkiv.[19] This had clearly devolved into a tit-for-tat exchange that was primarily harming civilians.

Ukrainian attacks on Russia had killed civilians. We count a total of 162 civilians and military killed in Russia from 11 May 2022 to 25 April

---

15   "Update: Death toll of Russia's mass air attack on Ukraine rises to 41," *The Kyiv Independent*, 30 December 2023. The count by regional reports in Wikipedia (29 December 2023 Russian strikes on Ukraine) adds up to 55 killed and 149 injured: 33 killed in Kyiv and 35 injured, 7 killed in Dnipro and 30 injured, 2 killed in Odesa and 15 injured, 1 killed in Lviv and 30 injured, 3 killed in Kharkiv and 13 injured, 9 killed in Zaporizhzhia and 13 injured, 9 people injured in Cherkasy Oblast, 3 people injured in Sumy Oblast. Wikipedia (29 December 2023 Russian strikes on Ukraine) says it was at least 58 killed and 160 injured.

16   From Air Force Command Facebook page.

17   Olena Ivanshkiv, "Nine Tu-9MS strategic bombers take off in Russia," *Ukrainska Pravda 25*, 29 December 2023 and Atle Staalesen, "Bombers from Kola Peninsula take center stage in terror bombing of Ukraine," *Eye on the Arctic*, 29 December 2023.

18   Volodymyr B., The Russians attacked Ukraine with North Korean ballistic missiles," *MilitaryNYI*, 4 January 2024 and John Hudson, "Russia fires missiles supplied by North Korea into Ukraine, says U.S. intelligence," *The Washington Post*, 4 January 2024.

19   Daria Shulzhenko, "Update: 5 killed, 130 injured in Russia's large-scale attack against Ukraine," *The Kyiv Independent*, 2 January 2024.

2025 (see Appendix II). In contrast, the United Nations has estimated that Ukrainian civilian dead from this war is at least 13,580 as of the end of June 2025, with June being the bloodiest in month in three years. As they point out, **"Long-range strikes with missiles and loitering munitions** in urban areas **caused the majority of civilian casualties in June (53 per cent)**… In June 2025, the number of missiles and loitering munitions launched by the Russian Federation into Ukraine was over **10 times higher** than in June 2024."[20] As of the third anniversary of the war (24 February 2025) some 210 civilians had been killed in Kyiv, according to Kyiv mayor and former heavy weight boxing world championship Vitalii Klitshko.[21]

On 6 June 2025, 452 drones and missiles were reported fired. It appears that 39 Shahed drones, 6 cruise missiles (Kh-101s) and one Kh-31P anti-radio location missiles got through Ukrainian defenses. The United Nations reported seven civilians killed and 53 wounded that night. June 9 and 10 was similar, with 57 Shahed drones and one cruise missile getting through Ukrainian defenses on those two days.

This process continued throughout the month, with another 472 drones and missiles fired on 17 June, 268 drones and missiles fired on 23 June, 371 drones and missiles fired on 27 June, and a record breaking 537 drones and missiles fired on 29 June.

The United Nations reported seven killed and 53 injured on 6 June, another 10 killed and 25 injured on 7 June, 29 killed and 152 injured on 17 June with the majority of casualties (27 killed and 132 injured) occurring in the capital, 12 killed and 53 injured on 23 June, and 21 killed and 256 injured on 24 June. United Nations reports are usually reasonably accurate, with them probably undercounting, especially in the early days of the Russo-Ukrainian War.

The drones and missiles fired at Ukraine in the month of June is summarized below.[22]

---

20 See: Ukraine: Protection of Civilians in June 2025 (Office of the High Commissioner, United Nations Human Rights, 10 July 2025) at Ukraine_protection_of_civilians_in_armed_conflict_June_2025_ENG.pdf.

21 Stepan Haftko, "201 civilians, including 11 children, killed in Kyiv over 3 years of war", *Ukrainska Pravda*, 24 February 2025.

22 Ukrainian Air Force Command Facebook page at https://www.facebook.com/kpszsu.

Drones & Missiles Fired (June 2025):

				P-800 Onyx		
				Kh-22, Kh-35		
				Kh-101, Kh-59/69	Kh-47M2	
			Kh-31	Kalibr, Iskander-K	Iskander-M	S-300
	Total	**Shahed-type**	**Air-to-surface**	**Cruise Missiles**	**Ballistic Missiles**	**Others**
1 June	479	472		4	3	
2 June	84	80		1	3	
3 June	112	112				
4 June	95	95				
5 June	104	103			1	
6 June	452	407	1	38	6	
7 June	215	206		7	2	
8 June	52	49		3		
9 June	499	479	2	14	4	
10 June	322	315		5	2	
11 June	86	85			1	
12 June	63	63				
13 June	59	55			4	
14 June	58	58				
15 June	194	183		8	3	
16 June	138	138				
17 June	472	440	1	29	2	
18 June	58	58				
19 June	104	104				
20 June	86	86				
21 June	280	272		6	2	
22 June	50	47			2	1
23 June	368	352		5	11	

24 June	97	97				
25 June	71	71				
26 June (08:00)	41	41				
27 June (09:30)	371	363		6	2	
28 June	23	23				
29 June (08:30)	537	477		46	11	3
30 June	107	107				
Totals	**5,677**	**5,438**	**4**	**172**	**59**	**4**
Daily Average:	189					

Mondays are in bold. All reports are given for 09:00 unless stated otherwise.

During this time, President Trump was regularly speaking to Vladimir Putin. They held their sixth phone call of the year on 3 July. Other phone calls had occurred on 12 February, 18 March, 19 May, 4 June and 14 June 2025. The night of 28 June to 29 June, Putin fired a record-breaking 537 drones and missiles at Ukraine. On the night of 3 to 4 July, after the phone call with Donald Trump, he fired another record-breaking volley of 550 drones and missiles at Ukraine. At least 72 of them got through and two people were killed and another 26 wounded.[23] It is pretty hard not to clearly see the message that President Putin was sending. On 5 July Russia fired another 322 drones and missiles.

Three days after the Operation Spider's Web attacks, on Wednesday, 4 June at 10:00(EST), President Trump had a 75-minute phone call with Vladimir Putin. President Trump said he had a "good" conversation with Putin, but that it was "not a conversation that will lead to immediate peace." They discussed Ukraine's Operation Spider's Web drone attacks, which had occurred on Sunday. As Trump noted "President Putin did say, and very strongly, that he will have to respond to the

---

23   Kateryna Hodunova, Dmytro Basmat, and Abbey Fenbert, "'Nothing but terror and murder' – Russia pounds Kyiv with record overnight drone, missile attack, 2 dead, 26 injured," *The Kyiv Independent*, updated 5 July 2025.

recent attack on the airfields." According to Russia, Trump "confirmed again that the Americans were not informed about this in advance." Trump posted his comments to his social media account *Truth Social*.[24]

On 24 June, President Zelenskyy stated in a speech to the Dutch Parliament that since the start of Russia's full-scale invasion, Moscow has launched 28,743 Shahed-type drones at Ukraine, with 2,736, roughly 9.5%, fired in June 2025 alone.[25]

Below is the list of attacks conducted in July.

Drones & Missiles Fired (July 2025):

			Kalibr Kh-59/69		
			Kh-101	Iskander-M	
			Iskander-K	Kh-47	S-300
	Total	**Shahed-type**	**Cruise Missiles**	**Ballistic Missiles**	**Other**
1 July	52	52			
2 July	118	114			4
3 July	52	52			
4 July (08:00)	550	539	4	7	
5 July (09:30)	322	322			

---

24 See: David Brennan and Meredith Deliso, "Trump says he had 'good' call with Putin but peace not 'immediate'," *ABC NEWS*, 4 June 2025. The *Truth Social* post said: "I just finished speaking, by telephone, with President Vladimir Putin, of Russia. The call lasted approximately one hour and 15 minutes. We discussed the attack on Russia's docked airplanes, by Ukraine, and also various other attacks that have been taking place by both sides. It was a good conversation, but not a conversation that will lead to immediate Peace. President Putin did say, and very strongly, that he will have to respond to the recent attack on the airfields. We also discussed Iran…" See: https://www.snopes.com/fact-check/trump-putin-phone-call-truth-social/.

25 Olena Goncharova, "Russia had launched over 28,000 Shahed drones at Ukraine since 2022, with nearly 10% fired in June along, Zelensky says, *The Kyiv Independent*, 25 June 2025.

6 July (08:30)	161	157			4
7 July (09:30)	105	101			4
8 July (08:00)	58	54			4
9 July (08:30)	741	728	7	6	
10 July (10:00)	415	397	6	8	4
11 July (13:00)	79	79			
12 July (10:00)	623	597	26		
13 July	60	60			
14 July (08:30)	140	136			4
15 July (13:00)	267	267			
16 July (08:30)	401	400		1	
17 July (08:30)	64	59 + 5			
18 July (08:30)	35	29 + 6			
19 July (10:30)	379	344	23	12	
20 July	no report				
21 July (09:30)	450	426	19	5	
22 July	42	42			
23 July	71	71			
24 July (11:30)	107	103	4		

25 July	63	61	2		
26 July (09:30)	235	208	15	12	
27 July (10:30)	83	83			
28 July (09:30)	331	324	4	3	
29 July	39	37		2	
30 July	78	78			
31 July	317	309	8		
Totals	**6,438**	**6,240**	**118**	**56**	**24**
Daily Average:	215 (the day with "no report" is not included).				

Mondays are in bold. All reports are given for 09:00 unless stated otherwise.

These charts are based solely upon Ukrainian Air Force Command data. The meaning of "intercepted" is open to interpretation, which is why we use the phrase "failed to reach target." The Ukrainian reporting at this does vary over time. So, for example they reported on 23 June that 354 (out of 368) targets were damaged. They then stated further down that it was 158 shot down and 196 lost location. The following day they report 78 destroyed (vice damaged) and further down they state that 63 were shot own and 15 lost location or "suppressed REB."

On 1 August they summarized the air defense activity for July as 6,262 air targets destroyed by anti-aircraft defense forces. We assume this means shot down, jammed, or got lost and didn't crash near a target. They broke the count out as 2,990 Shahed-type drones, 98 cruise missiles (65 Kh-101, 4 Kalibr, 9 Kh-59/69, 20 Iskander-K), 19 ballistic missiles (Iskander-M), 912 intelligence drones, and 2,242 drones of other types. Not sure why these do not match exactly with the summation from the daily reports, but they are close enough.

This 1 August report is useful in that it gives a count of the number of sorties the Ukrainian Air Force did during the month, some 790. Of those 550 were for aviation cover and guessing that most of those sorties were safely behind the front lines, but over 160 were for "fire and aviation support for the troops." We gather there were up to 80 sorties that were neither. Still, 160 ground-attack type sorties is impressive for an air force that faced overwhelming airpower since the start of the war.

The drone and missile activity from February 2022 to May 2025 is summarized in Appendix I. This is as reported by Ukraine, and it has not been possible to cross-check it with Russian reports. There is no reason to doubt the overall accuracy of these reports, even though there are certainly errors in each report each day. We do not think the overall counts are in any way inflated.

The decline in the percent that failed to reach the target in later reporting may be due to more stringent reporting on the part of the Ukrainian command as opposed to more effective Russian offensive capabilities and less capable Ukrainian defensive capabilities.

The number of drones and missiles launched on any given day appear to be tied to various political events and even conversations or statements made by Donald Trump. Just to flag a few of these:

Date	Event	Drones and missiles fired in response
23 May	Prisoner exchanges start	23 May: 176
		24 May: 264
		25 May: 367
		26 May: 364
1 June	Ukrainian drone attack	1 June: 479
3 June	Ukraine strikes Kerch Strait bridge	6 June: 452
3 July	Donald Trump talks to Putin	4 July: 550

Now, there is no clear evidence tying these strikes to specific events. It is assumed that most of the time these strikes are planned days ahead of time. For example, on 3 June Putin is reported in his talks with Donald Trump to be still planning a response for 1 June. It does not appear that this response occurred until 6 June. This implies at least a five-day lag between the event and the response. Therefore, the timing of some of these strikes could be simply spurious correlation. Still, if access is obtained to Russian planning and orders, this would be worth exploring as the appearance is that Vladimir Putin was specifically firing large volleys for the sake of making a political statement or in response to events. Even if this is not entirely the case, it is the appearance.

The 3 July Phone Call

Amid all this violence there was an hour-long phone call between Donald Trump and Vladimir Putin on Thursday morning, 3 July. This call is worth exploring as it demonstrates the posturing going and some significant shifts in relationships.

Trump later told reporters on the day of the call that he "didn't make any progress with him today at all" on Ukraine in his call with Putin.[26] This call came two days after the DOD had paused weapon systems shipments to Ukraine. Putin's foreign policy advisor said that the issue of U.S. weapons supply to Ukraine did not come up in the call. Trump also stated when he talked to reporters that the U.S. had not paused weapons to Ukraine with the qualification that 'we have to make sure we have enough for ourselves." The talks, according to Putin's foreign policy advisor, also included a detailed discussion on Iran and the situation in the Middle East. He also said that Putin told Trump that Russia is not going to give up on its goals in Ukraine and that Russia sees its peace talks with Ukraine as a bilateral issue that the U.S. should not be actively involved in.[27]

Now, one hates to get into all the history, polemics, double-talk and manipulations behind these statements, but the Budapest Memorandum on Security Assurances was signed in 1994 by Ukraine, Russia, the U.S. and Britian. The memorandum both disarmed Ukraine of nuclear weapons and provided security guarantees by all signing parties. Russia clearly violated the Budapest Memorandum in 2014, so it hard to understand how this now becomes only a "bilateral issue." But that is the argument that Russia was making.

On 4 July Russia fired 539 drones and 11 missiles at Ukraine. This was a new record. They had also damaged the Polish consulate in central Kyiv. It is reported that the Foreign Minister of Poland called the U.S. special envoy for Ukraine, Lt. General Keith Kellogg, in the early morning of 4 July to say that "Putin is mocking your peace efforts." He then requested "Please restore supplies of anti-aircraft ammunition to Ukraine." At the time, weapons deliveries to Ukraine had been frozen by the U.S. government two days earlier for reasons that were never entirely clear.

---

26   Tim Zadorozhnyy, "Putin tells Trump Russia won't back down from its war aims in Ukraine," *The Kyiv Independent*, 3 July 2025.

27   Barak Ravid, "Trump says he made no progress on Ukraine in his call with Putin," *Axios*, 3 July 2025.

Kellogg then called President Trump that morning and pushed for the resumption of Patriot air-dense missiles being sent to Ukraine. Trump agreed, and Kellogg called U.S. Secretary of Defense to tell him to resume deliveries to Kyiv. This pause in aid was rumored to have blindsided Trump, Secretary of State Marco Rubio and General Kellogg. It appears to have been a unilateral act by the Department of Defense. That same day Trump informed Volodymyr Zelensky that they would help with Kyiv's air defense.[28]

On Monday, 14 July, Donald Trump, after a weekend of posting about Russia and Ukraine on social media, announced the new supplies for Ukraine. The announcement included:[29]

1. The U.S. will sell around $10 billion in weapon to NATO allies. This certainly includes Patriot missiles.
2. Give Russia 50 days to agree to a ceasefire to avoid sanctions and tariffs.

This last point was unusual as it effectively gave Putin until 2 September before any sanctions were initiated. There was a sanctions bill about to be passed by the Senate which was then suspended. In the phone call of 3 July with Putin, it is rumored Putin said he was going to conduct offensive operations for the next 60 days. These dates do match up, leaving some to interpret the delay to mean that Trump was giving Putin a blank check to continue his offensives for two months.[30]

Now, selling $10 billion in weapons is very different from the last aid package done by the previous administration, which was $63 billion in direct aid or direct purchases that were then shipped to Ukraine. Since the war has begun, the United States had provided Ukraine with $175 billion in aid.[31] In effect, the United States had been providing Ukraine around $60 billion a year each year as had our NATO allies. The United States aid flow had stopped, but that is not the case for the other members of NATO.

---

28 Joe Barnes, "The full, untold story of Trump's U-turn on Ukraine," *The Telegraph*, 25 July 2025.

29 The full set of supplies are reported to include missiles, air defense systems and artillery shells.

30 Jamie McIntyre, "'I'm not done with him.' Trump gives Putin 50 days to complete the goals of his summer offensive in Ukraine," *Washington Examiner*, 15 July 2025.

31 Jonathan Masters and Will Merrow, "Here's how much aid the United States had sent to Ukraine," *Council on Foreign Relations*, 15 July 2025.

This was referred to as a "seismic policy shift" from Trump.[32] It was a change in policy, but far from a complete turnaround to the policy of the previous administration. It was more of a 90-degree turn than a complete 180-degree turn. It was not providing additional aid directly to Ukraine to the tune of over $60 billion a year as was done by the Biden administration. In fact, it was providing no direct aid to Ukraine. An additional $10 billion in weapons, paid for by other NATO countries, was still a big help. These supplies are a needed boost to Ukraine's defenses, and some of it had already been gathered near U.S. ports and was ready to ship.

A number of reports came out of those talks. First was that "Putin indicated over the next 60 days he would make a renewed push to occupy territory up to the administrative lines of the Ukrainian regions in which Russia has a significant foothold."[33] Now, as Russian had formally annexed the four provinces of Lugansk, Donetsk, Zaporizhzhia and Kherson back on 20 September 2022, then this implies that he intended to take the entirety of these four provinces. This would include the cities of Sloviansk and Kramatorsk, which he failed to take in the summer of 2022. It would also include the large city of Zaporizhzhia, which he has never been close to taking. Finally, it would include the city of Kherson, which Ukraine retook in November 2022 and is now well protected behind the Dnipro River. This is an ambitious effort for an army that in 2023 and 2024 was unable to take much more than a thousand square kilometers in any year. As of the date this book was sent to publication (October 2025), it does not appear that this has happened. If this was what Putin said in his call, then this appears to have been a very shallow bluff. Shortly after the call, Trump told French President Emmanual Macron that "He wants to take all of it."[34]

Putin's rather aggressive stance in the 3 July call, if true, appears to have finally forced Donald Trump to change his position. If so, that was a costly phone call for Russia. There may be no relationship but the strike by Ukraine on 1 June may have set the stage. There was a

---

32   The phase "seismic policy shift" is from *Axios*. This author does not consider it as such. See: Dave Lawler, Barak Ravid, "Trump to supply missiles to Ukraine, gives Russia 50-day ultimatum," *Axios*, 14 July 2025.

33   Barak Ravid, Marc Caputo, "Trump to announce 'aggressive' Ukraine weapons plan," *Axios*, 13 July 2025.

34   Barak Ravid, Marc Caputo, "Trump to announce 'aggressive' Ukraine weapons plan," *Axios*, 13 July 2025.

40-minute phone call with Zelenskyy the day after the call with Putin, on 4 July, where it was reported that President Trump told Ukrainian President Zelenskyy that the U.S. wanted to help Ukraine with air defense.[35] In April Russia fired at least 2,596 drones and missiles. In May Russia fired 4,127 drones and missiles. In June they fired 5,677 drones and missiles.

The other interesting rumor is that the shipment included long-range missiles that had the ability to reach as far as Moscow from Ukraine. This was amplified by the rumor that Trump asked Zelenskyy to strike at Moscow, so as to help force Putin to the negotiating table. Neither of these rumors have been confirmed.

With talks on hold, the drone activity quieted down in August. What does stand out is the lower interception rate. It was 85% the last two months (85.5% in June). Now it was 77% through 11 August.[36] Not sure what caused this difference other than drone strikes were more targeted and less aimed at large defended cities.

Drones & Missiles Fired (August 2025):

| | | | | Kalibr
Kh-101
Iskander-K
Kh-22 | Kh-47
Iskander-M | Unknown
S-300 |
| | | | | | | |
	Total	**Shahed-type**	**Air-to-surface**	**Cruise Missiles**	**Ballistic Missiles**	**Other**
1 August	72	72				
2 August	53	45 + 8				
3 August	83	76		1	1	5
4 August (11:30)	163	162			1	
5 August (08:00)	47	46			1	
6 August	45	45				

---

35 Barak Ravid, "Trump tells Zelensky he wants to help Ukraine with air defense, sources say," *Axios*, 4 July 2025.

36 Totals though 11 August is 903/693 = 77%. The interception rate did go up during the month, averaging 83% for the month.

7 August	112	112				
8 August (08:00)	108	104 + 4				
9 August	49	47		2		
10 August (08:00)	100	100				
11 August	71	71				
12 August	52	48			4	
13 August	51	49			2	
14 August	47	45				2
15 August (08:00)	99	97			2	
16 August (08:00)	86	85			1	
17 August	61	60			1	
18 August	144	140			4	
19 August	280	270		5	5	
20 August	95	93			2	
21 August	614	574		33	6	1
22 August	55	55				
23 August (08:30)	49	49				
24 August (08:30)	73	72			1	
25 August (08:00)	104	104				
26 August	59	59				
27 August	95	95				
28 August	629	598		20	11	
29 August (08:00)	68	68				
30 August	582	537		37	8	
31 August	142	142				
Totals	**4,288**	**4,132**		**98**	**50**	**8**

Air Defense Efforts (August 2025):

	Total	Failed to Reach Target	Percent Failed
1 August	72	44	
2 August	53	45	
3 August	83	61	
4 August (11:30)	163	161	
5 August (08:00)	47	29	
6 August	45	36	
7 August	112	89	
8 August (08:00)	108	82	
9 August	49	17	
10 August	100	70	
11 August	71	59	
12 August	52	36	
13 August	51	34	
14 August	47	24	
15 August (08:00)	99	63	
16 August (08:00)	86	61	
17 August	61	40	
18 August	144	88	
19 August	280	236	
20 August	95	63	
21 August	614	577	
22 August	55	46	
23 August (08:30)	49	36	
24 August (08:30)	73	48	
25 August (08:00)	104	76	
26 August	59	47	
27 August	95	74	

28 August	629	589	
29 August (08:00)	68	46	
30 August	582	548	
31 August	142	126	
Total	**4,288**	**3,551**	**83%**

Mondays are in bold. All reports are given for 09:00 unless stated otherwise.

With Trump saying he was going to take no real action until 2 September, Russia had a free hand to conduct offensive operations. These were insignificant, with them gaining only 218 square miles (564 square kilometers) of territory in July. This is an area less than half of the U.S. territories of Guam or Samoa, or a little more than half of Fairfax County in Northern Virginia. The areas taken in both May and June were similar.[37] This was not quite the massive offensive that Putin had hinted at. It had yet to take a major town, although Pokrovsk (pop. 60,127 in 2022 estimate), 43 miles (70 kilometers) northwest of Donetsk, was being threatened.[38] Russia was a fair way from taking any cities. Perhaps it was a negotiation ploy.

August also has not yielded any significant advances and Pokrovsk, in Donetsk Oblast, still remains under Ukrainian control, although it is severely threatened. Meanwhile Trump appeared to have moved the deadline for a negotiated settlement forward to 8 August. Then, on 8 August Trump announced on *Truth Social* that he and Putin would meet on Friday, 15 August in Alaska. Ukraine was not invited to this meeting.

It does appear that Russia deliberately backed down in August on the number of drones being fired, especially those being fired at cities. On 31 July Russia fired 371 drones and cruise missiles (8 reported) at Ukraine. Kyiv was heavily bombarded. According to reports at least 16 Ukrainians were killed in Kyiv in those attacks and at least 159 had been wounded.[39] Trump did again warn Russia that new sanctions would be imposed if such bombardments continued.

---

37 "How much territory did the Russian army capture in July 2025 in Ukraine?," *Zamin*, 3 August 2025.

38 It is estimated that the population of Pokrovsk in late July 2025 is 1,500 civilian residents. See: Andrew Osborn and Anastasiia Malenko, "Pokrovsk: why is Russia trying so hard to capture strategic city in Ukraine," *Reuters*, 23 July 2025.

39 Marc Santora, "Missiles and Drones hit Kyiv in Deadly Wave of Russian Strikes," *The New York Times*, 31 July 2025.

Russia then paused these bombardments, with only 72 drones fired on 1 August. Up through 15 August Russia only fired more than a hundred drones and missiles on only three days, with an average only 71 drones and missiles fired each day for the first 15 days of August. This compares to an average of 215 drones and missiles fired each day for July. Still was this hardly telling as for example, on the night of 14/15, just before Putin and Trump met, seven civilians were killed and 17 were injured.[40] The previous night, Ukraine had launched a drone strikes on Russia that hit an apartment building in Rostov-on-Don and a car in Belgorod Oblast. These strikes killed at least one person and injured at least 16 more. Ukraine also struck in Volgograd Oblast. Russia says they intercepted 44 Ukrainian drones.[41]

Donald Trump was quoted as saying twice on 14 July that "I go home, I tell the First Lady, 'You know, I spoke to Vladimir today. We had a wonderful conversation.' And she said, 'Oh really? Another city was just hit.'"[42] Apparently Russia finally got the message.

Meanwhile the battlefield heated up with Russian pushes around Pokrovsk getting more serious. This is a year-old battle that started back on 18 July 2024. But Russia was close to taking the town, in their attempt to further consolidate their holdings in the annexed Donetsk Oblast. On 12 August President Zelenskyy admitted in a press conference that the Russians had advanced 6 miles (10 kilometers) near the town of Dobropillia (pop. 28,170 in 2022 estimate). Dobropillia is 58 miles (94 kilometers) from the city of Donetsk and 12 miles (19 kilometers) almost due north of Pokrovsk.

This appears to have been infiltration by infantry as opposed to an actual mechanized breakthrough, but they had made a mark on the map with a 10-to-17-kilometer penetration. This does not appear to have been followed up by armor or heavy weapons. Still, it further threatened Pokrovsk and more important, reinforced the impression

---

40   Dylan Stableford, Andrew Romano and Katie Mather, "Trump-Putin meeting recap: No deal reached at Russia-Ukraine war summit in Alaska; leaders praise 'extremely productive' talks," *Yahoo! News*, August 16, 2025.

41   Filip Timotija, "Ukraine launches drone attacks on southern Russia ahead of Trump-Putin summit," *The Hill*, 14 August 2025.

42   Joey Garrison, "'Oh really?': Trump says his wife Melania has some thoughts on Vladimir Putin," *USA Today*, 14 July 2025. Melania Knauss (Trump) was born in 1970 in Slovenia and grew up there. At the time Slovenia was part of communist Yugoslavia. Yugoslavia was not a member of the Soviet-dominated Warsaw Pact.

that Russia was slowly winning this war. This was an important point make the days before the meeting between Putin and Trump in Anchorage Alaska.

Trump and Putin met on 15 August on Joint Base Elmendorf-Richardson near Anchorage, Alaska. This air base was a merger of the Cold War Air Force Base Elmendorf with the U.S. Army's Fort Richardson. It has two asphalt runways, one of 7,493 feet (2,284 meters) and one of 10,000 feet (3,048 meters). Elmendorf airfield began construction in 1940. It was a staging area for the U.S. World War II Aleutian Island campaign, transfer base for World War II Lend-Lease aircraft to the Soviet Union, and then became a major Air Force hub during the Cold War. There are 14 Soviet servicemen buried at Elmendorf, nine being pilots involved in the transfer of planes from the U.S. to the Soviet Union as part of U.S. Lend-Lease operations during World War II. President Putin did lay flowers at their graves and met with the American Archbishop Alexei of the Orthodox Church, American Diocese of Alaska.[43]

The meeting between Trump and Putin lasted for a little less than three hours for a meeting that was scheduled for four. Representing Russia in the talks was Putin (age 72), his Foreign Minister Sergey Lavrov (age 75) and foreign affairs adviser Yuri Ushakov (age 78). Representing the United States was Trump (age 79) and his Secretary of State Marco Rubio (age 54) and special envoy Steve Witkoff (age 68). Several other American officials were in Alaska, including the Secretary of Defense Peter Hegseth (age 45), Treasury Secretary Scott Bessent (age 62), and Commerce Secretary Howard Lutnick (age 64). It was the first face-to-face meeting between Trump and Putin in six years, although they had talked numerous times on the phone in that period. It appears there were additional items on the agenda above and beyond peace in Ukraine.

There does not appear to have been any significant outcome to the talks. While Trump stated the talks were "extremely productive," he added during the brief press conference that "there's no deal until there's a deal." Then, unusually for Trump, they ended the press

---

43 "Laying flowers at the graves of Soviet soldiers at the Elmendorf-Richardson military bases," *The International Affairs Journal*, August 16, 2025 at https://en.interaffairs.ru/article/laying-flowers-at-the-graves-of-soviet-soldiers-at-the-elmendorf-richardson-military-base/. Alexei was born in Delaware. His secular name is John Trader.

Also see Peter Smith, "US archbishop's meeting with Putin denounced as 'betrayal of Christian witness'," *AP*, 18 August 2025.

conference without taking questions after the two of them had only spoken for about 12 minutes. In the end it was clear that there was "no deal." They skipped the formal lunch. It was going to be green salad, filet mignon and halibut Olympia, with creme brulee for dessert.

During the meeting, Trump did hand deliver to Putin a letter from the First Lady. According to White House officials, this letter voiced concerns over reports of children being forcibly removed from occupied Ukrainian territories.[44] It was less direct than that. Putin immediately opened and read Melania Trump's letter in front of both delegates at the summit.[45]

Now, Putin is currently an indicted war criminal by the International Criminal Court (ICC) and the court has issued an arrest warrant for him for the unlawful deportation of children and the unlawful transfer of children from occupied areas of Ukraine to the Russian Federation.[46] The United States and Russia, along with about 70 other countries, are not members of the International Criminal Court. There are 125 countries that are, including all of our 31 NATO allies except Turkey. Ukraine is also a party to the ICC. The United States does not have a legal or treaty requirement to deliver any indicted people to the ICC. To date, this is the second indicted person who President Trump has allowed to visit the United States, as Israeli Prime Minister Benjamin Netanyahu has also been indicted by the ICC. While the United States does not have a legal obligation to detain these individuals, it does have the option to respect these arrest warrants from the ICC if it chooses to. Obviously, in both cases, its leadership chose not to.

Anyhow, this last step is unusual, as the First Lady in her letter is nominally addressing the exact issue that has led to an arrest warrant

---

44 Shane Galvin, "Melania Trump sends letter to Putin about abducted Ukrainian children," *New York Post*, 16 August 2025.

45 Rachel Dobkin, "Putin 'immediately' read Melania Trump' letter in front of delegates at Alaska summit, report claims," *Independent*, 16 August 2025.

46 The arrest warrant was issued on 17 March 2023 for the unlawful deportation and transfer of children during the Russo-Ukrainian War under articles 8(2)(a)(vii) an 8(2)(b)(vii) of the Rome Statue. See: "Situation in Ukraine: ICC judges issue arrest warrants against Vladimir Vladimirovich Putin and maria Alekseyevna Lvova-Belova," *ICC Press Release*, 17 March 2023.

for Vladimir Putin. The letter has been published and it does not address any specific issues.[47]

Melania Trump
First Lady of the United States of America
August 15, 2025

Dear President Putin,

Every child shares the same quiet dreams in their heart, whether born randomly into a nation's rustic countryside or a magnificent city-center. They dream of love, possibility, and safety from danger.

As parents, it is our duty to nurture the next generation's hope. As leaders, the responsibility to sustain our children extends beyond the comfort of a few. Undeniably, we must strive to paint a dignity-filled world for all — so that every soul may wake to peace, and so that the future itself is perfectly guarded.

A simple yet profound concept, Mr. Putin, as I am sure you agree, is that each generation's descendants begin their lives with a purity — an innocence which stands above geography, government, and ideology.

Yet in today's world, some children are forced to carry a quiet laughter, untouched by the darkness around them — a silent defiance against the forces that can potentially claim their future. Mr. Putin, you can singlehandedly restore their melodic laughter.

In protecting the innocence of these children, you will do more than serve Russia alone — you serve humanity itself. Such a bold idea transcends all human division, and you, Mr. Putin, are fit to implement this vision with a stroke of the pen today.

It is time.

Sincerely,

Signed Melania Trump

---

47   A copy of the letter is here: https://storage.ning.com/topology/ rest/1.0/file/get/13694527701?profile=RESIZE_710x.

Anyhow, the overall sense was this was not a particularly successful summit for the United States. As has often been the case when Trump meets with Putin, there was considerable criticism. The former British Prime Minister Boris Johnson stated in his newspaper column that "It's the most vomit-inducing episode in all the tawdry history of international diplomacy but it will have taught Trump this vital lesson…"[48] Later results in the peace negotiations will establish whether it was productive.

Melania's letter to Putin did have some effect, as in October Putin returned eight children who were reunited with their Ukrainian families.[49] The ICC does allege that "at least hundreds" of Ukrainian children were taken.[50]

On Monday 18 August in Washington D.C, Trump met with Volodymir Zelenskyy. This was the first in-person meeting since the rather contentious encounter on 28 February 2025. Zelenskyy was bolstered for this meeting by the attendance by the presidents and prime ministers of Germany, Britian, France, Italy, Finland, the European Commission President and the Secretary-General of NATO. This does represent the 3rd, 6th, 7th and 8th largest economies in the world coming to support Ukraine. In contrast, Russia is the 11th largest economy in the world as measured by nominal GDP, with its overall economy being less than half of Germany's and almost 1/15th the size of the U.S. economy.

Needless to say, the meeting was preceded by an increased bombardment of Ukraine, with 140 drone attacks and four ballistic missile attacks against Ukraine on the night of 17/18 August. These appeared to be targeted against civilians, with ten people killed, seven in Kharkiv and three in Zaporizhzhia. This was followed up the next

---

48   Boris Johnson, "Boris Johnson: It's the most vomit-inducing episode in all the tawdry history of international diplomacy but it will have taught Trump this vital lesson…," *Daily Mail*, 16 August 2025.

49   Darline Superville, "Melania Trump says 8 kids displaced by Russia-Ukraine War reunite with families after Putin talks," *AP*, 10 October 2025.

50   "Statement by Prosecutor Karim A. A. Khan KC on the issuance of arrest warrants against President Vladimir Putin and Ms Maria Lvovo-Belova, *International Criminal Court*, 17 March 2023. Also see Mark Landler, "Arrest Warrant from Criminal Court Pierces Putin's Aura of Impunity," *New York Times*, 17 March 2023 which states that Russia acknowledges transferring 2,000 children while Ukraine says they have confirmed 16,000 cases.

day with 280 drones and missiles. It appeared that Russia was back to their normal routine, after having given Ukraine a 17-day breathing spell. As was pointed by a Ukrainian-based newspaper, as of 19 August, a least 21 Ukrainians had been killed and 99 injured by Russia strikes since the Trump-Putin summit on 15 August.[51]

The meetings with Zelenskyy, Trump and the NATO allies were somewhat anti-climactic as it did not appear they produced any major results. But they were not contentious like the February meeting was. Everyone appeared on their best behavior even through it was clear that Ukraine and all of our major NATO allies held positions that differed from the current U.S. administration.

Before the Monday meeting was held, Trump posted on *Truth Social* on Sunday, 17 August at 9:17 PM: "President Zelenskyy of Ukraine can end the war with Russia almost immediately, if he wants to, or he can continue to fight. Remember how it started. No getting back Obama given Crimea (12 years ago, without a shot being fired!), and NO GOING INTO NATO BY UKRAINE. Some things never change!!!"[52] We gather this means that he feels that Ukraine should be ready to give up Crimea and that they would not be joining NATO. President Zelenskyy did respond that evening emphasizing that Crimea was part of Ukraine. But it does appear that Russia demands remained far more extensive than that.

This message by Trump, of course, undermines Ukraine's negotiating position, Unfortunately, the U.S. has done this before, over compromising on the Paris Peace Accords in 1973 over Vietnam and with the Doha Agreement negotiated by Donald Trump in 2020. In both cases, the two countries that we were supporting and had thousands of our soldiers die fighting for were conquered by the opposition around two years after the peace deal.[53] Not all peace deals are good peace deals.

---

51 Tim Zadorozhnyy, "Russian strikes killed 21, injured 99 in Ukraine since Trump-Putin summit," *The Kyiv Independent*, 19 August 2025. They specifically provide counts of five killed and 11 injured on 17 August, eight killed and 35 injured on 18 August and at least eight killed and 53 injured on 19 August.

52 Darryl Coote, "Trump tells Zelensky Ukraine will not regain Crimea, be NATO member," *UPI*, 18 August 2025 and https://truthsocial.com/@realDonaldTrump/posts/115047128460078066.

53 Specifically, the Paris Peace accords were signed on 27 January 1973 and South Vietnam fell by 30 April 1975, some 27 months later. The "Agreement for Bringing Peace to Afghanistan" was signed between

Not much did come out of these meetings, but having five NATO heads of state join Zelenskyy was definitely unusual, and the meeting was of a very different tone than the February meeting between Zelenskyy, Trump and Vance. Trump was pushing for a direct summit between Putin and Zelenskyy, but that did not appear to be happen. Not much else came out of this summit.

On 21 August, Russia hit Ukraine with its largest drone and missile attack yet, a staggering total of 614. This included 574 Shahed-type drones, 33 cruise missiles and six ballistic missiles. Ukraine reported that 546 Shahed-type drones were shot or "crushed" (deflected/ diverted) by air defense (95%), as were 30 of the cruise missiles (91%) and one of the six ballistic missiles (17%). They recorded strikes at 11 locations and damaging debris from shot down drones and missiles at three locations. At least one person was killed and 15 injured. An American-owned electronics factory in western Ukraine was also struck. Pretty hard not to imagine that was not deliberately targeted.

---

the United States and the Taliban in Doha, Qatar on 29 February 2020. Afghanistan had fallen by 30 August 2021, only 18 months later.

The war in Afghanistan had lasted 19 years, 10 months, 3 weeks and 2 days from 7 October 2001 to 30 August 2021. The war in Vietnam lasted 19 years, 5 months, and 29 days if you count it starting on 1 November 1955 and ending on 30 April 1975. The U.S. commitment of ground troops in an active ground combat role did not start until 8 March 1965 and we withdrew in March of 1973 in accordance with an article in the Paris Peace Accords. As one writer noted about the Paris Peace Accords: "This article proved…to be the only one… which was fully carried out" (see: Peter Church, *A Short History of South-East Asia* [John Wiley & Sons, Singapore, 2006], pages 193–194).

In both cases, the president who negotiated that agreement (Nixon and Trump respectively) was not in office two years later when the counties fell. It was Ford and Biden who would inherit these "peace agreements." I do consider both of these "peace agreements" to be an abandonment of a government and people we were allied with and supported for almost two decades. In the case of Vietnam, the United States lost 58,281 troops there, of which 47,434 were from combat. In the case of Afghanistan the United States lost 2,420 troops there and our NATO and other allies lost 1,159 troops. This does not included contractors. To completely lose both of these countries within almost two years of the signed agreement clearly shows how shallow and poorly conceived these agreements were. See my book *America's Modern Wars: Understanding Iraq, Afghanistan and Vietnam* (Casemate Publishers, Philadelphia & Oxford, 2015) for a more extended and nuanced discussion of these subjects.

The Flex Ltd. plant was located in Mukachevo, a town 382 miles (615 kilometers) southwest of Kyiv. It is in the corner of Ukraine that borders Poland, Slovakia, Hungary and Romania. This area, Carpathian Ruthenia, became part of Czechoslovakia in 1920. It was annexed by Hungary in 1938. It was incorporated into the Soviet Union after World War II. The town was half-Jewish before the war, but they had been exterminated or migrated. The Soviet Union expelled some of the Hungarian population.[54]

Two Russian Kalibr cruise missiles hit the factory at 04:30. The factory produced commercial items, plastic molding, components of electrical equipment, coffee machines, printer cartridge, electronic price tags, etc. Flex Ltd is a large Singaporean-American multinational manufacturing company with headquarters in Singapore and Austin, Texas. It was originally a California-based circuit board manufacturer, but in 1990 moved to Singapore. It has manufacturing operations in over 30 countries and employs 172,000 employees. The plant has been there for 13 years, employs 2,600 people and covers nearly 600,000 square feet. This is the first Russian strike on Mukachevo since the war started.[55]

One can probably interpret this attack by over 600 drones and missiles as a message from Moscow. One does get the impression from the tone of Trump's comments on 22 August that he had given up trying to negotiate a ceasefire or a peace deal between Russia and Ukraine. He gave Putin another two weeks ("I'll know within two weeks what I'm going to do"), which is close to the original 2 September date he gave over a month before after which he said he would take action against Russia. Trump left his options open on 22 August with the quote "Then I'm going to make a decision as to what we do, and it's going to be a very important decision. And that's whether or not it's massive sanctions or massive tariffs, or both, or do we do nothing and say, 'it's our fight'?"[56]

---

54 The 1921 census reported 21,000 people lived in Mukachevo. Of those, 48% were Jewish, 24% were Rusyn and 22% were Hungarian., In the 1966 census, 50,500 people lived there. 60% were Ukrainian, 18% were Hungarian, 10% were Russian and 6% were Jewish.

55 Anthony Blair, "Russian missiles hit US-owned factory in Ukraine days after Trump-led peace talks," *New York Post,* 21 August 2025.

56 Annie Linskey and Alexander Ward, "Trump give familiar two-week deadline for next steps to end war in Ukraine," *The Wall Street Journal,* 22 August 2025 and Steven Nelson, "Trump threatens 'massive' sanctions

On 22 August Russian only struck Ukraine with 55 Shahed-type drones. One does wonder if Russian was running low on drones and missiles. During July they expended at least 6,438 drones and missiles. This was 215 a day. They had also done similar high expenditures in May and June (4,127 and 5,677 respectively). From 1 through 20 August they only expended 1,818 drones and missiles, or only 91 a day.[57] They then did a 614-drone and missile strike on the 21st and then went back down to 55 drones on the 22nd. Did Russia expend its drone supply over the spring and summer in an attempt to pound Ukraine into submission? The next six days were relatively quiet (55, 49, 73, 104, 59 and 95 each day respectively). This ended the following day, 28 August, when Russia launched yet another record-breaking attack of 629 drones and missiles. This included 598 drones of which 563 were shot down or suppressed (94%), 20 cruise missiles of which 18 were shot down or suppressed (90%), and 11 ballistic missiles of which 8 were shot down or suppressed (73%). Ukraine recorded hits in 13 locations, are falling debris in 26 locations. This was followed up with a 582 drone and missile attack on 30 August. From 21–31 August (11 days), Russia averaged 225 drones and missiles a day.

Anyhow, the war continued through August with no significant additional events. Russia was unable to take Pokrovsk while Ukraine was able to only partially reduce what was probably only a battalion-size advance into their lines. Everything remained fundamentally stalemated with only limited advances along the front.[58]

---

and tariffs in two weeks if Putin and Zelensky don't meet: 'I'll see whose fault it is'," *New York Post*, 22 August 2025.

57   1,818/20 = 91 (through 20 August).

58   For practical concerns, we decided to end this discussion in August 2025. Not much has changed since then. See: "Putin says Russia had captured nearly 5,000 square km in Ukraine this year," *Reuters*, 7 October 2025.

Chapter 9

THE ATTACKS ON THE CRIMEAN BRIDGE

"This is an act of terrorism aimed at destroying critically important civilian infrastructure"

President Vladimir Putin
9 October 2022[1]

On 3 June 2025, at 04:44, Ukraine unleashed a second surprise attack against a vulnerable Russian target, the Crimean Bridge, also known at the Kerch Strait Bridge. This bridge connects Russia with Crimea. It goes from the Taman Peninsula in Krasnodar Krai to the Kerch Peninsula in Crimea. It is 12 miles (19 kilometers) long, making it the longest bridge in Europe or in Russia. It consists of two parallel bridges, one with a four-lane highway and the other with a double-tracked railway.

The Ukrainian SBU attacked one of the support pillars to the road bridge with 2,425 pounds (1,100 kilograms) of explosives. It was a single underwater explosion that Ukraine filmed and released. The actual means of delivery is not precisely known, but they were either hit by an underwater drone or planted by frogmen with possibly the help of an underwater drone to carry the explosives. The SBU stated at the time that mines were laid under the bridge over several months by its agents. This seems inefficient, with a high risk of discovery. Probably one Ukrainian-built underwater drone was used. There was at least one Ukrainian drone in the area filming the explosion.

While the explosion created great video, the damage was not extensive. The bridge was temporarily closed for three hours but

---

1   "Russia President Vladimir Putin accused Ukraine of Crimea-Russia bridge blast," *DOO News,* 9 October 2022.

reopened by 10:00 local time.[2] Some damage was done to the guard railing of the road bridge and some debris was left on top (see photo section). It was temporarily closed against later in the day.[3] There appear to have been no civilian casualties.

When Russian annexed Sevastopol and Crimea on March 2022, it was faced with a problem that these two areas were isolated from Russia. With Ukraine hostile to Russia, they were de facto islands, with Russia only being able to resupply them and move forces to these areas by boat, ferry or plane. They had no land connection with Sevastopol and Crimea.

They attempted to correct this by building a long and expensive bridge from the Taman Peninsula to the Kerch Peninsula. This project was started in 2015 and completed in May 2018 when it was opened to car traffic. The rail line was opened in December 2019. It cost $3.7 billion (227.92 billion rubles) to build this bridge. It gave Russia a road and rail connection to Crimea. This was fine as long as it was not interfered with.

The population of Sevastopol in 1989, when it was still part of the Soviet Union, was 356,123. Twenty-five years later, after being mostly under Ukrainian control, the population had grown to 393,304 in 2014. With the population of Russian and Ukraine being in continuous decline since the fall of communism, Sevastopol was unusual in that it was still growing. This was not the case with Ukraine's largest Black Sea port, Odesa, which had been in a slow decline since 1989. The population of Crimea, which was and still is administratively separate from Sevastopol, was 2,430,495 in 1989. This figure includes Sevastopol. In 2014, after the annexation, its population was 2,284,769.[4] This figure does not include Sevastopol.

The Russian seizure and annexation of Sevastopol and Crimea in 2014 meant that they had to support this de facto island of more than 2.6 million people by air and sea. The development of the Kerch Strait

---

2   According to Russian accounts, for three hours. See: "Russia claims no damaged after Ukrainian attack on Crimea bridge," *Aljazeera*, 3 June 2025; "Crimean Bridge Hit by Explosion," *Newsweek*, 3 June 2025 and Laura Gozzi, "Ukraine says it hit Crimea bridge with underwater explosives," *BBC News*, 2 June 2025.

3   Laura Gozzi, "Ukraine says it hit Crimea bridge with underwater explosives," *BBC News*, 2 June 2025.

4   Crimea's population in 2001 was 2,401,209. This figure includes Sevastopol.

bridge greatly helped and connected these areas directly to Russia. This whole issue was further complicated by the growth of population in these areas under Russian control. In 2021 the population of Sevastopol was given as 547,820 and of Crimea as 2,482,450. This is almost three million people. Added to that, it had now become a popular and preferred seaside resort for many people in Russia, with millions going there each year, with 9.5 million visiting in 2021.[5] This was a thin and limited causeway for supporting this many people.

This problem was solved for Russia in March 2022 when Russia took by force the southern parts of Zaporizhzhia and Kherson provinces. This connected Crimea by rail to Russia and by vehicle using overland roads. It also addressed the issue of being able to secure the water supply for Crimea, a problem that was an issue before the war.

On 30 September 2022 Russia annexed the entirely of the Zaporizhzhia and Kherson provinces. As of mid-November 2022 Russia had not controlled all the land or population in either province nor either of their capital cities. They still do not. This has lead Russia in the recent negotiations to claim that they want the entirety of both provinces. Needless to say, Ukraine is not going to surrender two major cities, Kherson (pop. 279,131 in 2022) and Zaporizhzhia (pop. 710,052 in 2022), to Russia as part of a peace deal.

It is the author's opinion that the reason Russian carried out this annexation and continues to forcefully make this claim, is not because they think this will ever happen, but because it gives them a stronger negotiating position that they can then back down from and instead claim only the southern part of those two provinces that they already control. This is a false compromise but would allow them to keep the land bridge directly connecting Russian to Crimea. Without this land bridge, Sevastopol and Crimea would be isolated again.

This was the third time that Ukraine has attacked this bridge. The first time was on 8 October 2022, in the first year of the war, when a truck driving across the bridge exploded. This large explosion collapsed two of the four lanes of highway. A railway tanker car on the railway bridge also caught fire, shutting down the rail bridge. Five people were

---

5   Yekaterina Mereminksaya, "The Symbolism of Russia's Bridge to
     Crimea," *The Moscow Times*, 10 October 2022. A similar theme is
     explored in Aleksandra Simonova, "The Crimean Bridge as a Symbolic
     and Military Object in Contemporary Russia," *Jordan Center, NYU*, 3
     December 2024.

killed in this attack. The attack occurred the day after the 70th birthday of Russia's President Putin.

This was particularly interesting, as it was a Ukrainian covert operation that loaded up a truck with explosives and then had it driven across the bridge. It foreshadowed other such operations, including Operation Spider's Web. Ukraine did not take responsibility for the attack until July 2023.

Russian investigation of the attack show that 50,200 pounds (22,700 kilograms) of explosives were transported according to the Russians on 22 pallets in the truck. According to Ukraine the explosives were wrapped in a container with large rolls of cellophane film with an explosive power of 21 tons of TNT.[6] The explosives were loaded at Odesa at the beginning of August 2022, and shipped through Bulgaria, Armenia and then Georgia to Russia. The explosive pallets were loaded at Ulyanovsk (pop. 613,786 in 2010) on 7 October into a truck bound for the Crimean capital city of Simferopol.[7] The truck driver was probably not aware of the load he was carrying. It is not known how the explosion was ignited, but it occurred when the driver was in the middle of bridge. In many aspects, this operation carried some similarities to Operation Spider's Web. Ulyanovsk is the birthplace of the founder of the Soviet Union, Vladimir Lenin.

The five people killed included four people in a car next to the explosion, including a judge at the Moscow Arbitration Court, Sergei Maslov, along with two tour guides-historians and a fitness trainer. They were perhaps heading to Crimea for a vacation, which is not something that is regularly done now. The fifth person killed was the truck driver, Russian citizen Machir Yusubov. The cargo was supposedly monitored by a Ukrainian intelligence officer Ivan Ivanovich.[8]

---

6   The Ukrainian account is from "SBU chief Malyuk on how Crimean Bridge was attacked – twice," *The New Voice of Ukraine*, 24 August 2023 at https://english.nv.ua/nation/sbu-chief-malyuk-on-how-crimean-bridge-was-attacked-twice-50348824.html.

7   "Russian special service detains eight people over attack on Kerch bridge," *iDNES.cz*, 12 October 2022 at https://www.idnes.cz/zpravy/zahranicni/ukrajina-rusko-valka-kercsky-most-podezreli.A221012_075856_zahranicni_misl and Niamh Cavanagh, "Russia arrests 8 people after Crimea bridge attack. Here's what we know.," *Yahoo! News*, 12 October 2022.

8   "Russian special service detains eight people over attack on Kerch bridge," *iDNES.cz*, 12 October 2022. The name Ivan Ivanovich sounds like a cover name.

By 12 October, Russia claimed that it had detained eight suspects, five Russian and three citizens of Ukraine and Armenia. Whether any of these people were actual Ukrainian agents is not known. They blamed Kyrylo Budanov for the attack and eventually a Moscow court issued an arrest warrant for hm on 21 April 2023. Of course, he was safely out of reach in Ukraine and still leads the SBU today.

With the bridge partially shut down, Russia reopened the ferry service across the Kerch Strait. The provided ferry service past the damaged portions of the bridge, with satellite photos showing hundreds of trucks being backed up for three or four days waiting to use the ferry in October 2022. Russia was able to repair the bridge and get the road bridge fully reopened on 23 February 2023 and the rail bridge on 5 May 2023. The rail bridge had continued in operation since October 2022, but running trains at reduced speed and reduced load. Now it was fully usable again.

Russia then initiated a series of drone and missile strikes on Ukraine cities, hitting civilian areas in Kyiv and other cities. According to Vladimir Putin, this was in retaliation for Ukraine's attack on the Kerch Strait Bridge. This new air campaign started on 10 October. In the previous 40 days (1 September – 9 October) Ukraine had claimed to have shot down a total of 173 planes, helicopters, cruise missiles and drones. In the last 20 days of October, due to increased activity, it was 403.

On the night of 8–9 October, at least 12 missiles were launched at the Ukrainian city of Zaporizhzhia, hitting residential buildings. Ukraine reported that thirteen civilians were killed, 60 people were hospitalized and at least 89 were wounded or injured.[9]

---

9   This article says 12 killed, but the secretary of Zaporizhzhia city council says it was 17 killed. See "Deadly Russian missile attack hits Ukraine's Zaporizhzhia city," *Aljazzera*, 9 October 2022. One notes that these attacks are not unusual, with at least 19 people dying in Zaporizhzhia on 6 October due to a Russian missile attack on apartment buildings.
     This article reports 13 killed and 89 injured: "Russian missile attack on Zaporizhzhia killed at least 13," *DOO News*, 9 October 2022.
     These attacks were followed up with additional attacks on 11 October that killed another 19 people and wounded 105 others. See: Jacob Knutson, "Biden condemns Ukraine attack as Putin claims it's retaliation for terrorism," *Axios*, 11 October 2022.

The next attack on the bridge occurred in the middle of 2023. The bridge had been fully reopened in May 2023. Putin had driven across it on 5 December 2022 in a Mercedes to publicly demonstrate that the bridge to Crimea was open to road traffic. On 17 July 2023 two explosions occurred next to the road bridge, causing that section to collapse. This was done by two newly developed maritime drones, which damaged two spans of the bridge. The attack killed two adults and wounded a child. The SBU has videos from the drones of this attack. They used what was called "Sea Baby" drones.

The "Sea Baby" drones are Ukrainian-designed and built naval drones that have been successfully used for a range of operations. They were independently developed by the Security Service of Ukraine (SBU) starting in mid-2022, in the early days of the war. The related Magura V sea drone is 18 feet (5.5 meters) long. The Sea Babies have a range of at least 621 miles (1,000 kilometers), and a maximum speed of 56 miles per hour (90 km/h). The newer version of these drones can carry a warhead of 1,874 pounds (850 kilograms) of hexogen.[10] This was a significant upgrade from the 238-pound (108-kilogram) warheads of earlier models.

These drones, like the Iranian Shahed drones, have the advantage of being affordable. They cost less than $300,000 each,[11] even though they are fairly sophisticated with a body made of radar-invisible material, multiple means of communication, and an ability to steer and pursue targets.

It took two days to sail them to the bridge. It was their first operational use of these new upgraded naval drones, although their initial successful use was in October 2022 in an attack against the Russian frigate *Admiral Makarov*.[12]

---

10   The Ukrainian account is from "SBU chief Malyuk on how Crimean Bridge was attacked – twice," *The New Voice of Ukraine*, 24 August 2023 at https://english.nv.ua/nation/sbu-chief-malyuk-on-how-crimean-bridge-was-attacked-twice-50348824.html.

11   8.5 million hryvnias according to one account. This is $239.844 in 2024 U.S. dollars. See: Alona Mazurenko, "Ukrainians donate nearly U.S. $7.71 million in record two days for Sea Baby drones," *Ukrainska Pravda*, 23 February 2024.

12   Roman Romaniuk, "Sea drones, Elon Musk, and high-precision missiles: How Ukraine dominates in the Black Sea," *Ukrainka Pravda*, 1 January 2024.

Russia also violently responded to this attack by withdrawing from the Black Sea Grain Initiative and launching a series of drone and missile strikes on Odesa.

This July attack was followed up on 12 August with a missile attack by three Ukrainian S-200 missiles. The Russians claimed to have shot down all three of the missiles. Russia did cover the bridge with white smoke to protect it. The bridge, shrouded in smoke, was temporarily closed.

The S-200 is an old Soviet SA-5 surface-to-air missile first deployed around 1966. It had a warhead weight of 478 pounds (217 kilograms) for the 5V28E variant. It was the same missile that Ukraine used to accidently shoot down a civilian Tu-154 over the Black Sea on 4 October 2001, killing all 78 people on hoard. The missile was officially retired from service in 2013, but clearly a few had been kept and were now used in a ground attack role. It was also the missile that was used to claim a Beriev A-50U, named "42 red", on 23 February 2024 over the Sea of Azov. Poland is reported to have provided Ukraine with S-200 missiles in 2023.

The Kerch Strait bridge was fully reopened on 14 October 2023.

On 3 June 2025, the Ukrainians damaged the bridge for yet a third time. This time a planted underwater explosion occurred near the support pillars. This was not as significant or damaging as the previous two attacks. The first explosive device was activated at 4:44 in the morning. There were no personnel casualties.

According to the SBU, the explosives were equivalent to 2,425 pounds (1,100 kilograms) of TNT.[13] The bridge was only temporarily closed and the Russians claimed that it was reopened by 07:00 the following day. A view of the video of the attack shows only limited damage to the bridge.

How the bridge was attacked is not exactly know. Some sources claim that the Ukrainian underwater drone Marichka made by AMMO was used for this attack. It is a 200-foot (six-meter) long and three-foot (one-meter) in diameter, submersible drone that the travel up to 621

---

13   According to one report, it was 2,200 kilograms. See Kateryna Zakharchenko, "'117 Drones and 2,200 kg of Explosives': SBU Chief Unveils Ukraine's Secret Ops," *Kyiv Post*, 23 June 2025. Specifically, he said "To be frank, the third time we hit the bridge, we used 1,100 kilograms of explosives – and another 1,100 kilograms. Two strikes against key supports." We have not seen clear evidence of that second strike.

miles (1,000 kilometers) and has a sizeable warhead. This submersible drone, first revealed in August 2023, costs around $400,000 to 430,000.[14]

It could have also been done using First Contact's VAL-1 Underwater Drone. According to First Contact their submersible drone has a working depth of 164 feet (50 meters), a cruising speed of almost 8 miles an hour (3.5 meters per second), a combat radius of over 500 miles (over 800 kilometers) and a payload of 2,204 pounds (1,000 kilograms). Their "end consumers" are the Naval Forces of Ukraine, Special Operations Forces of Ukraine, Security Service of Ukraine (SBU) and Main Intelligence Directorate of Ukraine (GUR).[15]

---

14   David Kirichenko, "Waiting for the Bridge to Blow Again," *Kyiv Post*, 5 July 2025; Vlad Litnarovych, "The Crimean Bridge was just struck underwater. Ukraine has a drone for that," *United 24 Media*, 3 July 2025 and Serge Havrylets, "Ukraine develops a kamikaze underwater drone to hit Russian bridges and warships (VIDEO)," *Euromaiden Press*, 25 September 2023.

15   See: https://firstcontact.biz/en/projects/val-1/. Further down the page they state "Thanks to a developed energy system, the vehicle is capable of delivering a combat load up to 750 nautical miles."

Chapter 10

THE UKRAINIAN AIR ATTACKS

"The number and scale of missile strikes on targets in Kyiv will increase in response to any terrorist attacks or acts of sabotage on Russian territory committed by the Kyiv nationalist regime."

Russian Ministry of Defense
15 April 2022[1]

All is not fair in war, but Ukraine has launched a number of drone and missile attacks on Russia. They are no way equal in size or extent of the Russian strikes, but often cleverly planned, and focused on military targets with considerably fewer civilian casualties. The first Ukrainian attack on Russia territory was on the second day of the war (Friday, 25 February 2022) with a missile attack on Russia's Millerovo air base. Photographic evidence shows one Su-30SM fighter destroyed on the ground.

Millerovo air base is located in Rostov Oblast just to the east of Ukraine, northeast of Mariupol. It is ten miles (16 kilometers) from the Ukrainian border. It has a concrete runway that is 9,764 feet (2,976 meters) long. It is home to the 31st Guard Fighter Aviation Regiment which had two squadrons of Sukhoi Su-30SMs (NATO designation: "Flanker-H") in 2022 and the 368th Assault Aviation Regiment equipped with Sukhoi Su-25s (NATO designation: "Frogfoot").

On the morning of 25 February Ukraine's 19th Missile Brigade fired two Tochka-U ballistic missiles at the air base and at least one hit the airfield.

---

1   "Russia pledges more strikes on Kyiv after missile attack," *Reuters*, 15 April 2022, and Pavel Polityuk and Elizabeth Piper, "Ukraine says fighting rages in Mariupol, blasts rattle Kyiv," *Reuters*, 15 April 2022.

Map 8: Map of Russia Oblasts.

A video showed the missile hitting the airfield and starting several fires on the runway.[2] It destroyed one Su-30SM out of the 130 or so Su-30SMs,

---

2   "February 25, 2022 Russia-Ukraine News," *CNN World*, 26 February 2002; "Ukrainian forces launch missile attack on Russia's military airfield," *Euromaidan Press*, 25 February 2022; "Russan military base

Russia's "4.5 generation" fighters.[3] Several people were wounded and one pilot was reported to have died later from his wounds.[4]

The Tochka-U is a Soviet-era ballistic missile, also known by the NATO designation as the SS-21 "Scarab B." It first entered service in 1975 (as the "Scarab A"). "The Scarab B" or Tochka-U was introduced in 1989. It has a range of 75 miles (120 kilometers) and a maximum speed of Mach 5.3. Its warhead size of not posted, but the "Scarab A" had a high explosive warhead of 930 pounds (420 kilograms).

The system was scheduled to be decommissioned by Russia in 2020 and replaced with the Iskander, but they were still in use by Russia in 2022 and were used to conduct multiple attacks against Ukraine. Russia still had around 200 missiles in 2022 and maybe 50 launchers. Ukraine still had an estimated 500 of these missiles and 90 launchers as of 2022.

There was also an explosion on a military air base in Taganrog in Rostov Oblast on 1 March 2022 that appears to have been caused by a Ukrainian missile. From the video it appears that an Il-76 transport plane was destroyed. There were no injuries reported.[5]

There were additional attacks reported in Russia on 23 March, 1 April, and 14 April 2022. The attacks in April were in the Belgorod Oblast, just north of Kharkiv, from a mix of weapon systems. Also on 14 April

---

blown up as Ukraine fights back," *Newsweek*, 25 February 2022; "Ukraine, in response to the shelling of Ukrainian cites, launched a missile attack on the Russian air base Millerovo – Butusov," *New Voice Ukraine*, 25 February 2022 at https://nv.ua/ukr/ukraine/events/vtorgnennya-rosiji-v-ukrajinu-zsu-zavdali-raketnogo-udaru-po-aviabazi-millerovo-novini-ukrajini-50220081.html; "Residents of the Rostov region reported the shelling of the Millerovo military airfield," *Kavkaz.Realii*, 25 February 2022 at https://www.kavkazr.com/a/voennye-sily-ukrainy-nanesli-udar-po-aerodromu-v-rostovskom-millerovo-smi/31722581.html.

3   "Ukrainian Missile Strike Destroyed Russian Sukhoi SU-30SM at Millerovo airbase," *Fighter Jets World*, 25 February 2022.

4   https://www.facebook.com/permalink.php/?story_fbid=153435673724716&id=105014091900208. According to this post this was a Ka-52 helicopter pilot Captain Vitaliy Voitsekhovsky.

5   "An explosion occurred at a military airfield in Russian Taganrog," *Zakhid.net*, 1 March 2022 at https://zaxid.net/u_rosiyskomu_taganrozi_stavsya_vibuh_na_viyskovomu_aerodromi_n1537224 and Mille Cooke, "Russian airfield in flames after 'missile attack' – claims," *EXPRESS*, 1 March 2022.

Ukraine sank the guided missile cruiser *Moskva*, the flagship and the largest warship of the Russian Black Sea Fleet. Ukraine fired two R-360 Neptune anti-ship missiles at the ship and one clearly hit, maybe both. That was enough. These missiles were Soviet-era Kh-35 anti-ship missiles that had been substantially upgraded with improved range and more modern targeting and electronics package. These new upgraded missiles were deployed less than a year before the war started, entering service in March 2021. It was a surprise to Russia and many in the West that Ukraine had developed this capability.

In response, Russia launched a retaliation attack on Kyiv the following day, striking a factory on the outskirts of Kyiv that made and repaired anti-ship missiles. This was apparently in direct retaliation for sinking the *Moskva*. As the Russian Defense Ministry was quoted as saying, "The number and scale of missile strikes on targets in Kyiv will increase in response to any terrorist attacks or acts of sabotage on Russian territory committed by the Kyiv nationalist regime."[6] A very clear quid pro quo had been established.

This was the largest missile strike made on Ukraine to date. By later standards this was extremely limited. Ukraine does not provide a count of missiles observed or that attacked it at this time, but it was reported that there were three impacts on the industrial building on the outskirts of Kyiv. On 15 April Ukraine claimed to have shot down two cruise missiles and three drones. So maybe a total of eight drones and missiles were fired at Ukraine that day. These attacks against Kyiv were done more than two weeks after the Russian army has withdrawn from the area.

This set the pattern, where when Ukraine did an attack or operation that embarrassed Russia, Russia would respond by attacking Kyiv. This was the first such attack in response, but this pattern would continue throughout the war.

The next big attack on Russia air bases came on 5 December 2022 when two bases, Dyagilevo and Engels-2, were attacked by Ukrainian drones or cruise missiles that morning.

The missile attacking Dyagilevo appears to have hit an oil truck, which exploded killing three soldiers and wounding four or six others. A nearby Tu-22M3 was probably damaged. It is claimed that

---

6   "Russia pledges more strikes on Kyiv after missile attack," *Reuters*, 15 April 2022, and Pavel Polityuk and Elizabeth Piper, "Ukraine says fighting rages in Mariupol, blasts rattle Kyiv," Reuters, 15 April 2022.

the bomber was armed with Kh-22 cruise missiles at the time of the attack.[7]

Engels-2 air base in Saratov Oblast was reported attacked at 09:00. Two people were injured and two Tu-95s were reported by the Russian Defense Ministry to have been slightly damaged.[8]

The following day a Ukrainian missile attack set an oil storage tank on fire near the Kursk-Khalino air base. The Kursk air base is only about 60 miles (90 kilometers) north of the Ukrainian border.[9]

These first two attacks were done by Ukraine using old Soviet-era drones, modified to be cruise missiles. Dyagilevo is 290 miles (467 kilometers) northeast of Ukraine. Engels is further away, at least 372 miles (600 kilometers) from the Ukrainian border. The missiles in these attacks probably came from Ukraine, rather than inside Russia.

The cruise missiles used were probably Ukrainian-modernized Tu-141 Strizh reconnaissance drone. Russia said they were Soviet-era drones, which these certainly are, being first fielded in 1979. The Russian civilians on the ground reported hearing turbine noises, and these are turbine-powered drones.[10] Ukraine was reported to have them in their inventory in 2022. No photos have been shown of the drone wreckage, but by default, they were probably the most convenient missile available for such a long-range strike, with Ukraine swapping out the reconnaissance equipment for explosives.

The Tu-141 Strizh (Swift) is a large drone, 47 feet (14.33 meters) long and weighing several tons (5,370 kilograms). It has a range of 620 miles (1,000 kilometers) with a cruise speed 620 miles per hour (1,000

---

7   Ivan Nosalsky, "Explosions at the Russian airfield 'Diaghilev': a satellite image of the consequences appeared," *RBK-Ukraina*, 5 December 2022 at https://www.rbc.ua/rus/news/vibuhi-rosiyskomu-aerodromi-dyagilevo-z-yavivsya-1670266283.html.

8   Natalia Yurchenko, "In Russia, explosions rang out at two airfield at once: what is known," *RBK-Ukraina*, 5 December 2022 at https://www.rbc.ua/rus/news/rosiyi-vidrazu-dvoh-aerodromah-prolunali-1670224662.html and Ilona Sviridova, "'Hit by Soviet drones.' Russia fantasized about a Ukrainian attack on airfields," *RBK-Ukraina*, 5 December 2022 at https://www.rbc.ua/rus/news/vdarili-radyanskimi-dronami-rosiyi-nafantazuvali-1670261753.html.

9   Pavel Polityuk and Sergiy Chalyi, "Ukraine appears to expose Russian air defence gaps with long-range strikes," *Reuters*, 6 December 2022, updated 28 February 2023.

10   "Who organized the drone strike on targets deep in Russia? Could it have been an attack from Russian territory?," *Meduza*, 7 December 2022.

kilometers per hour) along a route programmed into its memory. It is capable of flying its route as low as 164 feet (50 meters), making it difficult for air defense to spot and intercept it in a timely manner. The Soviet-era Swifts were produced at the Kharkov Aviation Plant, which is course now part of Ukraine. Up until production stopped in 1989, a total of 152 Swifts were built.[11] In October 2022 Ukraine announced that was developing its own heavy kamikaze drone with a range of a thousand kilometers and a warhead weighting 165 pounds (75 kilograms).[12] This unmanned air vehicle (UAV) should probably be considered a cruise missile rather than a drone.[13] Ukraine stated the drone was undergoing finals tests on 4 December. The two Russian air bases were struck on 5 December 2022.

Some reports said they were launched from Russian territory, but this is doubtful. They also said at least one of the strikes was carried out with the help of special forces close to the base. A number of Tu-95s had been operating out of Saratov and striking at Ukraine from the Caspian Sea area (as Ukraine says in its Air Force Command notes). This attack on Saratov might have served as an impetus for Russia to disperse their bombers to other bases.[14]

These attacks got Russia's attention, and they immediately launched a new wave of missile attacks on Ukrainian cities. On 5 December, by 16:00 Ukraine was reporting that 69 cruise missiles and one Kh31P air-to-surface missile had been fired. This included 28 Kh-101 cruise missiles carried on eight Tu-95MSs. They also fired 22 Kalibr cruise missiles from the ships of the Black Sea Fleet. The Tu-22M3s also attacked with three Kh-22s. Su-35 fighters fired six Kh-59 cruise missiles and one H-41P. Ukraine claimed to have intercepted over 60 of them (at least 87%). Two people in Zaporizhzhia were killed and three were wounded.[15]

---

11   "What is the Tu-141 'Strzh'," *Kommersant*, 26 March 2023 at https://www.kommersant.ru/doc/5252539.

12   "Who organized the drone strikes on targets deep in Russia? Could it have been an attack from Russian territory?," *Meduza*, 7 December 2022.

13   David Axe, "Ukraine pulled ex-Soviet recon drones out of storage, added bombs and sent them hurtling toward Russia," *Forbes*, 5 December 2022.

14   Pavel Polityuk and Sergiy Chalyi, "Ukraine appears to expose Russian air defence gaps with long-range strikes," *Reuters*, 6 December 2022.

15   Andrew Roth and Julian Borger, "Explosions rock two Russian airbases far from Ukraine frontline," *The Guardian*, 5 December 2022.

On 26 December at 01:35, Ukraine carried out a second attack an Engels air base.[16] The Russians claimed that the drone was shot down at low altitude while approaching the base. Three Russan servicemen were killed. One Tu-95 may have been damaged. The Russian accounts say the damage was due the fall of the wreckage of the drone. Russia also claimed to have shot down the two drones that attacked on 5 December and that their casualties were also caused by debris.[17] It is a little hard to imagine that fuel tanks will explode and the strikes will cause multiple fatalities just from falling debris. Most of the drones probably got clean hits.

As Ukraine probably had a limited supply of these Swift cruise missiles, this was probably the end of their operational use. The last one reported used was on 26 March 2023.[18] It does raise the question that if Ukraine targeted Engels air base twice in December 2022, why didn't they target the air base in their attacks in June 2025?

There were numerous attacks in and around Belgorod Oblast in 2022 and 2023, but these are best saved for a discussion on the fighting around Kharkiv. They did not generate another Russian bombardment of Kyiv. The first significant attack on Moscow during the war was on 3 May 2023 when two drones targeted the Kremlin in downtown Moscow in the early morning. The explosions over the Kremlin were caught on camera and beamed around the world. Over a year into the war and the Kremlin in the center of Moscow was being directly attacked.

Russia shot them down. No one was injured in this incident. Russia accused Ukraine of attempting to assassinate Putin but he was not in the Kremlin at the time. As Russia had already tried to assassinate President Zelenskyy multiple times, it appears that assassination was already considered very much of tool of this war from the beginning.

It is not known what drones were used, but they could have been launched from inside Russia.[19] Moscow is 280 miles (450 kilometers)

---

16   "Tu-141 Strizh, the improvised weapon Ukraine uses to attack Russian bomber bases," *Aviacionline*, 26 December 2022 at https://www. aviacionline.com/tu-141-strizh-the-improvised-weapon-ukraine-uses-to-attack-russian-bomber-bases.

17   "Three killed in second attack on Engels base deep inside Russia," *CNBC*, 25 December 2002.

18   "Three injured as Russia downs Ukrainian drone south of Moscow," *Reuters*, 27 Match 27, 2023.

19   According to one source, they may have been prototypes of the AN-196 Liutyi drone. This drone was developed by Ukroboronprom in October

from the Ukrainian border. The first drone exploded over the dome of the Senate building at 02:27, after which a fire broke out on the roof. The second drone's wreckage fell inside of the Kremlin at 02:43.[20] It appears that at least one drone was intercepted, damaged or disabled. Russia claimed that both drones were disabled using electronic radar assets.[21] Russian officials invariably called in a "terrorist attack" and compared the Ukrainian government to Al-Qaeda and the Islamic State. In just April 2023, Russian had launched at least 90 drones and 23 cruise missiles at Ukraine. Needless to say, Moscow vowed to retaliate.

One former dissident Russian politician, Ilya Ponomarev, has claimed that the drone attack was done by the Russia resistance.[22] There had already been a couple of attacks conducted inside of Russia by Russian dissidents. On 25 June 2022, the shadowy "Combat Organization of Anarcho-Communists" sabotaged a railway line near Moscow. On 4 January 2023 the same organization claimed responsibility for an explosion that damaged the Trans-Siberian Railway in Krasnoyarsk in the middle of Siberia. This organization has carried out no significant attacks since then but still maintains a website.[23]

It is possible that this attack was done from inside Russia by the SBU using Ukrainian agents. The Ukrainian government denies this. On 24 April an explosive-laden Ukrainian drone was found a short distance

---

2022. It has an operational range of 620 to 1,240 miles (1,000 to 2,000 kilometers) so could have reached Moscow from Ukraine. Its length is 14 feet (4.4 meters), its wingspan is 22 feet (6.7 meters) and it weighs 550–660 pounds (250–300 kilograms). Its warhead weight was probably 110 pounds (50 kilograms), upgraded to 165 pounds (75 kilograms) in November 2024 (see: Ivan Khomenko, "Ukrainian AN-196 Liutyi drone, dubbed 'Ukrainian Shahed,' receives major upgrade," *United24 Media*, 25 November 2024). They supposedly cost $200,000 each in early 2024 (see Vadim Kushnikov, "Ukrainian Peklo drone-missiles will be cheaper than Liutyi drones," *MilitarNYI*, 16 December 2024.

20   See https://archive.ph/20230503205901/https://www.kommersant.ru/doc/5967458?from=top_main_2. Also see Howard Altman and Joseph Trevitnick, "Drone Attack on the Kremlin in Moscow (Updated)," *TWZ*, 3 May 2023.

21   Will Vernon and Thomas Spender, "Kremlin drone: Zelensky denies Ukraine attacked Putin or Moscow," *BBC*, 3 May 2023.

22   Rob Picheta, Anna Chernova and Allegra Goodwin, "What we know about the murky drone attack on the Kremlin – and the questions that remain," *CNN*, 4 May 2023.

23   See: https://boakmirror.noblogs.org/.

from Moscow. It carried 37 pounds (17 kilograms) of explosives.[24] There is a picture of the drone and it is probably a UJ-22. The UJ-22 is a Ukrainian-built airplane-like drone powered by a small gas engine and driving a single three-bladed propeller at its front. It has a maximum range of 497 miles (800 kilometers) and can stay aloft for up to seven hours. Its fully loaded weight is 44 pounds (20 kilograms). This drone could hit Moscow from Ukraine, but it is not sure if this is what was done.

In February a UJ-22 drone had been found in the snow less than 70 miles (113 kilometers) southwest of Moscow.[25] It is clear that Ukraine has tried or tested their drone strike on Moscow multiple times before the strikes in May 2023.

Meanwhile, in January Russia upgraded the city's air defense with Pantsir air defense missiles mounted on top of multiple different government buildings in Moscow, including the Ministry of Defense and the Kremlin.[26] It is hard to believe that this upgrading of air defense occurred in a vacuum. Russia probably got some intelligence feed that indicated that Ukraine was going to strike at Moscow.

The Russian Pantsir (NATO name for the S-1 system is SA-22 "Greyhound") is a medium-range surface-to-air missile designed to provide point air defense. Three vehicles make up the system: a missile launcher, a radar truck and a command post. It was developed starting in 1990 as the Pantsir-S. Production started in 2008 but was only first deployed in 2012 as the Pantsir-S1. The modernized Pantsir-S2 entered service in 2015. There are multiple variants. The cost of a unit (all three trucks) is $13 to $15 million. The missiles are 168 pounds (76 kilograms) in launch weight and are a little over ten feet long (3.16 meters). There are 12 missiles mounted on the Pantsir and they can be reloaded. There are also two 30m autocannons. It is an effective air defense weapons system.[27]

---

24 Howard Altman and Joseph Trevitnick, "Drone Attack on the Kremlin in Moscow (Updated)," *TWZ*, 3 May 2023. The claim of the amount of explosives is according to the twitter account @front_ukrainian

25 Joseph Trevithick, "Ukrainian drone gets within 70 miles of Moscow," *TWZ*, 28 February 2023.

26 Joseph Trevithich, "Pantsir Air Defense Systems appear on Moscow rooftops," *TWZ*, 19 January 2023. This report recorded them on two buildings, but later Twitter accounts showed seven. See: Joseph Trevithick, "Ukrainian drone gets within 70 miles of Moscow," *TWZ*, 28 February 2023.

27 See: https://www.rusarmy.com/pvo/pvo_vvs/zrk_pantsir-s1.html.

Over 200 have been built, with the Pantsir-S1 most common. In January 2022 it was reported that 116 Pantsir-S21 and S2 units were in service.[28] According the website Oryxspioenkop, as of 27 July 2025, at least 34 Pantsir-S1s have been lost by Russia in the war.[29]

On 23 June 2025 Russia introduced an upgrade of the Pantsir, now carrying 48 "mini-missiles" to be used against drones. This was intended to spare more expensive missile for larger targets. It also provides more missiles so as to make it harder for attacking drones to overwhelm the system.[30] One now sees Russia adjusting to the cost trade-off game that is clearly a factor as this war continues to extend.

Russia struck back. On 3 May 2023 (as of 06:00) it had already launched at least 26 Shahed drones at Ukraine from the Bryansk Oblast and from the eastern coast of the Sea of Azov, effectively from both the north and the south. Ukraine claimed to have shot down 21 (81%). Another four drones were shot down later in the day (as of 17:00), two Lantsets, 1 Merlin-VR, and one unidentified drone.

On the night of 3/4 May by 06:00 Russia had launched another 24 Shahed drones. Ukraine claimed 18 were shot down (75%). Russian drone and missile attacks continued almost every day throughout the month, a total of over 600 attacks for the month of May 2023.

It is hard to pass on a large target like Moscow and on 30 May Ukraine attacked Russia's capital city again with at least eight drones. Russia claimed that five were shot down by Pantsir-S surface-to-air missiles while three others were suppressed by electronic warfare systems. Several of the drones hit around Moscow, causing minor damage. There were no warning signals or alarms. According to Viktor Sobolev, a Duma member, Russian radar was unable to detect the low-flying drones and trigger the air raid alarm. Several of the drones fell in the exclusive southwestern Rublyovka suburb where many senior officials live, including Vladimir Putin. Three of the drones were shot down over Moscow's exclusive Rublyovka suburb. No one in Moscow was seriously injured.[31] Two people suffered minor injuries according to

---

28 *The Military Balance 2022* (Routledge, UK. February 2022).

29 "Attack on Europe: Documenting Russian Equipment Losses During the Russian invasion of Ukraine," *Oryx*, checked 27 July 2025.

30 Boyko Nikolov, "Russia's Pantsir now uses 48 missiles to crush drone threats," *Bulgarianmilitary.com*, 23 June 2025.

31 Nadeem Shad and Robert Greenall, "Moscow drone attack: Putin says Ukraine trying to frighten Russians," *BBC News*, 30 May 2023.

the mayor of Moscow.[32] The attack went from around 06:00 or 06:15 to 07:00 in the morning.[33] Photos and videos from Moscow after the attack showed a few damaged upper stories on buildings. Three residential buildings were hit.[34] There are some claims that up to 25 drones were used.[35]

The drones used were Ukrainian long-range UJ-26 Bobers (Beavers) developed by Ukrjet. This is the same Kyiv-based company that built the UJ-22.[36] A public fundraising campaign for these drones was started in December 2022 and the drones were first publicly seen in action on 11 May 2023. The drone has a canard layout with the tail in front of the main wings and using a pusher propeller in the rear. The drone has a range of 620 miles (1,000 kilometers) and carries a payload of 44 pounds (20 kilograms).[37]

Meanwhile, Ukraine had been undergoing several days of heavy bombardment. Every day from 25 May to 30 May Russia fired between 36 and 76 drones and missiles at Ukraine, for a total over those five days of 187 Shahed and Shahed-type drones, 50 cruise missiles, seven S-300 missiles and three other drones. An apartment in Kyiv was hit early morning of the 30th leaving one person dead and three wounded.[38]

The following week Ukraine initiated its much-anticipated but unsuccessful spring ground offensive.

Kyiv then initiated a campaign to regularly bombard Moscow with drone attacks in June, July, August and September. In May, June and July there were 20 separate reported attacks against Russian cities, Sevastopol

---

32   Christopher Miller and Max Seddon, "Vladimir Putin vows retaliation for drone attack on Moscow," *Financial Times*, 30 May 2023.

33   Andrew Roth and Pjotr Sauer, "Large-scale drone attack hits Moscow for first time in Ukraine war," *The Guardian*, 30 May 2023.

34   Thomas Spencer, Olga Robinson and Jake Horton, "Moscow drone attack: What we know about the strikes," *BBC*, 31 May 2023.

35   Tim Hanlon, "Moscow under siege by drone strikes with explosions in wealthy parts of Russian capital," *Mirror*, 30 May 2023. These claimed has Russia downing 15 of the 25 drones.

36   See www.ukrjet.ua.

37   H. I. Sutton, "Guide to Ukraine's Long Range Attack Drones," *Covet Shores*, 6 July 2025 at http://www.hisutton.com/Ukraine-OWA-UAVs.html.

38   Andrew Roth and Pjotr Sauer, "Large-scale drone attack hits Moscow for first time in Ukraine war," *The Guardian*, 30 May 2023.

and Crimea.[39] Of particular interest were the reported attacks against Moscow on 21 June, 4, 24, 28 and 30 July, and finally on 1 August. On 21 June, Russia claimed a UAV attacked was thwarted near a military base outside of Moscow. On 4 July, Russia claimed it intercepted five drones over Moscow. Four were claimed to be intercepted by air defense while one was suppressed by electronic warfare. There were no casualties. Some flights had to be diverted at one of Moscow's four commercial airports.[40] Early in the morning on 24 July, Ukraine hit two non-residential buildings in Moscow. There were no casualties. The Russian Ministry of Defense said that the two drones were "suppressed by electronic warfare means and crashed." One of the buildings hit was near the Ministry of Defense headquarters.[41] Russia clamed to destroyed another UAV in the Moscow region by air defense on 28 July.[42] On 30 July the Russian Defense Ministry claimed that three drones were intercepted over Moscow, with one drone was shot down and two suppressed by electronic warfare. At least one building was damaged. A security guard was reported wounded. One commercial airport was shut down for an hour.[43] On the same day, the Russian Defense Ministry claimed that 25 UAVs were fired at Russian-occupied Crimea. They claimed to have shot down 16 of them and forced nine others to crash into the Black Sea by signal jamming.[44] A Russian non-residential building was hit again on 1 August. Russia claimed to have shot down two drones while third drone was intercepted, lost control and crashed. It hit the same building

---

39 Joshua Berlinger, "What we know about recent drone strikes in Russian territory," *CNN World*, 1 August 2023.

40 Olga Voitovychj, "Russian military says it shot down 5 drones in attempted 'terrorist' attack near Moscow," *CNN World*, 4 July 2023 and Olga Voitovych, "Moscow mayor says attempted Ukrainian drone attack forces airport to divert flights," *CNN World*, 4 July 2023.

41 John Pennington, "Ukraine carried out drone attack on Moscow, officials say," *CNN World*, 24 July 2023.

42 Olga Voitovych and Alex Stambaugh, "Russia says Ukraine launched drone attack on Moscow region overnight," *CNN World*, 28 July 2023.

43 John Pennington, Mariya Knight, Zahra Ullah and Heather Chen, "Zelensky says war 'returning to Russia' after Moscow drone attack," *CNN World*, 30 July 2023 and "Ukrainian drone attack on Moscow wounds one, shuts airport," *Aljazeera*, 30 July 2023.

44 John Pennington, Mariya Knight, Zahra Ullah and Heather Chen, "Zelensky says war 'returning to Russia' after Moscow drone attack," *CNN World*, 30 July 2023.

that was struck on 30 July. That building, in the financial district of the city, houses government offices. The Russian Ministry of Digital Development may have been targeted.[45]

This was a total of 15 UAVs attacking Moscow between 21 June and 1 August (inclusive). Of those, eight were shot down, five were thwarted by electronic warfare and two we are not certain of. We do not know what Ukrainian cruise missiles or drones were used. In these six drone attacks, there were no casualties reported.

More drone attacks against Moscow occurred on 3, 6, 7, 9, 10, 18, 19, 20, 21, 22, 23 and 26 August 2023. On 3 August, six drones were shot down over Kaluga on the way to Moscow. Kaluga is 124 miles (200 kilometers) southwest of Moscow.[46] On 6 August drones were shot down on the outskirts of Moscow, and on 7 August another seven drones were shot down near Kaluga. On 9 August two drones were shot down heading for Moscow, was also the case the following day.[47] On 18 August one drone was shot down at 04:00 but it crashed into a building, with debris falling on the buildings in the city's Expo Cetner complex.[48] On 19 August another UAV was reported shot down.[49] On 20 August a single drone was suppressed by electronic warfare systems to the south of Moscow and crashed in an unpopulated area. It still forced the temporary closure of two airports.[50] On 21 August two people in Moscow were reported injured when parts of a drone fell on a house in the Moscow region. Russia said it jammed one Ukrainian drone and destroyed another. All four Moscow

---

45   Olga Voitovych, Anna Chernova and Vasco Cotovio, "Russia called second drone strike on Moscow skyscraper 'terrorist attack'," *CNN World*, 1 August 2023.

46   "Russia shoots down drones heading to Moscow," *The Telegraph*, 3 August 2023.

47   "Russia shoots down two armed drones headed for Moscow," *Aljazeera*, 9 August 2023 and "Russia says 13 Ukrainian drones down on way to attack Sevastopol, Moscow," *Aljazeera*, 10 August 2023.

48   "Ukraine combat drone damages building in central Moscow, Russia says," *Aljazeera*, 18 August 2023 and "Drone shot down over central Moscow, no injuries reported," *The Independent*, 18 August 2023.

49   Hafsa Khalil and Adrienne Vogt, "August 19, 2023 – Russia-Ukraine news," *CNN World*, 21 August 2023.

50   "Russian authorities reports attempted drone attacks on Moscow and Rostov region," *Meduza*, 20 August 2023.

commercial airports were temporarily closed down.[51] On 22 August two drones were reported shot down to the west of Moscow. Air traffic was again temporarily shut down at all of Moscow's commercial airports.[52] On 23 August two UAVs were shot down outside of downtown Moscow while another one was electronically disabled over central Moscow. It crashed into a building in downtown Moscow early in the morning. Air traffic was yet again halted at Moscow's commercial airports. This was the sixth day in a row of drone attacks.[53] Another drone was reported downed near Moscow on 26 August once again prompting the closure of Moscow's commercial airports.[54]

On 19 August, amid all the other Ukrainian attacks on Moscow, Belgorod and Crimea, there was a drone attack on the Soltsy-2 air base in Novgorod Oblast in northwestern Russia. A Tu-22M3 bomber was clearly set on fire rather dramatically. Russia claimed that the drone was detected by the airfield's observation post and was then hit by small arms fire. It still managed to "damage" a plane. It is hard to argue with the picture of the plane engulfed in flames: it was destroyed (see photo section). The plane was part of the 52nd Guards Bomber Aviation Regiment. This may have been a targeted revenge strike, as a Tu-22M3 from that regiment had hit a block of apartments in Dnipro in January, killing 30 civilians. This Ukrainian attack took place at 10:00 Moscow time in wet and overcast conditions. Soltsy-2 is around 400 miles (650 kilometers) from the Ukraine border. The Russian Ministry of Defense described the drone as a "copter-type UAV."[55] This probably means a drone with one or more overhead propellors and it may have been flown from inside of Russia.

On 27 August, the SBU launched 16 drones in an attack on a military air base in Kursk. Ukraine claimed that it destroyed four Su-30 and

---

51   "Two injured in Ukrainian drone attack in Moscow region, nearly 50 flights disrupted," *Reuters*, 21 August 2023.

52   "Russian air defences down two drones near Moscow, mayor says," *Aljazeera*, 22 August 2023.

53   "Russia downs 3 combat drones in latest attempted raid on Moscow," *Aljazeera*, 23 August 2023.

54   "Russia destroys drone near Moscow in latest attack on Russian capital," *Aljazeera*, 26 August 2023 and Uliana Horoshko, "Moscow temporarily shuts down all airports," *The Kyiv Independent*, 26 August 2023.

55   Graeme Baker, "Ukrainian drone destroyed Russian supersonic bomber," *BBC*, 22 August 2023 and "Drone attacks military airfield in northwestern Russia," *The Moscow Times*, 19 August 2023.

one MiG-29 fighters. They claimed the radar systems for the S-300 missile system and two Pantsir missile systems were also hit. There is not much confirming evidence, with the Russians reporting a drone strike on an apartment building in Kursk. This building was near military facilities. The SBU claimed that three drones were shot down by Russian air defense while the Russian claimed two drones were destroyed. Ukraine claimed 13 explosions were recorded.[56] It is debatable if any planes were damaged or destroyed.[57] There had been a few other attacks in the Kursk region, on 15 May, 4 August, and 20 August. The attack on 20 August hit the Kusk railway station. Five people sustained minor injuries from glass fragments.[58]

On 30 August there was another airfield attack, this time on Pskov air base near the Estonian border. It is claimed that two Il-76s were destroyed and two others were damaged. Russia said that four planes were damaged. One of the few cases where both sides kind of agree as to losses. Photographic evidence clearly shows one plane destroyed (see photo section). This raid was launched from inside of Russia, according to Kyrylo Budanov, the head of the Ukrainian HUR.[59] While Pskov is far from the Ukrainian border, some 434 miles (700 kilometers), it is right next to the Estonian border, a NATO member and strong supporter of Ukraine. Budanov clearly needed to say if was fired from inside of Russia so as to not bring untoward suspicion on the small former-Soviet Union nation of Estonia or nearby Latvia.

These attacks from 3 August to 30 August 2023 on Moscow included at least another 30 drones. Of those, at least 27 were reported as shot down or destroyed while only three were reported to be suppressed by electronic warfare. In the three attacks on air bases in August, two or three drones were shot down, 13 may have gotten through, one drone

---

56 "Ukrainska Pravda: SBU sources confirm drone attack in Russia's Kursk region," *The Kyiv Independent*, 27 August 2023; "Source in Ukraine intelligence reports drones attack on military airfield in Kursk region," *Meduza*, 27 August 2022; Maryna Shashkova and Chris York, "Kyiv claims 5 Russian fighter jets hit in drone attack on Kursk airfield," *Kyiv Post*, 27 August 2023 and "Night explosions in Kursk: Russians claim drone hit multi-story building," *RBC-Ukraine*, 27 August 2023.

57 Olina Ganyukova, "Satellite images of the Kursk airfield after a drone attack by SBU counterintelligence appear," *OBOZ.UA*, 28 August 2023.

58 Abbey Fenbert, "Russin official claims drone attack on Kursk railway station," *The Kyiv Independent*, 20 August 2023.

59 Robert Greenall, "Ukraine war: Drone attack on Pskov airbase from inside Russia – Kyiv," *BBC News*, 1 September 2023.

was damaged or downed by small arms fire and four or more drones were unaccounted for. It does appear the Russian air defense efforts around Moscow were effective. Air base defense was less effective.

The attacks against Moscow continued in September but only three were recorded. There was an attack on 1 September by a single drone against a factory in Lyubertsy on the outskirts of Moscow. That factory manufactures microchips used in missile production. The mayor of Moscow claimed that Russia shot down the drone, but a plume of smoke was seen rising out of the suburb. It does appear that the factory was hit. A picture of the drone shows a canard airframe, most likely a UJ-26 Bober.[60] On 17 September, one drone was shot down over Moscow.[61] Finally there was an attack on 18 September on Chkalovksy air base. Chkalovsky air base is 19 miles (31 kilometers) northeast of Moscow. This last attack was conducted by saboteurs, not drones. The individuals managed to place and detonate explosives at the airfield, seriously damaging an An-148 passenger jet, an Il-20 ground attack aircraft and an Mi-28 attack helicopter.[62] This attack is all based upon Ukrainian claims, and we have not been able to verify this last report.

Probably the most interesting attack was that on Khalino air base in Kursk Oblast on 24 September 2023. The previous month Ukraine had carried out a drone strike on the Kursk railway station which slightly injured five people. On this day, Russia reported a drone strike on an administrative building in the center of the city. Informal Ukrainian reports said it was an FSB building. Kursk is about 56 miles (90 kilometers) from the border with Ukraine. That strike occurred in the morning, and a few hours later, a second explosion occurred in the city as a drone hit an oil refinery near the local airfield.

Ukraine reported a drone strike on a building at the Khalino air base near Kursk. The Ukrainian military intelligence (GUR) claimed that the regiment commander of the 14th Guards Fighter Aviation Regiment, one of his deputies, an intelligence officer and a group

---

60   "US hails 'notable progress'; in counter-offensive," *The Telegraph*, 1 September 2023 and Will Steward and Rachel Hagan, "Major Russian missile factory goes up in flames after latest Ukrainian drone strike," *The Mirror*, 1 September 2023.

61   "Russian forces destroy 7 Ukrainian drones over Moscow and Crimea: Defense Ministry," *Iran Press TV*, 17 September 2023 via globalsecurity. org.

62   Jake Epstein, "Saboteurs 'blew up' aircraft at a Russian base in the latest in a string of attacks, causing 'hysteria', Ukrainian military intelligence reports," *Business Insider*, undated.

of aviators and air base employees were killed or wounded.[63] Hard to say how the GUR knew such details but one of the people killed is named as Lt-Colonel Aleksandr Gal. He is listed as the regiment deputy commander of military and pollical work, with a birth date of 1 January 1975, making him 48 years old. He was born in the Kursk region. According to the description of this account:[64]

> At the airfield "Khalino" in the Kusk region, a Ukrainian drone was landed by Russian electronic warfare systems on the runway. When the leadership of the aviation regiment and FSB officers arrived for closer inspection drone exploded. As claimed, the following were killed or injured during the explosion:

- Commander of the 14th aviation regiment
- One of his deputies [we believe this must refer to Gal];
- A group of aviator officers;
- A representative of the FSB military counterintelligence;
- Airport employees.

It is a good story. Whether it is true we have no way of confirming, but we gather the death of Lt-Colonel Aleksander Gal is not disputed.

The Khalino air base, or Kursk Vostochny Airport, is located four miles (seven kilometers) east of Kursk. It is primarily a military air base but has been utilized before as a commercial airport. Its runway is 8,200 feet (2,500 meters) long. All commercial activity was banned there starting at 03:45 on 24 February 2022, the day the war started. There have been several strikes against this air base, which is well within range of many Ukrainian weapons. This included a drone strike

---

63   "Ukrainian Drone Strikes Russia's Kursk – Official," *The Moscow Times*, 24 September 2023; Dinara Khalilova, "Media: Russian air regiment command hit in drone attack near Kursk," *The Kyiv Independent*, 25 September 2023 and Sofia Telishevska, "Babel's source in the Main Intelligence Directorate: A drone attacked the command of the Russian air regiment in Kursk," *Babel*, 26 September 2023 at https://babel.ua/news/98812-dzherelo-babelya-v-gur-dron-atakuvav-komanduvannya-aviapolku-rosiyan-u-kursku.

64   See https://topcargo200.com/1070/. Also see "'Air regiment leaders' killed as drone self-destructs on Russian airfield," *Newsweek*, 25 September 2023; Vadim Kurshnikov, "Consequences of the attack on the Russian Khalino air base become known," *Military NYI*, 25 September 2023 and Anna Paskevych, "An attack on an airfield in Kursk killed one of the leaders of the air regiment: details have surfaced. Photo," *Oboz.UA*, 11 December 2023.

on 6 December 2022 on the airport's oil storage, an unverified report of an attack on several aircraft there on 2 June 2023, and now this attack.[65]

There were no Ukrainian drone attacks on Moscow in October, although Ukraine was attacking Belgorod, Sochi, Kursk. Smolensk, Novorossiysk and other places. The same for most of November until the 26th when Ukraine fired 24 drones at Moscow, Tula, Kaluga, Smolensk and Bryansk, according to Russian reports. In addition, Russia claimed that it intercepted 53 drones over Ukrainian areas under Russia control. No one was injured in Moscow but one person in Tula received a slight cut after one of the drones there crashed into an apartment building. The Russian Defense Ministry identified 17 of the missiles as HIMARS and also claimed to have shot down two S-200 anti-aircraft missiles.[66] One Russia Pantsir-S booster broke through the wall of a residence in the Moscow region. No one was injured.[67] While we think the vast majority of the drones went towards Moscow, we did not get a count of the number spotted over Moscow vice other areas of Russia.

On 25 November Russia had fired around 75 Shahed drones at Ukraine, mostly at Kyiv.[68] The Ukrainian attack on the 26th may have been part of the tit-for-tat response that now seemed to be regularly occurring.

This was the last attack on Moscow for a while.

There was also a series of attacks against Russia air bases. The attack on Millerovo air base on 25 February 2022 and the attack on Engel-2 on 5 December 2022 are described above. On 10 April 2023 a drone carrying a bomb crashed into a fence at Belgorod airport. This was a

---

65   The source of the report for the 2 June 2023 attack was the twitter account @NEOLreports. They stated: "Needs verification. But based on preliminary info, in Kursk, Russia, several Su-34 jets were reportedly damaged. Also a Pantsir-1C air defense missile system was destroyed. This due to an unknown strike, carried out today at an airfield in the Kursk region, possibly Vostochny." This has still not been verified.

66   Yulia Kesaleva, Alex Stambaugh, Darya Tarasova and Radina Gigova, "Russia destroyed Ukrainian drones including over Moscow, defense ministry says," *CNN*, 26 November 2023.

67   Tetiana Lozovenko, "Russian air defence system breaks through wall of house near Moscow during drone attack," *Ukrainska Pravda* 25, 27 November 2025.

68   Maria Kostenko, Daria Tarasova Marchkina, Jessie Yeung and Hafsa Khalil, "Russia launches biggest drone attack against Kyiv since start of the war, Ukrainian officials say," *CNN World*, 25 November 2023. Ukraine claimed to have intercepted 71 drones.

commercial airport that had been closed since 24 February 2022. No casualties were reported.[69] On 2 July 2023 a Ukrainian missile was shot down near Primorsko-Akhtarsk air base, leaving a rather impressive 10-meter wide by 4-meter deep crater 200 meters from the airfield. There were no casualties.[70]

And then on 19 August 2023 was the drone strike on Soltsy air base, also described above. On 25 August a Ukrainian S-200 missile was shot down near Shaykovka air base near Kaluga, not far from Moscow. Then on 27 August came the large 16-drone strike against Khalino air base near Kursk followed by the successful drone attack on 30 August against Pskov, the sabotage attack on 18 September on Chkalovsky air base near Moscow and the drone strike on Khalino airfield that killed or wounded a number of commanders. These attacks are described above. There was also a drone strike on Sochi airport on 20 September that set a fuel storage tank on fire.

The next attacks included multiple drones attacking Adler air base in Sochi on 1 October, and an attack on 18 October 2023 against Khalino air base near Kursk using SBU-launched drones,

This is not much considering how many times Ukraine has been hit by drones, missiles and aircraft. This is thirteen air base attacks in the first 22 months of the war and maybe five planes destroyed (a Tu-22M3, an Su-30SM and three Il-76s).

The campaign against Moscow was then ended and no more drone attacks against Russia's capital city were recorded until 1 September 2024. This was a ninth-month break.

Ukraine did conduct a sabotage attack against Russia helicopters at an air base in the Moscow region on 21 July 2024 that claimed to have damaged two helicopters, an Mi-28 and a Ka-226.[71] They also did another sabotage attack the same day in Samara Oblast which destroyed an Mi-8 helicopter. Ukraine did another sabotage attack in Moscow on 24 July when a GRU officer and his wife were wounded by a bomb planted under their car. On 21 August 2024 11 drones intercepted on the way to Moscow.

---

69 "Russian media report 'drone attack' on Belgorod airport," *The New Voice of Ukraine*, 11 April 2023.

70 Alexander Khrebet, "Explosion reported near airfield in southern Russia," *The Kyiv Independent*, 2 July 2023.

71 Yulia Akymova and Oleksandra Bashchenko, "Ukrainian intelligence damages 3 helicopters on Russian territory, sources say," *RBC-Ukraine*, 27 July 2024.

The attack against Moscow on 1 September 2024 was the first major drone attack on the city in nine months, since 26 November 2023. It was part of a massive launch by Ukraine of over a hundred drones against multiple targets in Russia. It was Ukraine's first strike of over a hundred drones in this war. In contrast, up until 1 September 2024, Russian had conducted at least seven attacks against Ukraine of a hundred or more drones and missiles.[72]

This attack was repeated on 10 September 2024, when Ukraine launched 144 drones against nine regions of Russia, of which 20 were downed in the Moscow region, where one Russian was reported killed in this attack and eight wounded (three hospitalized).[73]

These were the last attacks against Moscow until 10 November 2024, when at least 34 drones were launched. The previous night they had launched an attack 120 miles (190 kilometers) south of Moscow on the Aleksin Chemical Plant in the Tula province using at least 13 drones.[74]

These were the last attacks against Moscow in 2024 and no attacks have been made against Moscow for 2025 through the end of August 2025. Three assassinations were attempted in Moscow during that time, all three successful.

Meanwhile in 2024, attacks against air bases continued. On 3 January 2024 a Ukrainian saboteur set fire to a Su-34 fighter-bomber at Chelybinsk Shagol Airport. The plane probably only suffered minor damage.[75]

---

72 This includes 16 December 2022 (103), 29 December 2023 (158), 2 January 2024 (134), 22 March 2024 (151), 29 March 2024 (101), 1 June 2024 (100) and 26 August 2024 (236). It may have also included 15 November 2022 (96), 10 February 2023 (96+) and 1 January 2024 (99). These counts are based, of course, on Ukrainian reporting. See Appendix I.

73 "A woman is killed near Moscow after more than 140 Ukrainian drones target Russia, officials say," *AP*, 10 September 2024; Dmytro Basmat and Olena Goncharova, "Moscow claims Ukraine launched 'massive' 144-drone attack on Russia, casualties reported," *The Kyiv Independent*, 10 September 2024; Yuri Zoria, "Russia claims it downed 144 drones on their way to Moscow," *Euromaidan Press*, 10 September 2024; and "Ukraine Launches 144-drone barrage on Russia, targeting Moscow and key regions," *Kyiv Post*, 10 September 2024.

74 "Attack on Russian chemical plant gets new details," *RBC-Ukraine*, 9 November 2024.

75 *Aviation Safety Network*, 4 January 2024 at https://asn.flightsafety.org/wikibase/349609 says it was "minor" damage. Also see: David Axe, "A

On 23 February 2024 Ukraine shot down a Beriev A-50U over the Sea of Azov. It was operational A-50U, named "42 red." It was probably done with a Polish-provided S-200 surface-to-air missile.

The Ukrainians had retired their S-200s in October 2013. They had four active batteries in 2010. It was old and obsolete and had high maintenance costs. It was the missile that Ukraine had used to accidently shoot down a Russia Tu-154 passenger jet over the Black Sea on 4 October 2001, killing all 78 people on board. The S-200 surface-to-air missile system, the SA-5 "Gammon," was developed by the Soviet Union in the 1960s as a long-range high-altitude missile. The Poles had done a refit of the S200VE (Vega-E") system between 1999 and 2002 to create the S-200C "Vega." In 2023 Poland provided Ukraine with twelve of its S-200 systems, which they were intending to retire, along with twenty missiles. Poland had maintained three batteries of these missiles. It has a range of 186 miles (300 kilometers) and warhead of 478 pounds (217 kilograms).[76] Ukraine also restored some of the systems and missiles that they had retired a decade earlier. They also repurposed the missile to do ground attack.[77] We have seen three of them used in a surface attack role on 12 August 2023 against the Kerch Strait Brigade, again on 25 August 2023 to attack the Shaykovka air base in Kaluga province, and on 26 November 2023 Russian claimed to have shot down two S-200s that were attacking Moscow.

Anyhow, the crew of ten went down with the plane, including five majors.[78] As Russia only has a half-dozen of these AEW&C plane operational, this was a significant coup. It was reported that five other planes were recalled from combat operations after the A-50 was shot down.

Ukrainian saboteur traveled 900 miles to a snowy Russian airfield and, in the dead of night, lit a Russian Sukhoi fighter-bomber on fire," *Forbes*, 4 January 2024. This article provides the video of the fire on the plane, but it is not too convincing.

76   "Poland Delivers Soviet-made S-200 surface-to-air missiles to Ukraine," *Defense News Army 2024*, 6 June 2024 and "Ukrainian Military may have received S-200 air defense systems from Poland," *Defense Express*, 5 June 2024.

77   Thomas Newdick, "Is Ukraine using old S-200 SAMs in the land-attack role?," TWZ, 10 July 2023.

78   Roman Kravets and Roman Petrenko, "10 Russians, including 5 majors, killed in down A-60 aircraft – Ukrainska Pravda sources," *Ukrainska Pravda 25*, 24 February 2024. The article does list all ten crew members by name.

On 5 April 2024 Ukraine conducted a large attack of 53 drones against four air bases in western Russia. This included at least 44 drones fired at Morozovsk air base in Rostov province. This is only 81 miles (130 kilometers) from the Ukrainian border, although it is further from the front lines. It has a concrete runway 8,100 feet (2,472 meters) in length. Open-source intelligence shows that the air base housed 26 Su-34s and three Su-035 on 4 April.[79]

Russian claimed it intercepted 44 drones before they reached the base, but there were clearly multiple explosions in and around the air base. The Ukrainians claimed six aircraft destroyed, eight substantially damaged and 20 personnel killed or wounded.[80] It does not appear that any of these plane losses were validated.[81] We assume personnel losses were 20 killed or injured, although this has also not been confirmed. Russian reports say that eight were injured not far from the aerodrome.[82]

Russia reports intercepting six drones over Krasnodar region, and one drone each over Saratov, Kursk and Belgorod.[83] In the case of Engels-2 air base in Saratov, there were explosions reported at 05:00. Ukraine claimed that seven airmen were killed and three Tu-95MS were damaged, although Russia said there were no losses.[84] We suspect the Russian reports are true in this case. Engels is around 466 miles (750 kilometers) from the Ukrainian border. It has a concrete runway of 11,483 feet (3,500 meters) and then large revetments for protecting

---

79   Kateryna Zakharchenko and Alisa Orlova, "Kyiv confirms Ukrainian drones destroyed 6 Russian planes at air base, as many as 3 sites blasted," *Kyiv Post*, 5 April 2024. They reference OSINT researcher MT Anderson @MT_Anderson on twitter (now known as X).

80   "Ukrainian drones target Russian airfield in Rostov, described as one of Kyiv's largest air operations of the war," *SOFX*, 6 April 2024; and Olena Ivashkiv, "Ukrainian drones attack military airfield in Russia's Rostov Oblast en masse – video, *Ukrainska Pravda 25*, 5 April 2024. This last source reports more than 60 explosions and provides video.

81   Olena Ivashkiv, "ISW finds no visual evidence of Russian aircraft being hit at airbases," *Ukrainska Pravda 25*, 6 April 2024.

82   Robert Greenall, "Ukraine war; six Russian planes destroyed by drones, says Kyiv," *BBC News*, 5 April 2024. This article also has a video of a light plane converted to a UAV striking in Tatarstan on 2 April.

83   Anna Chernova, Victoria Butenko and Sophie Tanno, "Ukraine claims major drone strike on Russian airfield, killing servicemen and destroying aircraft," *CNN World*, 5 April 2024.

84   "Ukraine organizes attack on three Russian airfield, Tu-95MS damaged," *RBC-Ukraine*, 5 April 2024.

their planes. Friedrich Engels was the communist philosopher who co-authored books with Karl Marx.

In the case of Yeysk airport in Krasnodar, explosions were reported at 03:00 at the airfield.[85] Yeysk, on the Sea of Azov, was only 24 miles (39 kilometers) from the Ukrainian border at the start of the war. It is claimed that four people were killed there and two Su-25s were destroyed.[86] We also assume that these reports are not correct. Yeysk was a concrete runway also of 11,483 feet (3,500 meters), although we gather it was extended to this length around 2024.

Open-source satellite imagery showed on 4 April that Engels air base had five Tu-95s, one Tu-22, three Tu-160s and an Il-76 transport plane. Yeysk air base had 10 L-39 trainers, five An-26 transports, one An-74 transport, one An-12 transport, four Su-27 fighters, four Su-25 ground attack planes, one Su-30 fighter, and several Ka-52 and Mi-8 helicopters.[87]

This was the first time Ukraine attempted strikes on multiple air bases in Russia. They may have also attempted to target a fourth air base in Kursk Oblast.

The S-200 struck again on 19 April 2024 when Ukraine shot down a Tu-22M3 over Stavropol Krai in the North Caucasus region of southern Russia. The bomber was returning to base (Engels-2 in Saratov?). Ukraine claimed to have shot it down at a range of 308 kilometers. Two of the four crew were killed or missing. Russia claimed, of course, that it was a technical malfunction.[88] This was the second Tu-22M3 that Ukraine has

---

85   Anna Chernova, Victoria Butenko and Sophie Tanno, "Ukraine claims major drone strike on Russian airfield, killing servicemen and destroying aircraft," *CNN World*, 5 April 2024. There are reports of more than 10 explosions over Yeysk.

86   "Ukraine organizes attack on three Russian airfields, Tu-95MS damaged," *RBC-Ukraine*, 5 April 2024.

87   Olena Ivashkiv, "ISW finds no visual evidence of Russian aircraft being hit at airbases," *Ukrainska Pravda 25*, 6 April 2024.

88   "At least nine killed in Ukraine strikes as Kyiv says it downed Russian warplane," *France 24*, 19 April 2024; Kateryna Hodunova, "'Air Force' Ukraine downs Russian Tu-22M3 bomber for first time," *The Kyiv Independent*, 19 April 2024; Kateryna Zakharchenko, "Kyiv destroyed Russian long-range bomber used in Odesa attack," *Kyiv Post*, 19 April 2024; and Thomas Newdick and Howard Altman, "Russian Tu-22M3 Backfire shot down with S-200 missile: Ukraine's spy chief," *TWZ*, 19 April 2024. These last two articles provide video of the bomber going down.

destroyed, the previous one (set on fire) on 19 August 2023 at Soltsy-2 air base in Novgorod. This was slowly attriting the Russians' bomber force, which they did not have the ability to easily replace.

Also starting in January 2024, Ukraine went on an air campaign against Russian oil facilities. This also relied primarily on drones. These strikes occurred widely across Russia, including in St. Petersburg, Volgograd (previously known as Stalingrad), Belgorod, Kursk, Ryazan, and a wide range of other targets, including even in Tatarstan, some 807 miles (1,300 kilometers) from the Ukrainian border. This campaign against the oil refineries and other facilities ran for a month, starting on 9 January and appearing to have ended with their last big strikes on 9 February. This story deserves further exploration as it was Ukraine's attempt at a coordinated strategic air campaign.

Before the strikes in January, there had been a number of attacks against oil depots and refineries. These were scattered in time and location.[89] In January, multiple major strikes were attempted. This started on the afternoon of 9 January with several drones attacking "facilities of a fuel and energy complex" in Oryol. A drone hit the Orelnefteprodukt oil depot and another drone struck the building of local energy provider Oryolenergo. Three people were reported injured, but only one was hospitalized. It appears that at least three drones were involved in this attack.[90]

The attacks continued with a drone attack on the oil terminal in St. Petersburg on 18 January, a drone attack on an oil depot in Bryansk Oblast on 19 January, a drone strike on a gas terminal in Leningrad Oblast on 21 January, drones attacking the Tuapse oil terminal in Krasnodar Krai on 25 January, another drone attack on St. Petersburg against an oil refinery on 31 January, a drone attack on 3 February on

---

89   Attempted strikes include: 25 April 2022 in Bryansk, 22 June in Rostov, 15 October in Belgorod, 16 November in Oryol, 28 February 2023 in Krasnodar, 4 March in Belgorod, 4 May in Rostov, 11 May in Bryansk, 28 July in Samara, 17 September in Oryol, and 29 October in Krasnodar. They tended to be focused on oil depot (19 cases) and oil refineries (20 case). See Appendix II.

90   Dinara Khalilova, "Drones reported hit oil deport, energy provider in Russia's Oryol region," *The Kyiv Independent*, 9 January 2024. The article also reports explosions on 8 January at a railway track by an oil depot at Nizhny Tagil (in Sverdlovsk Oblast in Siberia) and a fire at a substation in Moscow on 4 January. Not sure if these are due to Ukrainian action.

the Volgograd Refinery in Volgograd Oblast, and on 9 February drone attacks against the Ilsky Oil refinery in Krasnodar Kai that set it on fire.

Meanwhile, starting in June 2024, the campaign against the air bases began again with a drone strike on 8 June on Akhtubinsk in Astrakhan Oblast. Two Su-57 fighters may have been damaged, with one of them clearly severely so. It may not have been repairable.[91] Russia also claimed to have shot down three Ukrainian drones near an air base near Mozdok in North Ossetia.

The Russian Defense Ministry claimed it downed 40 Ukrainian drones that night. Two struck an electronic warfare facility in Chuvashia, over 373 miles (600 kilometers) east of Moscow. In Voronezh Oblast, 25 drones were intercepted. One damaged a gas pipeline, sparking a small fire according to Russian official reports.[92]

On 14 June Ukraine attacked Morozovsk air base in Rostov Oblast with at least 70 drones. This was probably the single biggest drone strike done to date by Ukraine. It was claimed by Russian unofficial sources that 6 were killed and 10 wounded. Two Su-34s were damaged. After-action satellite photos clearly show the base was hit and it appears that two Su-34s suffered some damage. This base was about 174 miles (280 kilometers) from the front lines and housed Su-34s, fighter-bombers, and Su-24 and Su-24M fighters.[93] Russia claimed to have destroyed 87 drones that day: Belgorod (2 drones), Voronezh (6 drones), Kursk (6 drones), Rostov (70 drones), Volgograd (2 drones) oblasts, and one drone shot down over Crimea. In the Voronezh Oblast some fuel tanks were damaged.[94]

Ukraine then continued its efforts with another attack on Yeysk air base on 21 June. Then there was a sabotage attack by the Freedom of Russia Legion on 18 July against Bolshoye Savino airport in Perm out in Siberia. This base hosts MiG-31 fighters, but it appears that no planes were damaged, although two KAMAZ trucks were seen burning in videos. The Freedom of Russia Legion are Russians fighting

---

91   Howard Altman and Tyler Rogoway, "Su-57 Felon struck deep inside Russia, Ukraine's spy agency claims (update)," *TWZ*, 9 June 2024.

92   Haye Kesteloo, "Russia unleashes record 479-drone barrage on Ukraine, escalating aerial warfare," *Dronexl*, 9 June 2025.

93   Yuri Zoria, "At least two Russian Su-34 bombers damaged in Ukrainian drone attack at Morozovsk airfield," *Euromaidan Press*, 15 June 2024.

94   Abbey Fenbert, "Drone attack in Rostov Oblast causes blackouts, fire," *The Kyiv Independent*, 14 June 2024.

against the current government of President Putin, freedom fighters or traitors, depending on your point of view. This may have not been in coordination with Ukraine. Still, Ukraine continued targeting air bases in July and August. On 20 July Millerovo air base in Rostov Oblast was hit by a drone strike that generated 16 explosions and a rather impressive fire. The Russian governor of Rostov Oblast said the Russian air defense shot down 26 drones that night.[95] The following day Ukrainian GUR saboteurs attacked a helicopter facility in Moscow at 03:00 in the morning and also the Kryazh air base in Samara. It is claimed they damaged two helicopters in Moscow, an Mi-28a and a Ka-226 and destroyed an Mi-8 in Samara.[96]

Attacks continued with drone attacks on Olenya, Engels and Dyigilevo on 27 July. These were two of the five targets of Operation Spider's Web. The drones attacked all three air bases and also an oil refinery in Ryazan Oblast. The attack on Dyagilevo airfield occurred at 06:00 with three explosions reported. The attack on Engels airfield occurred at 08:00. The attack on Olenya took place at 15:47. Two Tu-22Ms were damaged on Olenya. Russia reported that a total of twelve drones were shot down in Kursk, Belgorod, Rostov, Bryansk and Lipetsk regions.[97]

This was followed up by a major drone attack on Morozovsk air base in Rostov Oblast on 3 August. They also hit fuel storage facilities in Kamensky and Morozovsky districts. Fuel tanks were hit and some fires were reported, including one at the air base.[98] This does not appear to be near as big of an attack at the one using at least 70 drones on 13 June.

---

95   Olha Hlushchenko, "Russians claim large-scale UAV attack on Rostov Oblast, airfield on fire – videos," *Ukrainska Pravda 25*, 20 July 2024.

96   "Ukraine's intelligence hits three helicopters in Russia – source," *Ukrinform*, 27 July 2024. Mi-8 destroyed appears to be confirmed. See Aviation Safety Network at https://asn.flightsafety.org/wikibase/414382 which references this picture on twitter (X): https://x.com/MarcinRogowsk14/status/1828225802921484794.

97   Daryna Vialko, "Two Tu-22M3 bombers damaged during strike on Olenya airfield – Defense Intelligence of Ukraine," *RBC-Ukraine*, 30 July 2024 and Uliana Bezpalko and Oleksandra Bashchenko, "Ukrainian drones attack oil refinery and air bases in Russia, damaging Tu-22M3," *RBC-Ukraine*, 27 July 2024.

98   Abbey Fenbert, "Drones hit warehouses, fuel tanks in Rostov Oblast, official says," *The Kyiv Independent*, 3 August 2024.

This was followed on 8 August with a large drone attack on Lipetsk air base, which is 186 miles (300 kilometers) from the Ukrainian border. Multiple explosions were observed and a fire broke out. Lipetsk usually has two dozen or more Su-34s, Su-35s and MiG-31s there, although there were no reports of any planes lost. One source reported that nine people were injured while the governor of Lipetsk reported that six people had been injured.[99] A number of buildings were hit and set fire, and supposedly more than 700 bombs were destroyed. Russia said that it intercepted 75 different drones over six different oblasts and Crimea. They also said that seven naval drones in the Black Sea had been intercepted.[100]

On 14 August 2024 a massive attack by 117 drones was conducted against four air bases. These were Savaleyka air base in Nizhny Novgorod Oblast, Khalino air base in Kursk Oblast, the Voronezh Malshevo air base (also called the Baltimore air base) in Voronezh Oblast, and Borisoglebsk air base in Voronezh Oblast. Russia claimed they destroyed four Tochka-U missiles and 117 drones. They reported 37 drones and four tactical missiles destroyed over the Kursk Oblast, 37 drones destroyed over the Voronezh Oblast, 17 drones destroyed over the Belgorod Oblast, eleven drones destroyed over the Nizhny Novgorod Oblast, nine drones destroyed over the Volgograd Oblast, three over the Bryansk Oblast, two over the Oryol Oblast and one over the Rostov Oblast.[101] The attacks over Nizhny Novgorod were spotted at 06:00.[102] This was the largest drone attack by Ukraine since the war began. The figure of 117 drones has no particular significance as this was the Russian claim of what they shot down. The number of drones fired may have been more.

---

99 Ruxanda Iordache, "Ukraine unleashes large drone attack on Russian airfield as Kyiv's offensive continues," *CNBC*, 9 August 2024; and "Ukraine's General Staff confirms strike on Russian Lipetsk air base – video," *Ukrainska Pravda*, 9 August 2024.

100 Nate Ostiller, "Updated: 700 bombs destroyed in Ukrainian strike against Russia's Lipetsk airbase, source says," *The Kyiv Independent*, 9 August 2024.

101 Telegram channel for Minister of Defense of Russia on 14 August 2024 at https://t.me/mod_russia/42135; and Constant Meheut, "Ukraine Captures Russian Town, Zelensky Says," *The New York Times*, 15 August 2024.

102 "The largest attack. 11 drones were shot down in the sky over the Nizhny Novgorod region," *NNRU*, 14 August 2024 at https://www.nn.ru/text/incidents/2024/08/14/73955750/.

The damage to the air bases seems fairly limited for what was an attack by 117 drones and four missiles. Eleven drones hit Savasleyka air base. Eleven MiG-31 K/I fighters, an Il-76 transport, five Mi-8 and Mi-24 helicopters were based there at the time of the 13 August strike conducted the previous day.[103] It appears that one MiG-31 K/I fighter was destroyed along with two Il-76s transports, with five other planes damaged, although this has not been confirmed.[104] The Ukrainian General Staff stated on their Facebook page that "The main objects of the attack were the warehouses of fuel-oil materials and means of attack [we assume this means stored bombs and missiles]."[105] At Borisoglebsk air base, photos show two hangers had been struck. There appears to be damage to two fighter aircraft. At Savasleyka air base the damage appears more limited.[106]

On 22 August Marinovka air base in the Volgograd Oblast was attacked by drones. This resulted in six to ten reported explosions at 03:30 and a fire at the base. Ukraine claimed to hit a fuel warehouse and bomb storage. On 19 August, satellite footage showed nearly 30 warplanes at the base and eight trucks.[107] After that, there were no more air base attacks for a few weeks, although the Ukrainians were back to striking at oil depots and facilities, with oil depots and refineries hit on 18 August in the Rostov Oblast, on 26 August at Omsk, on 28 August at Rostov Oblast, on 28 August at Kirov Oblast, on 1 September with massive 100+ drone strike on a power station in Tver Oblast and a

---

103 Kateryna Denisova, "Ukraine destroys 3, damages around 5 Russian aircraft in recent attack, source says," *The Kyiv Independent*, 21 August 2024.

104 "Russian Savasleyka airbase attacked by drones: Ukrainian intelligence reveals aftermath of strike," *RBC-Ukraine*, 21 August 2024. The video provided in the article is not definitive.

105 Facebook page for General Staff of the Armed Forces at https://www.facebook.com/GeneralStaff.ua/posts/ pfbid05kqUx7YtawpKgMaGVGtfdxqbp8mt YKL6xS5rirdKFjpgvyzcaPoVWA5tVNj8sukXl.

106 Samya Kullab and Hann Arhirova, "Zelenskyy says Ukrainian troops have taken full control of the Russian town of Sudzha," *AP World News*, 15 August 2024.

107 Olena Goncharova and Matin Fornusek, "Updated: Ukraine hits fuel and bomb warehouses in Russia's Volgograd region airfield, source says," *The Kyiv Independent*, 22 August 2024 and Kateryna Serohina, "Drone attack reported in Volgograd region that caused fire at airfield," *RBC-Ukraine*, 22 August 2024.

refinery in Moscow. Ukraine then switched to two attacks on 18 and 21 September on ammunition depots. This does all seems to be a thought-out and coordinated series of campaigns, but one does wonder if they would have been better served to concentrate everyone on a single type of target, like oil refineries.

The attacks on air bases were renewed with another attack on 3 October, Borisoglebsk air base in Voronezh Oblast and 10 October on Khanskaya air base in the Republic of Adygea. On 14 November drones attacked Krymsk air base in Krasnodar. Russian claimed they shot down 51 drones.[108]

On 20 January 2025 they actually went after airplane production capability with a drone attack hit the Tu-160 plant in Kazan, Tatarstan. The large Gorbunov Kazan Aviation Plant is about 620 miles (1,000 kilometers) from the Ukrainian border. Several explosions were observed but local Russian sources state that damaged was minimal.[109] Russia reported shooting down 31 Ukrainian drones in Tatarstan and five other regions. Regional authorities in Bryansk region said that 14 drones and four HIMARS missiles were destroyed.[110] The plant produces around two Tu-160s every one or two years, if that.[111] This was the only active strategic bomber production facility in Russia.

This all had added up to some attrition of the Russian Air Force. These attacks probably resulted in 10 or 11 planes destroyed. This includes: one Su-30SM fighter destroyed on 25 February 2022, an Il-76 transport on 1 March 2022, a Tu-22M3 set on fire on 19 August 2023, one or two Il-76s on 30 August 2023, on 23 February 2024 Ukraine shot down a Beriev A-50U over the Sea of Azov with a S-200 missile, a second Tu-22M3 shot down over Russian on 19 April 2024 by an S-200, an Mi-8 destroyed by sabotage on 21 June 2024, and maybe a MiG-31 destroyed on 14 August 2024 along with another two Il-76s. Of those,

---

108 "Russia says UAVs attack their military airfield in Krasnodar territory," *Ukrinform*, 15 November 2024.

109 "Explosions rock Russian nuclear aviation plant after massive drone raid," *Newsweek*, 20 January 2025.

110 "Ukrainian drones target industrial plants in Russia's Tatarstan," *The Moscow Times*, 20 January 2024.

111 Ivan Khomenko, "Russia's Tu-160 bomber factory see major activity. Here's what satellite images show," *United 24 Media*, 29 June 2025. They produced one or two bombers in 2022, and two more in 2024. The plans are to build a total of 50 new Tu-160M2s.

seven or eight planes or helicopters were destroyed at bases in drone attacks, one by sabotage and two shot down by missiles.

Seven to eight planes were destroyed in at least 43 air base attacks by drones or missiles through the end of January 2025. At least 352 drones were fired in those attacks, along with at least eight missiles. This is 45 drones or missiles fired per plane killed (assuming eight destroyed). To put that in perspective, Operation Spider's Web fired 117 drones (shipped 150) and killed 13 planes, or nine drones per every plane destroyed (or 11.5 based upon the number shipped).

Russian losses from a variety of aerial operations were significant. According to one list, Russian combat jet aircraft lost in the war through July 2025 was 92.[112] Three of those were from drone attacks.

Ukraine has also conducted limited ground operations of some significance. First was the offensive into the Russian Kursk Oblast in August 2024. This ended up taking 2.84% of the Oblast, or over 1,000 square kilometers, by September 2024. Its control was reduced to 1.48% by November 2024 and they were still holding onto 1.20% as of March 2025. They were then completely driven out of the province due to Russian and North Korean pressure. They also control 4% of Belgorod Oblast.[113]

The drone and missile war heats up (2025)
The air war to date had been an uneven exchange. Just in the last four months of 2022 Russia had fired at least 1,234 drones and missiles at Ukraine or over ten a day. The tempo definitely increased on 10 October and after. From 1 September through 9 October, they fired an average of five (4.7) drones or missiles a day. From 10 October through 31 December, Russia fired an average of around thirteen (12.5) drones or missiles a day.

In contrast, from the beginning of war for 2022 (for more than ten months) we record for Ukraine only 49 attacks on Russia (this does not

---

112 See Wikipedia "List of aviation shootdown and accidents during the Russo-Ukrainian War." This count includes destroyed (not damaged) MiG-31s (3), Su-24s (9), Su-25s (32), Su-27s (3), Su-30s (12), Su-34s (25), Su-35s (7), Su-57s (0 – 1 damaged) and Il-22Ms (1 destroyed and one listed as damaged, although it was most likely destroyed). The list includes the three jets destroyed by drone attacks and the Il-22 shot down. The Wikipedia listing does not include the MiG-31 lost on 14 August 2024, or the Il-76 lost on 1 March 2022, or the two Il-76s lost on 14 August 2024.

113 Again, all these statistics are from War Mapper.

include seized territory in Ukraine including Crimea), consisting of at least 6 drones and 15 missiles fired at Russia. These attacks did kill 22 people and wounded or injured at least 49 more. Losses caused by Russian attacks were much higher. In 2022 alone Russia fired at least 2,273 drones and missiles at Ukraine.

In 2023 Russia had fired at least 4,598 drones and missiles at Ukraine. This was around thirteen (12.6) drones and missiles a day. The last four months of the year it had increased to around eighteen (17.8) a day. In contrast, for 2023 Ukraine conducted only 118 attacks, firing more than 253 drones and missiles (21 or more missiles). This resulted in Russia reporting the deaths of at least 42 Russians and at least 157 injured.

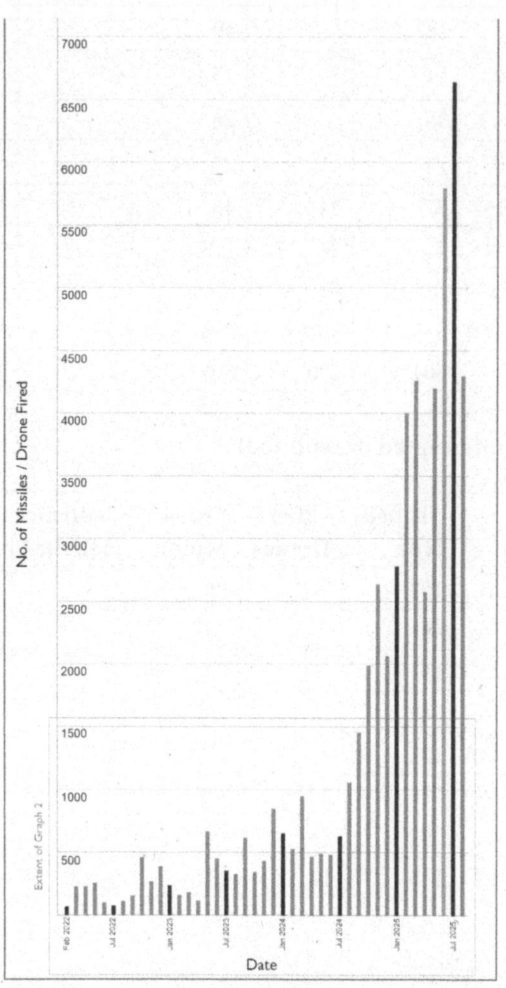

Graph 1: Russian drones and missiles fired at Ukraine.

Totals for 2022 (intercepted or reported):

		Drones	Shahed	Cruise Missiles	Ballistic Missiles	Other Missiles	Helicopters & Planes
January	N/A						
February	67	1		25	-	-	41
March	197 + 25 = 222	40		62	-	-	120
April	220	105		51	-	-	64
May	249	183		49	-	-	17
June	94 + 6 = 100	71		25	2	-	2
July	74	45		26	-	-	3
August	97 + 10 = 107	74		24	2	-	7
September	137 + 15 = 152	57	24	46	-	1	24
October	42 + 403 = 445	6	243	168	-	-	28
November	220 + 40 = 260	14	64	176	-	-	6
December	295 + 82 = 377	8	99	235	-	32	3
2022	**2,273**	**604**	**430**	**887**	**4**	**33**	**315**

Totals for 2023 (intercepted or reported):

	Total	Shahed-type	Other Drones	Cruise Missiles	Ballistic Missiles	Other Missiles	Helicopters & Planes
January	210 + 21 = 231	108	9	96	-	-	18
February	137 + 19 = 156	48	3	102	-	-	3
March	112 + 64 = 176	86	1	72	-	15	2
April	100 + 13 = 113	76	14	23	-	-	-
May	495 + 151 = 646	407	48	170	8	12	1
June	401 + 38 = 439	195	43	174	16	4	7
July	330 + 14 = 344	202	43	92	6	-	1
August	262 + 55 = 317	165	14	121	7	8	2

September	490 + 109 = 599	497	15	84	1	2	-
October	257 + 76 = 333	281	15	22	6	9	-
November	325 + 94 = 419	377	7	19	5	11	-
December	645 + 180 = 825	623	-	130	23	41	7 + 1 ship
2023	**4,598**	**3,065**	**212**	**1,105**	**72**	**102**	**41 + 1**

Totals for 2024 (intercepted or reported):

	Total	Shahed-type	Other Drones	Cruise Missiles	Ballistic Missiles	Other Missiles	Helicopters & Planes
January	420 + 213 = 633	362	-	157	57	55	2
February	365 + 149 = 514	377	-	79	16	29	13
March	731 + 193 = 924	650	4	173	29	66	2
April	346 + 107 = 453	287	21	90	17	37	1
May	427 + 51 = 478	357	12	83	7	19	-
June	407 + 60 = 467	333	9	108	16	1	-
July	523 + 88 = 611	429	83	78	21	-	-
August	875 + 156 = 1,031	790	24	159	46	12	-
September	1300 + 165 = 1,465	1,337	-	64	38	26	-
October	1,991	1,916	4	35	23	13	-
November	2,615	2,363	-	224	19	9	-
December	2,074	1,850	-	177	28	19	-
2024	**13,256**	**11,051**	**157**	**1,427**	**317**	**286**	**18**

Totals for 2025:

	Total	Shahed-type	Other Drones	Cruise Missiles	Ballistic Missiles	Other Missiles	Helicopters & Planes
January	2,701	2,629	-	49	18	5	-
February	4,000	3,902	-	71	25	2	-
March	4,280	4,198	-	52	21	9	-
April	2,598	2,476	-	87	25	10	-
May	4,127	4,005	-	73	47	2	-
June	5,677	5,438	-	172	59	8	-
July	6,438	6,240	-	118	56	24	-
August	4,288	4,132	(12)	98	50	8	-
September							
October							
November							
December							
2025							

In 2024 Russia had fired at least 13,256 drones and missiles at Ukraine. This a massive growth in offensive bombardment power, almost three times the drones and missiles fired at Ukraine the previous year. This massive increase was almost entirely due to the Iranian Shahed drone and Russian-manufactured versions of the same drone. Russia fired at least 11,051 of these drones at Ukraine. This made up 83% of their activity. More to the point, in 2023 Russia fired 1,105 cruise missiles at Ukraine and in 2024 they fired 1,427. The increased bombardment was almost entirely due to Shahed drones, with at least 22 fired in 2022, at least 3,065 fired in 2023 and a jaw-dropping 11,051 or more fired in 2024.While a Shahed drone is intercepted or deflected over 90% of the time, and they have a much smaller warhead than Russian cruise and ballistic missiles, it is still more than 11,000 of those drones fired at Ukraine. Hard to ignore.

Ukraine fired back at Russia only a little over 1,300 drones and missiles in 2024. There were also civilian casualties on both sides, which Ukrainian losses being much higher than Russian losses. By our incomplete count (see Appendix II), Russians injured from Ukrainian drone and missile strikes in Russia was 22 killed and 49 wounded in 2022, 42 killed and 157 wounded in 2023 and 99 killed and 210 wounded in 2024. We have not yet assembled a list of Ukrainian losses from Russian drone and missiles attacks but expect that it will be at least ten times higher.

Graph 2: Ukraine drones and missiles fired at Russia.

But Ukraine has ramped up its drone production significantly. This exercise in industrial engineering is worth a detailed examination, but it appeared by 2025 that Ukraine was building over a million drones a year and was ramping up production to build four million a year. This increase in bombardment platforms began to show up on the field of battle. In 2024 Ukraine fired an average of four (3.6) drones and missiles per day at Russia. In January 2025 it was 14 a day.

On 11 March 2025, Ukraine fired at least 337 drones at Russia. Russia was recorded that day only firing 126 drones and one missile back. This was probably the first time since the start of the war that Russia had been significantly outshot by the much poorer and smaller Ukraine.[114] This has now happened repeatedly. In particular on 7 May 2025,

---

114 As was noted in the article "Almost 10,000 drones used by Ukraine to attack Russia since start of war", *Novaya Gazeta Europe*, 13 March 2025, Ukraine had now fired at least 9,700 drones at Russia since the start of

Ukraine fired 524 drones at Russia. Russia that day fired 187 Shahed drones and five ballistic missiles at Ukraine. For the month of May, Ukraine fired at least 1,280 drones and 14 missiles at Russia. This was probably the heaviest month of bombardment done by Ukraine. Still, Russia had more weight, firing at Ukraine that month 4,127 drones and missiles. But the increased Ukrainian bombardment was making itself felt, and it was no longer a completely one-sided exchange.

Russia was also building up its drone manufacturing capabilities. It had a range and supply of drones at the start of the war, but these were mostly used for reconnaissance and artillery spotting. They had an extensive collection of cruise missiles and ballistic missiles, something that the Soviet Union had developed and Russia continued to use. But Russia had not built a large collection of "kamikaze" drones. These are one-strike weapons, much like cruise and ballistic missiles. Russia's first large collection of "kamikaze" drones was the Iranian Shahed drone that first showed up on the battlefield in September 2022. They purchased large numbers of them from Iran and also made arrangements with Iran to build their own. Russian stood up several factories to manufacture the Iranian Shahed drones, sometimes calling them the Geran-2. Eventually, between Iranian Shahed drones, Russian-built Shahed-type drones and their extensive collection of cruise missiles and ballistic missiles, they built up to the point where they fired at least 17,706 of these at Ukraine in the first five months of 2025.

This appears to be an air war defined by the number of weapons that could be launched at the other. It appears that Ukraine had ramped up

---

the war, including 343 this day (the number if slighter higher than the one I use). As they noted in the following chart:

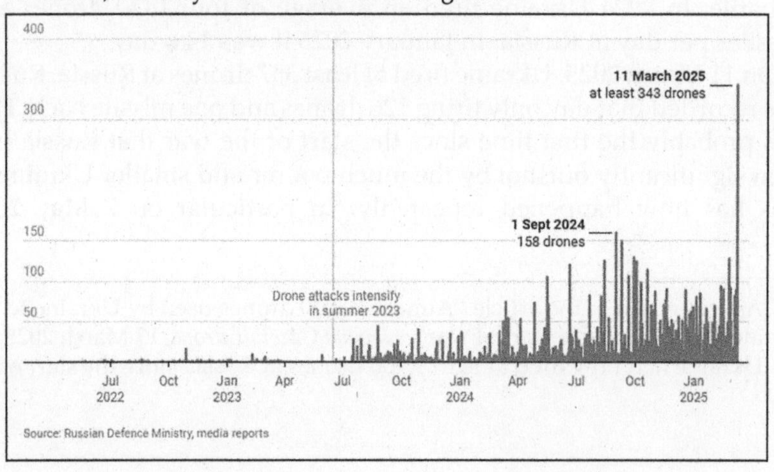

its production. They probably will not be able to out-produce Russia in these weapons, but their numbers have become significant. This is no small feat for the country that has an economy one-tenth the size of its opponent's.[115]

The Oil War

In 2024, Ukraine had launched at least forty attacks against Russian oil depots, fuel depots, oil pipelines and oil refineries.[116] This was a frequent target but did not appear to be the primary focus of their drone campaign. However, in January 2025 it appears that a systematic and organized bombing campaign against Russian oil facilities was started. This included at least seven attacks against oil depots (8 January in Saratov, 14 January in Saratov, 15 and 16 January in Voronezh, 17 January in Kaluga, 18 January in Tula, 20 January in Voronezh) and at least six attacks again oil refineries (11 January in Tatarstan, 15 January in Volgograd, 23 January in Ryazan, 26 January in Ryazan, 29 January in Nizhny Novgorod, 31 January in Volgograd). The Ryazan facility was shut down by these attacks.[117] They also hit power stations and power plants (24 January in Kursk and Ryazan). On 29 January Russia claimed Ukraine attacked a nuclear power plant in Smolensk Oblast, although there was no damage.[118] It also included attacks against the gas pipeline (13 January in Krasnodar) which would eventually become

---

115 The 2025 IMF estimate for the nominal GDP of Russia is $2.076 trillion, making it the 11th largest economy in the world. Ukraine is estimated at $206 billion, making it the 55th largest economy in the world.

116 We have the count, drawn from Appendix II, as at least two attacks in 2022 (on 22 June and 16 November), at least ten attacks in 2023, and at least 40 attacks in 2024. Some articles give higher counts. See: Coalan Magee, "Satellite images reveal how Ukraine has left Russia's oil industry in flames: Ukraine has launched more than 80 strikes on Russian oil facilities," *The I Paper*, 24 February 2025.

117 Abby Fenbert, "Russia's Ryazan oil refinery suspends operations after drone strike, Reuters reports," *The Kyiv Independent*, 28 January 2025. The Ryazan oil refinery was attack on 23 (or 24) and 26 January 2025 and had previously been attacked in May 2024. Also see Sonya Bandouil, "Fire reported at oil refinery in Russia's Ryazan Oblast amid drone strike," *The Kyiv Independent*, 24 January 2025; and Lucille Brizard, "Ukraine Strikes 84 Russian Oil facilities in 2024, Reaching 1,500 km Behind enemy Lines," *United24 Media*, 27 January 2025. No attempt has been made to resolve the differences in these counts.

118 "Russia claims nuclear plant targeting during massive Ukrainian drone attack," *Aljazeera*, 29 January 2025.

an issue for Hungary and Slovakia. At the time of the strike, Russia accused Ukraine of "energy terrorism." Ukraine had halted the transit of Russian gas through Ukraine on 1 January 2025. It had continued to allow natural gas to pass through the pipelines going through the country during the almost three years of war. They were now cut off. At this point, European users of Russian gas had been reduced to primarily Hungary and Slovakia. Ukraine targeted the TurkStream pipeline with nine drones. It attacked a gas compressor station in the village of Gia-Kodzor near the Black Sea coast. Russia said that all the drones were shot down and gas deliveries were unaffected. The TurkStream pipeline runs for 580 miles (930 kilometers) under the Black Sea from Russia to northwestern Turkey and then connects to overground pipelines that run through the Balkans to western Europe. After this attack, Hungary called for its 'security and operability" to be "respected by all." Hungary receives gas through this pipeline.[119]

February was similar with two attacks on oil depots (5 February in Krasnodar and 15 February in Belgorod) and nine attacks on oil refineries (3, 8 and 15 February in Volgograd, 10, 17 and 26 February in Krasnodar, 11 February in Saratov, 19 February in Samara, 24 February in Ryazan), a gas processing plant in Astrakhan on 3 February and an oil pumping station in Krasnodar on 17 and 20 February. The Kropotkinskaya pumping station hit on 17 February was part of the Caspian Pipeline Consortium (CPC) which carries Kazakh oil across southern Russia to the port of Novorossiysk. From there tankers travel across the Black Sea to Western Europe. It is a 930-miles (15,000-kilometer) pipeline. Drones (seven reported) clearly hit the pumping station but the staff prevented the attack from causing an oil spill.[120] On the 20th the Ukrainian drones hit a substation that powers the Novovelichkovskaya oil pumping station. This pipeline provides oil to two refineries.[121]

March was similarly active with nine attacks on oil refineries (3 March in Bashkortostan, 4 and 10 March in Samara, 8 March in Leningrad, 9 March in Chuvashia, 11 March in Moscow, 14 March in Krasnodar, 17 March in Astrakhan, 23 March in Volgograd) during the month.

---

119 By AFP, "Russia Accuses Ukraine of 'Energy Terrorism' Over Alleged Pipeline Strike," *The Moscow Times*, 13 January 2025.

120 By AFP, "Ukrainian Drones Hit Major Pipeline in Southern Russia, Disrupting Oil Supplies," *The Moscow Times*, 17 February 2025.

121 Valentyna Romanenko and Stanislav Pohorilov, "Ukrainian Security Service drones hit substation supplying oil to two large Russian refineries," *Ukrainska Pravda 25*, 22 February 2025.

Ukraine also did another couple of attacks on oil pipelines (4 March in Rostov, 11 March in Oryol). On 14 March Ukraine also targeted two natural gas compressor stations, Davidovskaya (Tambov Oblast) and Novopetrovskaya (Saratov Oblast).[122] On 19 March Ukraine hit the Kavkazskaya oil pumping station on Krasnodar Krai.[123]

On 19 March, as part of President Donald Trump's peace initiative, both sides had agreed to pause attacks on energy infrastructure for 30 days. While Russia agreed to the halt starting 18 March, Ukraine did not immediately agree. On 21 March someone attacked the Sudzha gas pumping and metering station in Kursk Oblast, with both sides claiming the other one was responsible.[124] If this attack was done by Ukraine, it would have violated that agreement. This was a non-functioning station, although the attack did produce a huge fire. There was then a claim on 23 March that Ukraine attacked an oil refinery in Volgograd Oblast with drones.[125] Then the Sudzha gas metering station in Kursk oblast was attacked again by somebody on 28 March. Russia accused Ukraine of firing HIMARS rockets and more than dozen drones at the station. Ukraine said that Russian forces had fired on the non-operating station. Russia also claimed that an oil refinery was attacked by 19 drones in Saratov Oblast, but there was no confirming evidence of this.[126] Then attacks on Russian energy structures finally ceased, as was also the case in Ukraine. The next attacks did not start up again until June. There were no Ukrainian attacks in April or May against Russian energy facilities.

On 1 June 2025 Ukraine conducted Operation Spider's Web. On 2 June peace negotiations in Istanbul ended. On 3 June Ukraine attacked the Kerch Strait Bridge for the third time. On 6 June Ukraine again started

---

122 Video attack is here: "SBU Drones Strike Russian S-300/S-400 Missiles Deport and Gas Facility," *Kyiv Post*, 14 March 2025.

123 Tim Tadorozhnyy, "Ukrainian drone strike halts operations at Russia's Krasnodar Krai oil station, authorities claim," *The Kyiv Independent*, 22 September 2025.

124 "Russia and Ukraine Trade Blame for Attack on Gas Pumping Station in Kursk Region," *The Moscow Times*, 21 March 2025.

125 Kateryna Serohina, "Explosions in Volgograd: Russians claim attempt to attack oil refinery," *RBC-Ukraine*, 23 March 2025.

126 "Russian Army Accused Ukraine of Attacking Sudzha Gas Metering Station," *The Moscow Times*, 28 March 2025. Also see "APU bombed objects in Saratov at night and Engels residents counted more than 30 explosions," *EAD*, 28 March 2025.

striking oil refineries and fuel and oil depots. It was not much activity, only two strikes against oil refineries (6 June in Saratov and 27 June in Samara), three strikes against fuel and oil depots (6 June at Engle-2 air base in Saratov, 16 June in Tambov and 26 June in Bryansk oblasts), and a sabotage attack against a power station on 14 June in Kaliningrad, the isolated part of Russia next to Poland and the Baltic States.

In July the number of attacks against energy facilities remained low. This included on 7 July an attack against an oil refinery in Krasnodar Oblast, an attack against a fuel depot on 24 July in Krasnodar, a drone attack on a power substation in Moscow on 3 July, a sabotage attack on a gas pipeline along the Sea of Japan in Primorsky Oblast on 5 July, another sabotage attack on a gas pipeline in Tyumen Oblast, and a drone attack on 23 July against a power plant in Rostov Oblast.

August was a lot more active. It included 14 attacks against oil refineries (on 2 August against oil refineries in Ryazan and Samara, 3 August in Nizhny Novgorod, 7 August in Krasnodar, 10 August in Saratov, 10 August in Komi, 14 August in Volgograd, 15 August in Samara, 21 August in Rostov, 24 August in Samara, 28 August in Krasnodar, 28 August in Samara and on 30 August attacks in Krasnodar and Samara).[127] An attack against the Adler oil depot in Krasnodar on 3 August generated a massive fire. There was also an attack on the Ust-Luga gas processing complex on 24 August.

As one source noted:

> The capacity of the refineries attacked in August is about 77 million tons of oil processing per year. At the same time, the actual damage affected capacities of about 58.7 million tons, which is equivalent to 18.7% of Russia's total oil refining capacity.[128]

---

127 This list was drawn from multiple sources but also see: Evgeny Makarchuk, "Attacks on the Russian energy system in August 2025," *iSANS*, 5 September 2025. The attack on the Afipsky oil refinery in Krasnodar Krai on 7 August is not included in the *iSANS* account (see "Unknown drones strike Russia's Krasnodar region: Oil refinery and military base in flames," *RBC-Ukraine*, 7 August 2025).
There was a drone shot down over the Slavyansk-on-Kuban oil refinery in Krasnodar Krai on 13 August. This is not included in this count.

128 Evgeny Makarchuk, "Attacks on the Russian energy system in August 2025," *iSANS*, 5 September 2025. Note that this estimate is based upon 12 oil refineries attacked in August. We count one additional oil refinery attacked in August, the Kstovo oil refinery in Nizhny Novgorod on 3 August. We also count the Afipsky oil refinery attacked a second time on 3 August.

Map 9: Ukrainian attacks on Russian oil refineries in August 2025.

The attacks against oil refineries and other installations continued into September. According to one accounting by 23 September, Ukraine had attacked 16 of Russia's 38 oil refineries since the start of August.[129]

---

129 See on X (Twitter), account @ChistopherJM, 9/23/25 at 13:09. The full statement is "Sixteen of Russia's 38 refineries have been hit since the start of August, some of them multiple times, including one of Russia's largest fuel-processing facilities, the 340,0000 barrel-a-day plant at Ryazan, close to Moscow." The author, Christopher Miller, is the UK-based *Financial Times* chief correspondent in Kyiv.

Other people also use the figure of 38 major refineries. See on X (Twitter) @Tatarigami_UA who references BBC. See Olga Robinson, Matt Murphy and Yaroslava Kiryukhina, "Surge in Ukrainian attacks on oil refineries sparks Russian fuel shortages," *BBC*, 2 October 2025. They state: "Some 21 of the country's 38 large refineries . . . have been hit since January, with successful attacks already 48% higher than the whole of 2024." And "Our analysis shows reported attacks reached a record level in August, with 14 refineries targets by Ukrainians drones, and eight

It does appear that Russia has over 30 major oil refineries and dozens of smaller ones, totaling according to one source to 74.[130]

Ukraine also conducted a campaign against the Russian oil and gas pipelines and their facilities. There were attacks against pipelines on 13 August in Bryansk (Druzhba pipeline) and Rostov, and the Nikolskoye oil pumping station in Tambov on 18 August. This last attack also degraded the Druzhba pipeline.[131] That day the Hungarian Foreign Minister complained about Ukrainian attacks on the Druzhba oil pipeline as his country is a major recipient of that oil. Both Hungary and Slovakia reported the cessation of oil supplies for about a day.[132] This was then followed up with attack on pipelines on 21 August in Rostov and Bryansk. In Bryansk they went after the Unecha oil pumping station. This generated rather impressive pictures of a blazing inferno from multiple fuel tanks. It is said that these attacks cut off oil to Hungary and Slovakia for five days.[133] On 26 August a blast destroyed a trunk oil pipeline in Ryazan that provided petroleum to Moscow. On 29 August an oil pumping station in Bryansk. This is seven different attacks, including at least three against the Druzhba pipeline.

---

in September." They provide a nice graph of attacks on oil refineries by month from January 2024 through September 2025 and a map of the strikes.

On the other hand, Evgeny Makarchuk, "Attacks on the Russian energy system in August 2025," *iSANS*, 5 September 2025, shows 12 refineries attacked in August 2025 out of 74 refineries in Russia.

130 "How Many Russian Oil Refineries Has Ukraine Damaged So Far, and Where?," *United24 Media*, 5 September 2024 and Evgeny Makarchuk, "Attacks on the Russian energy system in August 2025," *iSANS*, 5 September 2025.

131 "Druzhba oil pipeline halts operations after Ukrainian strike on Nikolskoye pumping station in Russia," *Ukrainska Pravda*, 18 August 2025.

132 Ulyana Krychkovska and Valentyna Romanenko, "Hungarians foreign minister accuses Kyiv of attack that halted Russian oil supplies to Hungary," *Ukrainska Pravda 25*, 18 August 2025; and Evgeny Makarchuk, "Attacks on the Russian energy system in August 2025," *iSANS*, 5 September 2025.

133 Emily Crane, "Ukraine obliterates critical part of Russai's Druzhba oil pipeline as attacks ramp up after Trump-Putin summit," *New York Post*, 22 August 2025. Note that the Bryansk governor stated that Ukraine fired HIMARS rockets and drones at the site.

In an attack that got many people's attention, on 24 August Ukraine attacked the Kursk nuclear power plant. This plant is just 38 miles (60 kilometers) from the Ukraine border. It is said that Russian air defense shot down a drone just after midnight that detonated near the plant. It damaged an auxiliary transformer and forced a 50% reduction in the operating capacity of reactor No. 3. This is the only one of four reactors at the plant that is generating power at this moment. Radiation levels remained normal. Ukraine also attacked the Ust-Luga gas terminal near St. Petersburg.[134]

One can argue the primary difference between Ukraine and Russia is oil. Ukraine's primary export is wheat. Russia's primary export is oil. Per capita income of Ukraine in 2021 was 4,776. Per capita income of Russia is 2021 was 12,522.[135] This glut of energy resources, both oil and gas, allowed the Russian economy to boom starting in 2000. It allowed Putin to win democratic election after democratic election, effectively being in power continuously since 1999. It has allowed Russia to implement a flat tax, one of the few countries able to do so.[136] The booming economy and the tax structure resulted in Russia having the second highest number of billionaires in the world, even though its per capita income is a fraction of most European countries. It allowed the government to be funded primarily by oil and gas revenues, rather than tax receipts.

It was estimated when oil was in the $80 to $100 range that oil and gas revenues made up half of Russian government revenues. If the price

---

134 Guy Faulconbridge and Lidia Kelly, "Ukraine drone hits Russian nuclear plant, sparks huge fire at Novatek's Ust-Luga terminal," *Reuters*, 24 August 2035.

135 This is per capita income based upon GDP (nominal). Sources: https://www.macrotrends.net/datasets/global-metrics/countries/ukr/ukraine/gdp-per-capita and https://www.macrotrends.net/global-metrics/countries/rus/russia/gdp-per-capita. These are "pre-war" figures. Per capita income for Ukraine, 2025 IMF estimate, is 6,261. For Russia, 2025 IMF estimate, it is 14,258. Just for comparison, United States is 89,105 and UK is 54,949. Some people prefer to use GDP (PPP) for this comparison.

136 Russia introduced a flat tax rate of 13% in 2001. It added a second higher rate of 15% in 2021. It finally had to create a progressive tax rate in 2024 to pay for the war. See Chrstopher A. Lawrence, "The end of the flat tax in Russia," *Mystics & Statistics*, 13 June 2024.

Ukraine also has a flat tax at a rate of 19.5%. No Western European country or major country in the Western Hemisphere has a flat tax (Belize and Bolivia are the notable exceptions).

of oil was above $80 a barrel for Brent crude, the Russian government ran at a surplus. It the price of oil was below $80 a barrel, the Russian government ran at a deficit.[137] Therefore, once the war started, the U.S. policy was to try to keep the price of oil below $80, sanction Russian oil exports, and convince Europe to divest itself of Russian oil and gas. Over time that has happened. Most of Europe is now divested of Russian oil and gas, the notable exceptions being Slovakia, Hungary and Turkey. Russian exports have been limited and they are often selling it below market price. And the price of oil has remained below $80 a barrel for most of the duration of the war, although this is as much due to market forces as opposed to any active U.S. policy efforts. But, in the end Russia's war with Ukraine is funded by oil. Therefore, if Ukraine can reduce or degrade Russia's ability to refine and export oil, it can reduced Russia's ability to fund the war.

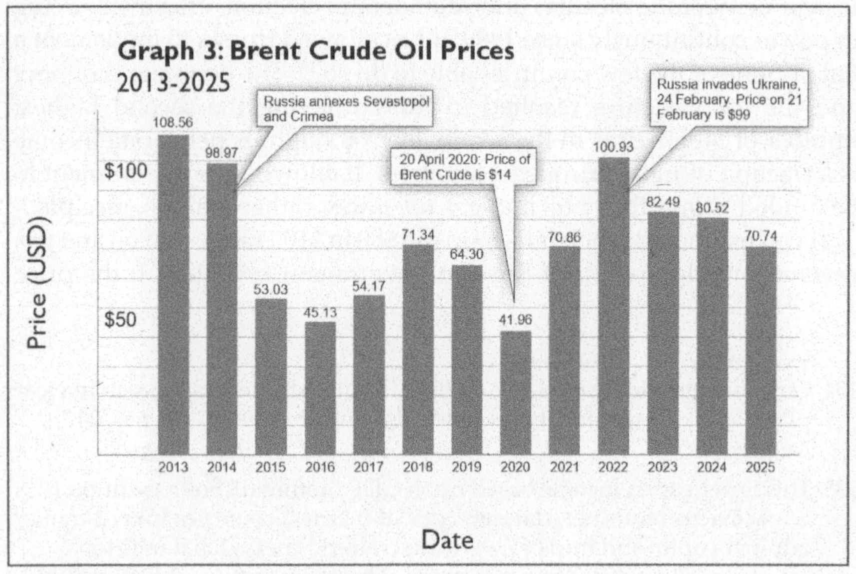

Graph 3: Price of Brent Crude Over Time.

The Ukrainian offensive against the Russia oil industry began in force starting the second week of January 2025. In the last three weeks of the month, they did at least 17 attacks against oil depots, oil

---

137 Christopher A. Lawrence, "Russia Plans for $40 Oil," *Mystics & Statistics*, 15 October 2016.

refineries, power plants and other such targets. This included at least seven attacks against oil depots and at least seven attacks against oil refineries or processing plants.

February was similar with at least 13 attacks, including nine attacks against oil refineries. In the first half of March, there were another six attacks against refineries. In the first ten weeks of the year, at least 21 oil refineries had been attacked.[138] Up until the end of 2024, only around 20 had been attacked before.

Ukrainian attacks against oil facilities and occasional airfields continued after the 1 June Operation Spider's Web attack. On 9 June 2025 Ukrainian special operations reportedly hit two Russian fighter jets with long-range drones at Savasleyka airfield in Novgorod Oblast, 404 miles (650 kilometers) from Ukraine's border.[139] On 19 July they conducted a drone attack on Rostov.

The attacks that got international attention were the repeated strikes on the Druzhba oil pipeline. The Druzhba pipeline, also called the "Friendship Pipeline" (Druzhba means friendship), is one of the world's longest and largest oil pipeline networks. It first began operation in 1964 during the Soviet era and before the war carried oil over 2,500 miles (4,000 kilometers) from the eastern part of European Russia to Ukraine, Belarus, Poland, Hungary, Slovenia, the Czech Republic and Germany. Over the intervening years Germany, Poland and others have stopped receiving oil from Russia, no longer wanting to fund the Russian war against Ukraine. Germany ceased buying oil in January 2023 and Russia ceased to supply oil to Poland the following month. Germany began using the pipeline in December 2023 to import oil from Kazakhstan. This oil travelled through Russia and Ukraine on the way to Germany. On the other hand, Hungary and Slovenia have not ceased purchasing Russian oil.

Now, the pipeline to Hungary and Slovenia passes through Ukraine. In July 2024, Ukraine stopped the transportation of oil from the Russian company Lukoil through the pipeline to Hungary and

---

138 Other people are also counting these: Kateryna Serohina, "How many oil refineries in Russia were attacked since beginning of 2025," *RBC-Ukraine*, 18 February 2025. Because she did not give dates of the attacks, it is hard to cross-check it with my listing in Appendix II.

139 Haye Kesteloo, "Russia unleashes record 479-drone barrage on Ukraine, escalating aerial warfare," *Dronexl*, 9 June 2025 and "Ukraine destroyed MiG-31L, Su-30/34 at Russia's Savasleyka airfield, 650 km from Ukraine," *DeepNewZ*, 9 June 2025.

Slovakia. Ukraine had put Lukoil on its sanctions list, although this did not stop all Russian oil from going to Hungary and Slovakia. The two countries did complain to the European Union (EU), but the EU took no action. Hungary and Slovakia are both in the EU and in NATO. They have also been the two countries in those organizations that have been opposed military aid to Ukraine during this war.

In August 2025 Ukraine began attacking the pipelines in Russia. On the night of 12/13 August Ukrainian drones operated by the Defense Intelligence of Ukraine attacked the Unecha junction (linear production and dispatch station) and pumping station at the town of Vysokoye in Bryansk Oblast. The Unecha junction is about 36 miles (58 kilometers) from the Ukrainian border just north of Chernihiv. On 17 August the drones attacked the Nikolskoye pumping station. This second attack shut down the pipeline but it was restored on the 20th. On 21 August Ukrainian drones again hit the junction and pumping stations at Unecha, again shutting down the pipeline. This one produced a dramatic video of the pipeline burning. The Bryansk governor claimed that two Ukrainian fixed-wing drones had been destroyed with "no casualties or damages" but the picture of the burning pipeline argues otherwise.[140] The attacks on 21–22 August were done by the Ukrainian 14th UAV Regiment. These attacks affected the oil supply to Hungary, Slovenia and Belarus. It was initially predicted that the oil pipeline would be shut down for five days.

On 22 August the Hungarian and Slovenian Prime Ministers sent a joint letter to the EU complaining about the attacks. The President of Hungary, Viktor Orban, wrote a letter to President Trump about the attacks, who responded that he was "very angry about it." There did not seem to be much support for Hungary's complaint in the EU with the Polish foreign minister saying "You have as much solidarity from us as we have from you."[141] Hungary has vetoed many aid packages for Ukraine, while Poland has strongly supported Ukraine.

---

140 Yuri Zoria, "Ukraine drones turned Russia's Druzhba oil lifeline into fire – second hit in Bryansk's Unecha this month (video)," *Euromaidan Press*, 22 August 2025.

141 Sandor Zsiros, "Hungary and Slovakia demand EU action after Ukraine hits key oil pipeline again," *MSN*, 22 August 2025; and Pavel Polityuk, Anita Komuves and Vera Dvorakova, "Ukrainian attack suspends Russia oil flows to Hungary, Slovakia," *Reuters*, 22 August 2025. Also see John Hudson and Isabelle Khurshudyan, "Zelensky, in private, plots bold attacks inside Russia, leak shows," *The Washington Post*, 13 May 2023.

Chapter 11

IMPACT ON RUSSIA

"I have said many times that I consider the Russian and Ukrainian people to be one nation. In this sense, all of Ukraine is ours.
We have a saying, or a parable: Where the foot of a Russian soldier steps, that is ours."

Vladimir Putin
20 June 2025[1]

The attack on 1 June 2025 destroyed thirteen planes and damaged a few more. This is up to 28 damaged according to some Ukraine estimates. Probably realistically it was less than a dozen other planes damaged. The Ukrainian SBU estimated that they caused $7 billion in damage. Maybe, but that sounds high. How does one assign a value to planes that have not been produced since the 1980s? The Russian annual defense budget in 2024 was $149 billion, so this was 5% of their annual defense budget destroyed in a single day, if these figures are correct.[2]

The real problem was that Ukraine took out eleven planes that are not easily replaced. There are no open production lines for the Tu-95MS or the Tu-22M3. There is for the T-160, but it is very slow, producing about one or two planes every two years. So this a net loss to their strategic bombing force. This is also a loss to part of their nuclear Triad, reducing the number of launchers and bomber from 587 to 576, or a

---

1   Sarah Hooper, "Putin claims the whole of Ukraine as Russian in speech," *MSN*, 21 June 2025.

2   Do not know the basis for the $7 billion damages claim. The 2024 Russian defense budget comes from the Stockholm International Peace Research Institute. See: https://www.sipri.org/sites/default/files/2025-04/2504_fs_milex_2024.pdf#page=2.

2% decline. This is for all practical purposes, a permanent loss. The strategic bomber force has been reduced from 71 to 60 bombers.

Still, this does not really have any clear immediate impact on the war. Russia was still able to launch more than 400 drones and missiles in one night on 1 June, 6 June, 9 June and 17 June, close to 400 on 23 and 27 June and over 500 on 29 June. It is a slight degradation in capability, but very far from crippling.

The real value of this attack was psychological. For the Ukrainians it showed that they indeed had some "cards to play." The morale boost in Ukraine and among Ukraine's supporters internationally was significant. In this David versus Goliath story, every stone that hits inspired them to load another one in their sling.

For the Russians, it showed that they were vulnerable everywhere. Ukraine simultaneously struck at one air base north of the Arctic Circle near Murmansk and at another in the middle of Siberia near the legendary Lake Baikal. This means that nominally Russia has to establish air base defense at every air base in the country, regardless. It is an additional cost.

It clearly showed Russia's vulnerability. Ukraine has already fired drones into Moscow and crossed the border into Kursk Oblast. For better or worse, they have briefly taken the war home to the average resident of Russia. The Russian populace, unlike Ukraine, has been pretty detached from this war and its effects. The stick-to-it-ness of Russia in wars is a mixed record. While the Soviet Union suffered the most losses of any nation in World War II and stayed with the war until victory in September 1945, its track record in other wars has not been as good. In the middle of the Russo-Japanese War of 1904–05, there was a large series of protests, strike and uprisings starting in January 1905 that continued until 1907. In the case of World War I, Russia was the first major nation to drop out of that war and surrender territory (including Ukraine) to its opponents. The Soviet Union withdrew from Afghanistan after a nine-year commitment with maybe 15,000 (or more) killed. Their losses and level of commitment were a fraction of what the U.S. suffered in Vietnam before it withdrew.

Ukraine also attacked the Kerch Bridge for the third time, although this latest attack was not particularly effective. Still, it does strongly signal that Ukraine has the ability to attack the bridge and at some point may bring all traffic on the bridge to a complete halt.

This war was effectively started in 2014 over control of Crimea and Sevastopol (and Luhansk and Donetsk). Ukraine has been rather systematically threatening Crimea throughout this war. The Ukraine naval campaign for control of the Black Sea and the areas around Crimea have been very effective. From sinking the largest Russian warship in the Black Sea in April 2022, to the retaking Snake Island in June 2022, to the first bombing of the Kerch Bridge on 8 October, to the drone attacks on the Black Sea Fleet in Sevastopol harbor on 29 October 2022, to the subsequent attacks on Sevastopol harbor on 13 September 2023 that damaged two Russian warships, and the missile attack against Black Sea Fleet headquarters on 22 September 2023 (Operation Crab Trap), and the regular missile and drone attacks on Crimea in 2034 and 2024, Ukraine has managed to systematically deprive Russia of control of the west half of the Black Sea and of the use of the port of Sevastopol. Russia's protected harbor in Sevastopol Bay is now as much of an internment camp as it is a military base. Many Russian naval assets are now based at the port of Novorossiysk and points east, not at Sevastopol or others part of Crimea.

Crimea is turning into a ghost town. In 2021 Crimea had 9.5 million tourists. Even in 2022 it had 5 million. Now, nothing. There are now trenches and foxholes on the beaches of Crimea, and not many tourists.

Ukraine is slowly isolating Crimea. If they cut the bridge, then this isolation increases. This leaves the only the overland route as viable, and that is in considerable danger if Ukraine can initiate an effective ground offensive in that area.

Now Russia has been responding to the problem. First, they have extensively defended the Kerch Strait Bridge. This multi-layer defense includes underwater barriers and air defense systems. This includes a line of boom barriers made up of 21 barges. They have installed piers and metal fencing around the bridge's foundations. It has been reported in the Russian media that divers and trained dolphins are involved in guarding the bridge.[3] The old ferry that pre-dated the bridge has been re-established.

Additionally, Russia has expanded the rail lines going overland from Russia to Crimea. This has included the new Tavrida-2 rail line. It goes from Rostov-on-the-Don to Taganrog in Russia, to Mariupol (was part of Ukraine) to past the Azov sea port of Berdiansk to Melitopol and down into Dzhankoi in Crimea. This is a significant additional rail line. It is some 310 miles (500 kilometers) long. It was probably completed by the end of 2024.

---

3   David Kirichenko, "Waiting for the Bridge to Blow Again," *Kyiv Post*, 5 July 2025.

Ukraine can attack this new rail line. On 24 May 2025, Ukrainian sent at least three drones to hit a Russian military train near the village of Molochansk, just north of Melitopol.[4]

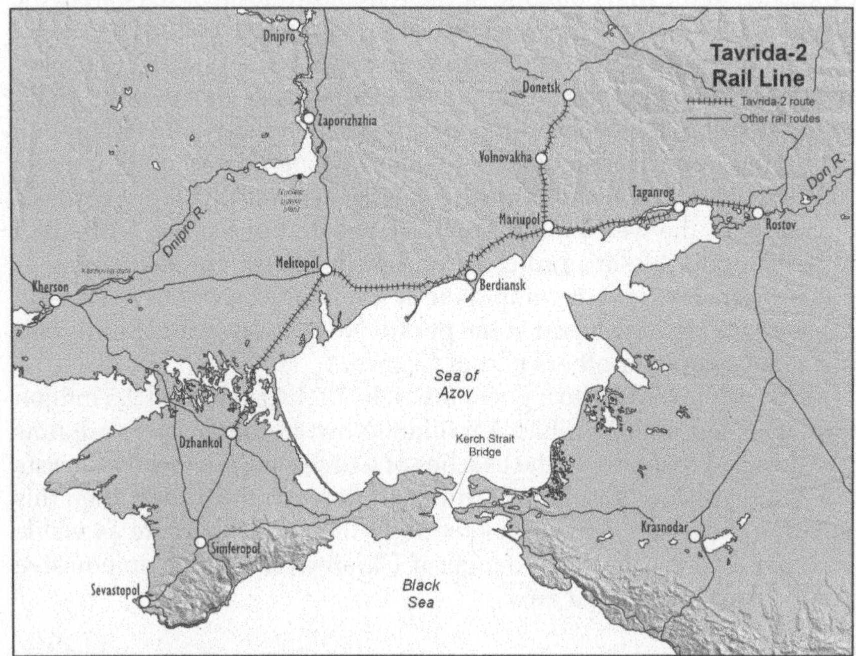

Map 10: The Tavrida-2 rail line.[5]

All this costs money. It costs money to prosecute the war, maintain an army, repair bridges, and build new rail ways. In 2024 the Russian defense budget was $149 billion. This made up 7.1% of Russian GDP. It is possible to spend a higher percent of GDP on defense, Ukraine does, but it is a burden to the taxpayers. The Russian economy is not doing great. It is only the 11th largest economy in the world, behind Brazil and Canada. It is under sanctions, and the economy is still built substantially around gas and oil sales. It is much larger than the

---

4   Good video provided in Juliana Cruz Lima, "Off the Rails: Heartstopping drone footage shows Ukrainian assault on Russian war train leaving it a burning wreck," *The Sun*, 25 May 2025.

5   Image from Cristian Segura, "Russia finalized train line to connect to the occupied Ukrainian territories in the Sea of Azov and Crimea," *El Pais*, 21 June 2024.

Ukrainian economy, but Ukraine receives a considerable amount of outside aid that affects this relationship.

But the Russian economy continued to grow in 2023 and 2024, up 4% in 2024. This had confounded the people who thought Russia could be tamed and brought to the negotiation table by economic pressure. They are running 10% inflation and the central bank interest rates are 21%, so it is challenged. The economy is only expected to grow by 1 or 2% in 2025.[6]

All this means is that Russia can sustain this war for potentially several more years, even though it has been hurt by it.

---

6   See Alexander Libman, "The Russian Economy Three Years after the Full-Scale Invasion of Ukraine," *Jordan Center NYU*, 13 May 2025.

Chapter 12

THE POLITICS
OF THE STRIKES

"War is merely the continuation of policy by other means."

General Carl von Clausewitz

@ 1831[1]

It is hard to get away from the political aspects of these strikes. Clearly Russia was sending its strikes to make a point at various times about its lack of willingness to compromise in negotiations and its desire to force Ukraine into compromising. The most telling of these was the 550 drones and missiles strike on 4 July, the day after the conversation between President Trump and President Putin. The strike of 616 drones and missiles on 20 August, after Putin's meeting with Trump in Alaska on 15 August and after Trump met with Zelenskyy and the European leaders on 18 August, appears to have been done to send a message. It appears they specifically targeted an American-owned factory in Ukraine.

A famous theorist said once that war is politics by another means (he actually said "policy"). In this case, the war was being used to make political statements and score political points. Of course, Ukraine was doing the same.

The real value of the Ukrainian drone strike was that it 1) showed that Russian bombers were vulnerable, 2) showed that Ukraine can outsmart and hurt Russia, and 3) boosted Ukrainian morale because it showed that Ukraine could strike back. In a meeting on 28 February 2025 between President Donald Trump, President Zelenskyy and U.S.

---

1   Carl von Clausewitz, *On War* (Princeton University Press, Princeton, New Jersey, 1976).

Vice-president James David Vance, Trump made the argument to that Ukraine had "no cards to play." This apparently was a reference to Ukraine having limited military options to continuing the war with Russia and was probably an attempt to browbeat the President of Ukraine into making more concessions for the sake of making peace with Russia.

It does appear that the attack on 1 June did indeed show that at least politically, Ukraine did still have some cards to play. Ukraine has made that point before back in 6 August 2024 when it invaded Russia near Kursk and took a thousand square kilometers in one day. The power of this political statement was significant and was probably not missed by a lot of people.

But political statements do not win wars. In the end wars are won by having more people, more equipment, more ammunition, stronger economy, better strategy, better tactics and better morale and training than your opponent. That is still being fought over and that fight may continue for years.

Chapter 13

THE PROBLEMS OF AIR DEFENSE

"The lesson of history is that no one ever learns any lessons from history"
Anonymous, but adopted by this author as being
particularly relevant to his profession

Before Operation Spider's Web Ukraine appeared to be at best firing 45 drones or missiles per plane destroyed. There are lots of assumptions in this calculation. Was it eight planes that were killed or only seven (which would make it 51 drones or missiles)? Were three planes not destroyed in the attack on 14 August 2024 (which could make it as low as 90 drones or missiles per plane destroyed)? Have we recorded all air base attacks (I assume we have missed a couple)? Did we count all the drones (probably not)? Still 45 to 90 drones or missiles per plane destroyed sounds a little inefficient. In contrast, Operation Spider's Web fired 117 drones and killed 13 planes, or nine drones per every plane destroyed. Of course, that is not counting the failed attack on Ukrainka air base or any other air base that was not reported. But we don't think 45 to 90 drones per plane destroyed is out of the ordinary. This leads us to a historical discussion on air base defense.

This attack raises the question of how one defends an air base in the modern world of drones and missiles. Air bases have been an object of attack since aerial warfare first developed. We are not sure when the first such attack was conducted, but British pilot Louis Strange does describe these actions in mid-November 1914 against his base:

Just at dusk, a German machine flew over at a very low height and dropped three bombs, one of which hit a small building on the edge of the aerodrome that served as a combination of bomb store, watch hut and guard room. I saw the machine quite plainly when it came over and recognized it as exactly like those I had observed in the hanger in the morning. I think the bomb must have been a petrol one, as it started a fire immediately. When it fell, "Litle Tich," the sentry by the gate close to the guard room, leapt or was blown up high into the air, but came down safely, while the guards turned out none the worse for their rude disturbance.

Anyhow, there was a good old blaze, and when the rifle ammunition in the building went off and Verey lights of all colours started to shoot through the windows, we voted it a very fine sight . . .

The next morning we were well told off by the commanding officer, who reminded us in plain language that there was a war on, and as we had to take what he gave us lying down, we decided to work off our "hate" by passing on his reminder to our opposite numbers in [the German] Fives Aerodrome, on whom we swore to drop every sort of bomb we could scrape together . . .

We kept up the bombing of Fives Aerodrome for ten days, from the entries in my diary I find that I dropped a total of 336 bombs during that time. I do not know the total dropped by our flight, but evidently we made things hot for our opposite numbers.

This bombing of enemy bases was occurring during the very first months of the Great War. It became a common event throughout the war, although they had limited effects. To start with the ordnance was smaller. The largest of the bombs used were only 110 pounds (50 kilograms) with 46% of the weight being TNT. Often they were using grenades for bombing this early in the war.[1]

Keep in mind, this was what was developing in aerial warfare, a little over ten years after the invention of the airplane. Drones have been around for a lot longer than that.

The idea of conducting aerial strikes against air bases became a standard way to open a war or a campaign. It was common in World War II with the most successful initial strike being at the start of Operation Barbarossa in June 1941, when Nazi Germany attacked the Soviet Union.

---

1   Lt-Col. Louis Arbon Strange, *Recollections of an Airman* (Casemate, Philadelphia & Oxford, 2016, originally published in 1933), pages 72–5.

It was also effective at Pearl Harbor on 7 December 1941. In that case, the Japanese struck with 354 carrier aircraft and ended up destroying 188 American aircraft. This was a devastating first-day strike. Another 159 aircraft were damaged out of the 390 aircraft that the Americans started with. The attacks on the air bases were magnified because many of the aircraft were parked close together to make them easier to protect against sabotage. This, of course, maximized the effectiveness of the Japanese attack. We are amused that some Russian commentators compared the Ukrainian drone strike to Pearl Harbor. That is, as they say, a reach.

This was also done at the start of the Battle of Kursk in 1943, with the Germans initiating an airfield attack north of Kursk on 5 July 1943 and the Soviets initiating an airfield attack south of Kursk on 5 July 1943. The Soviet attack in the south was not successful. The Soviets committed 207 planes to the effort including 90 Ilyushin Il-2 Shturmoviks. By the end of the day, from both the morning strike and later the later air-superiority fight in the air, the Soviets had lost 189 airplanes, including 109 Il-2s, while the Germans had lost 19 to 27 airplanes.[2] Not all air base attacks were successful.

On the other hand, the Israeli Air Force attack against Egypt and Syria at the start of the June 1967 Six Day War was highly successful. Using around 120 aircraft in multiple waves, they destroyed around 300 Egyptian aircraft on the ground, including over 200 MiG-17s, MiG-19s and MiG-21s, their entire force of 30 Tu-16 bombers and over 30 transport planes. Israeli lost 19 aircraft.[3] It did help that they, like the Germans in June 1941 and Japanese in December 1941, had the advantage of strategic surprise.

One can certainly argue that the drone is the new poor man's air force. If that was entirely the case, then there would not be a big difference between sending a 117 drones to strike an airfield and 117 airplanes. But, they are not the same. To start with the multiple armaments carried on a plane vastly exceeds the munition or two carried on most drones. They can also do multiple passes and have a human involved in the effort that can steer and direct and redirect the aircraft. In the

2   *Aces at Kursk*, pages 55, 59 & 63.

3   Colonel Trevor N. Dupuy, *Elusive Victory: The Arab-Israeli Wars 1947-1974* (HERO Books, Fairfax, VA, USA, 1984), pages 245–6. *Operation Focus* is discussed in more detail on Wikipedia. They claim 304 Egyptian aircraft destroyed in the first two waves of attacks.

end, no planes were destroyed on Dyagilevo airfield. If it was done as an airstrike, then there probably would have been.

The Vietnam War (1955–75) is known for multiple and continuous attacks on U.S. air bases by the Viet Cong and the North Vietnamese Army (NVA). One of the most famous were the attacks on Long Bihn. Long Bihn was a sprawling logistic and aviation facility and the largest U.S. Army base in Vietnam, In 1968 it had over 20,000 people.

The U.S. Army's First Aviation Brigade was headquartered at Sanford Army Airfield at Long Bihn as was the 12th Aviation Group. At its peak in the late 1960s the First Aviation Brigade consisted of six aviation groups consisting of up to 16 aviation battalions that were scattered across bases in southern Vietnam. For example, the 269th Aviation Battalion was part of the 12th Aviation Group and located at the Cu Chi Base Camp, among other bases.[4] Each of these aviation battalions consisted of three or four companies with a total of 21 to 30 helicopters in each company.

In the first days of the Tet Offensive, from 31 January to 2 February 1968, Long Binh and the nearby Bien Hoa air base were attacked by the Viet Cong. Ben Hoa was the home of over 500 aircraft belonging to U.S. Air Force and the Republic of Vietnam (South Vietnam). The Viet Cong opened first during the night with approximately 100 82mm mortar rounds and 90 122mm rockets on Bien Ha air base the Long Bihn post. It was coordinated with ground attacks.

The Viet Cong suffered heavy losses. The 190 mortar rounds and rockets ended up destroying two airplanes, an A-37 and an F-100, and damaging 17 others. USAF losses were four killed in action. The Viet Cong did manage the penetrate into the ammunition dump and ignited three pallets of artillery shells, causing a massive explosion. There were no significant aviation losses at Long Bihn.

These attacks, while a significant failure on the part of the Viet Cong with a very negative lopsided exchange ratio, did force the U.S. armed forces to consider upgrading air base defenses across South Vietnam. This included improved bunkers and heavier defensive armament. It also led to the Department of Defense approving 165 "Wonderarch" roofed aircraft shelters at the major bases. In addition, airborne "rocket watch" patrols were established in the Saigon, Bein Hao and Long Bien areas to reduce attack by mortar and rocket fire. This is what the

---

4   The author's father was the battalion commander for six months.

United States armed forces was doing in 1968.[5] Probably needs to be considered by the Russian armed forces now.

The weapon used in most of these attacks was the mortar. They were often snuck to within 5 or 10 kilometers of the base in question, and from cover fired multiple rounds at the air base. These sometimes fell harmlessly on the base, but sometimes hit and damaged and destroyed valuable aircraft. The mortar crews would then slink away, usually otherwise unspotted, and usually escape.

This is an attack very similar to this drone attack, where the attacker moves close to the air base in question, fire multiple rounds (vice a box of 27 to 30 drones), and then withdraws to safety. In all reality, this drone attack is more similar to these mortar attacks, although nominally more effective.

What is clear it that while this was a new technology applied to base attack, what it was not was something that was doctrinally different than what had been done before. It was a particularly clever application of technology to allow an inside intelligence operation to attack Russian airfields. There are other ways that this could have been done, but probably none with as good results, or with the same level of security for the perpetrators. This attack and the capabilities demonstrated does not significantly change the nature of future war or of air base defense, but it does expand the capabilities and the means for attacking them.

So what is needed to defend air bases against such attacks? There are probably three elements to consider. First, the area five to ten kilometers out from the air base needs to be observed or patrolled. This can be done with armed patrols, cameras, or even other drones. This is something that needs to be done whether the attacker is using mortars or using drones.

Second, some means of intercepting incoming drones needs to be developed. This can be cheaply done with kinetic energy weapons like manned machine guns and autocannons posted at points around the air base. Perhaps machinegun towers. This will probably not be of use against mortars but can certainly be of use against drones. It probably needs to have night vision capability. The Russians seem to rely heavily on the Pantsir air defense system. The Pantsir-S air defense systems

---

5   See Roger P. Fox, *Air Base Defense in the Republic of Vietnam, 1961-1973* (Office of Air Force History, Washington D.C., 1979).

does have a dozen surface-to-air missiles, two 30mm autocannons and electronic jamming.

Third, there needs to be a means of protecting the planes against drones. The traditional way of protecting aircraft is to put them in revetments. Also spreading them out helps (it certainly would have at Pearl Harbor). There were around 40 revetments at two of the air bases attacked. They did not appear to help against drones. They would certainly help against attacking planes and mortars. The problem is that the drones landed right on the aircraft, so only overhead cover would help. Therefore, to project aircraft against drones would require placing them in covered revetments or closed hangers which offer proper overhead protection and keep the planes entirely out of view of anything flying over the airfield.

There was an attempt at static overhead protection in the form of rubber tires and rubber mats placed on the planes. As can be shown by the pictures of these from the drones, they were not particularly effective. It is not known if they helped confuse, misdirect or obfuscate any of the attacks against these aircraft, but to date, we have no evidence that they did. This is probably best to be considered a failed defensive effort and other means should be considered. Perhaps covered revetments.

And then there is electronic warfare (EW).

Anti-drone Electronic Warfare Systems

Ukraine has a broad drone defense system called Pokrova. It was first revealed in late 2023. When activated, it interferes with all satellite navigation systems through most of the nation. It either shuts down their signals or causes them to display inaccurate data. This, of course, affects civilian GPS, GLONASS (a Russian GPS-type system) and similar navigation systems as well.[6] It is a mesh network of hundreds of thousands of jammers installed throughout the country.[7] Russia is developing a similar system for deployment called Sfera. It is a system

---

6   "Pokrova EW system is a real game-changer in Ukrainian fight against Shahed-136 drones and cruise missiles, that renders PGS receivers useless," *Defense Express*, 4 November 2023. Also see Valerii Zaluzhnyi, "Modern Positional Warfare and How to Win In It," UDC-355 at https://drive.google.com/file/d/1D_Sf1FesVQcEvN5rPIpN23oX54AAj0Qc/view, not dated but late 2023. Zaluzhnyi was the Commander-in-chief of the Armed Forces of Ukraine.

7   "The Invisible Russia-Ukraine Battlefield," *Wired*, 23 December 2024.

that can jam or interfere with navigation signals for areas as large as cities.[8]

The Shahed-136 drones uses satellite navigation paired with a simple inertial navigation system. If the signal is lost, the drone will maintain a straight course towards the target, but will not make further adjustments because of wind. Without satellite navigation, the drones deviation is potentially 5% of the distance to be traveled. So a drone still ten kilometers away will potentially miss by 0.5 kilometers. The jamming does have to occur for the duration of its flight to the target to be effective. Still, this greatly decreases its likelihood of hitting a target. Part of Russia's response to this is the Kometa-M systems which make the drones interference-resistant. Ukraine claims to have already countered this system.

The spoofing of signals has also allowed Ukraine to gently bring down these drones, which can then be cannibalized for parts. According to one report, the spoofing has resulted in more than 100 Shahed drones flying back into Russia.[9]

The Pokrova system also works against cruise missiles, but because they use a more advanced inertial navigation, including terrain following, it is not as effective.[10]

Counter-EW efforts include systems that regularly hop or change frequencies and systems that fly using terrain mapping (like the U.S. Tomahawk cruise missile developed in the 1980s).

One problem with their various electronic warfare systems is that some require the disabling of mobile internet access temporarily in areas of the country. For example, the Russian government ordered the mobile 4G (LTE) networks to be switch off at night in northwest Russia,

---

8   "Anti-drone Sfera: Russians crated a massive EW system to shield entire cities," *Defense Express*, 23 December 2024.

9   "The Invisible Russia-Ukraine Battlefield," *Wired*, 23 December 2024.

10   "Pokrova EW system is a real game-changer in Ukrainian fight against Shahed-136 drones and cruise missiles, that renders PGS receivers useless," *Defense Express*, 4 November 2023. Also see Valerii Zaluzhnyi, "Modern Positional Warfare and How to Win In It," UDC-355 at https://drive.google.com/file/d/1D_Sf1FesVQcEvN5rPIpN23oX54AAj0Qc/view, not dated but late 2023. Zaluzhnyi was the Commander-in-chief of the Armed Forces of Ukraine.

between 25–30 January 2024 in the areas of Leningrad, Novgorod and Pskov.[11]

The LTE wireless broadband and the Russian electronic-warfare units both operate on the same frequencies. The electronic warfare can interfere with cellphone data and we gather vice versa. For example GPS data in Poland and the Baltic region was disabled in Poland on 10 and 16 January 2024 and in the south Baltic Sea on 25 and 27 December. This was possibly as a result of Russian electronic-warfare exercises.[12]

One is left to conclude that drones have created a new means to attack airfields, but the defensive measures to counter them are already in place. It is just a matter of implementing them. The problem is the large number of targets that need to be defended, which is a burden.

---

11   See www.kommersant.ru "the Internet is switched to protection," *Kommersant*, 29 January 2024 at https://www.kommersant.ru/doc/6478262.

12   Tom Porter, "Russia's electronic warfare is so intense, it may be messing up GPS signals in nearby countries: ISW," *Business Insider*, 19 January 2024.

Chapter 14

CONCLUSIONS

"Trust me, Wilber. People are very gullible. They'll believe anything they see in print."

E.B. White, from the book *Charlotte's Web*, 1952.

The Russo-Ukrainian War dramatically moved back and forth from February 2022 to mid-November 2022. These nine months of war were full of maneuver, armor actions, and moving front lines, leading to many operations and many dramatic turns of events. Since 11 November 2022 the war has been effectively stalemated, with movements on the ground limited and contained. Advances have been incremental. None are achieving breakthroughs, pushing forward dramatically and taking any cities. No cities (places with a population in excess of 100,000) have changed hands since mid-November 2022. This is now three years of stalemate.

There has been a dramatic drone and missile war. It started in 10 October 2022 with Russia's air campaign against Ukraine's power gid. That campaign went from 10 October 2022 to 9 March 2023 and at one point, had reduced Ukrainian electricity almost in half. Still, it failed, not having enough weight to complete the job. Ukraine then responded with its own attacks against Moscow starting in May 2023 and continuing until 26 November 2023. They then stopped. Meanwhile, Russian responded with their own campaign against the cities, starting in earnest around May 2023 and never really ending. Russian also conducted a second campaign against the power grid, starting on 21 September 2023 and ending it in the Spring of 2024. Ukraine did respond with its own campaign against Russian oil facilities starting on 9 January 2024 and temporarily wrapping it up on 9 February. Since then they have continued this campaign. All the while Russian continued it rather intense combat campaign against

Ukraine and Ukraine responded on 6 August 2024 with the invasion of Kursk Oblast, the first time a foreign power had occupied any territory in Russia since 1945.

Finally, Ukraine initiated a campaign against Russian air bases, starting seriously around 8 June 2024 and culminating in the attack on 1 June 2025 that is the subject of this book.

Many people equate this war with the Great War or World War I, in that it has extended entrenched lines with limited forward movement for years. In the case of the Great War, in the west the front line moved dramatically back and forth for a little over the first six weeks of the war, until the end with the Battle of the Marne (5 to 14 September 1914). After that, the war then stagnated for the next four years. Only late 1918, as the Germans were slowly being pushed across Belgium by primarily American offensive forces,[1] did the Germans' morale collapse and they then asked for an armistice.[2]

The Great War lasted for four years, 3 months and 14 days. For four of those years, in the west, it was a stalemated front. Many people already see this as a valid historical comparison to this war. But, perhaps a better comparison would be the Iran-Iraq War of 1980–8. This often-ignored conflict is the longest and bloodiest conventional war since World War II. In consisted of Iraq invading Iran on 22 September 1980, taking significant parts of Khuzestan province in southwest Iran, and then the offensive stalling out by early December 1980. They were then being pushed out of Iran in June 1982. So a back-and-forth period of around 21 months. After that the two sides dug in and continued fighting in a stalemated position for the next six years, until 20 August 1988. Eventually, the war devolved into the a "war of cities" between Iran and Iraq, where they regularly fired missiles as each other cities

---

1   While American only extensively fought for the last six months of this four-year war, we did end up putting the final nail in the coffin.

2   Specifically on 29 September 1918, the de facto Commander of the German Army on the Western Front, Erich Ludendorff, along with the Supreme Commander, Paul von Hinderburg, asked the Kaiser to obtain an immediate armistice. There is considerable irony in that only five year later, General Ludendorff, allied with Adolf Hitler, led a coup against the Bavarian government. The Nazi Party repeatedly claimed that Germany lost World War I because it had been "stabbed in the back." Yet, Ludendorff was the person who declared the war was lost back in 1918 and initiated the process that led to its ending.

each day, while their front lines remained stationary, although not without period of considerable bloodshed.

This is more like the scenario we are seeing play out between Ukraine and Russia, with a stagnated front line, and extended bombing campaign, and a war that drags on year after year. It does open the question, is this the future of this war? This war has now lasted 42 months, up though August 2025.[3] World War I lasted 51 months. This is clearly going to continue through most of 2025 and perhaps beyond. It may extend longer than the Great War. It may be longer than World War II which lasted 72 months and one day. Is its real historical antecedent the Iran-Iraq War which lasted 95 months?

We did stop this book as of the end of August. There was certainly plenty to write about in September, with 19 Russian drones flying into Poland, but we will save that for another day (or another book). The Operation Spider's Web strike on 1 June occurred in the middle of rather contentious peace negotiations between Ukraine and Russia as mediated by the United States. These negotiations were punctuated by record breaking drone and missile bombardments throughout the process. By 22 August, it is became clear to President Donald Trump that no peace deal could be negotiated. This appears to be a good point to end this book. Unfortunately, it does appear that the war will continue for many more months if not years. The drone and missile war between these two parties is only looking to escalate over time.

---

3   I count the war as starting on 24 February 2022. Some people choose to count it from late February 2014.

Satellite image from Maxar Technologies of Olenya air base.

Drone photo of a Tu-95MS after being hit at Olenya airfield (SBU).[8]

____

8   Screenshot from Charlie Hancock, "We Analyzed New Drone Footage of Ukraine's Operation Spider's Web," *The Moscow Times*, 4 June 2025.

Results of drone attacks against Tu-95MSs at Olenya airfield (SBU).[9]

---

9   See "The SSU showed unique footage of the special operation . . . ," *Sluzshzhba Bezpeki Ukraini*, 4 June 2025.

Attack on Olenya airfield (SBU).[10]

---

10   Screenshot taken from "Ukraine attacked strategic bombers bases in the Murmansk and Irkutsk regions with drones brought on trucks," *The Moscow Times*, 1 June 2025.

Photo analysis done by the Telegram site "AviVector" dated 31 May. It is showing the locations of Tu-95MS, Tu-22M3S and Tu-160s on the base the day before the strike.

Annotated image of the Belaya air base taken on 4 June 2025 that shows the seven destroyed aircraft (Planet Labs PBC).

A Tu–22M3 at Belaya airfield (Maxar Technologies, Stephen Wood).

Two destroyed Tu–22M3s at Belaya airfield (Maxar Technologies).

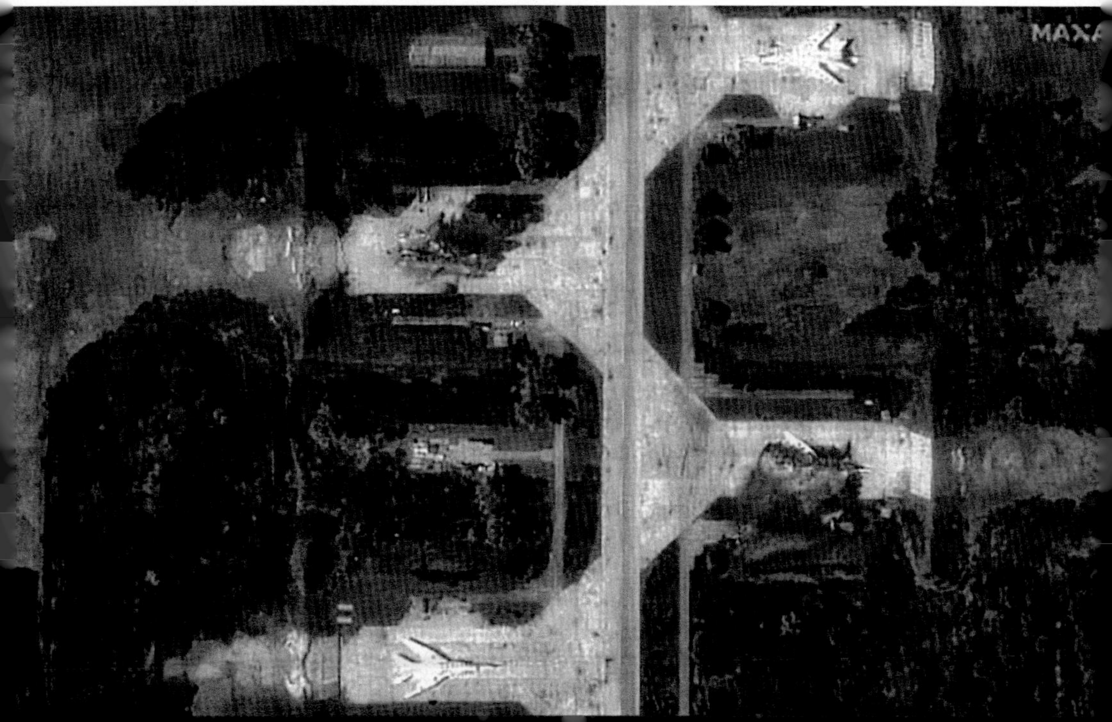

Two destroyed Tu-95MS at Belaya airfield on 4 June 2025 (Maxar Technologies, Stephen Wood).

Photo of Belaya air base after the attack on 1 June 2025 (Social Networks).[11]

____

11   Picture from "Ukraine carried out a series of attacks on airfields based on Russian strategic aviation," *Vazhnyie Istorii*, 1 June 2025.

A Tu–22M3 about to be struck (SBU).[12]

12   The four screenshots from the SBU videos were drawn from article Thomas Newdick, "Confirmed Losses of Russian Aircraft Mount After Ukrainian Drone Assault," *The War Zone*, 4 June 2025.

A Tu–22M3 about to be struck (SBU).

A Tu–22M3 with tires and rubber matting on the wings (SBU).

A drone closes in on the wing of a Tu–95MS on Belaya airfield (SBU).[13]

____

13 This and the following screenshot are from Charlie Hancock, "We Analyzed New
    Drone Footage of Ukraine's Operation Spider's Web," *The Moscow Times*, 4 June 2025.

A plane burns on Belaya airfield next to an Il–76 (SBU).

A Tu-95MS about to be struck. It is armed with a Kh-101 cruise missile (SBU).

A Ukrainian drone over Belaya air base, 1 June 2025 (SBU).[14]

---

14 Screenshot taken from Taras Safronov, "Spiderweb Operation: Drone Strikes Destroyed Russian Bombers in $7 Billion Attack," *MilitaryNYI*, 4 July 2025.

A drone photo from Dyagilevo airfield showing a Tu–22M3 under observation and the grass on fire behind it (SBU).[15] There are no photos of damaged aircraft from Dyagilevo.

---

15 This screenshot is from Charlie Hancock, "We Analyzed New Drone Footage of Ukraine's Operation Spider's Web," *The Moscow Times*, 4 June 2025.

First attack on Kerch Strait Bridge, 8 October 2022 (photo by Roman Dmitriyev, AFP).[16]

---

16   Drawn from David Kirichenko, "Waiting for the Bridge to Blow Again," *Kyiv Post*, 5 July 2025

Third attack on Kerch Strait Bridge, 3 June 2025.

Damage to the roadway from the third attack, 3 June 2025. (Photo from the Security Service of Ukraine, via X. (twitter) account @EuromaidanPress on June 3, 2025).

The Sea Baby drones used in the second attack on the Kerch Strait Bridge on 17 July 2023 (poster released on 16 August 2023).

The Val-1 submarine (First Contact).

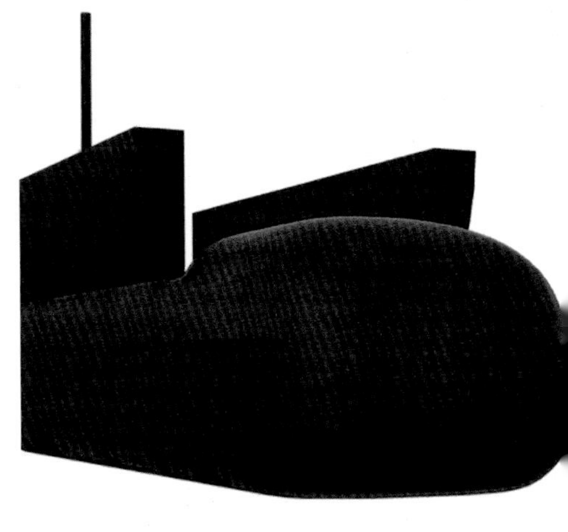

Marichka drone (Andrey Rusanov, ITC.ua)

The Marichka underwater drone, from a video taken in August 2023.[17]

____

17 Serge Havrylets, "Ukraine develops a kamikaze underwater drone to hit Russian bridges and warships (VIDEO)," *Euromaiden Press*, 25 September 2023.

CCTV footage showing Colonel Ivan Voronych outside his apartment shortly after 09:00.[18]

____

18 We do believe this is public domain. The picture was taken from Aleks Phillips, "Ukrainian intelligence officer shot dead in Kyiv," *BBC*, 12 July 2025. It is a local close circuit footage provided to the press by the Ukrainian government. Same for the next picture.

The masked assailant running away after shooting Colonel Ivan Voronych five times.

First Ukrainian strike on an air base. A Tochka-U hits Millerovo air base in Rostov Oblast on the morning of 25 February 2022.[19]

____

19 "Ukrainian forces launch missile attack on Russia's military airfield," *Euromaidan Press*, 25 February 2022.

Aftermath of the attack on Dyagilevo airfield on 5 December 2022 (@RALee85).

The Tu-141 Strizh cruise missile at Monino Central Air Force Museum in Moscow,
22 August 2006 (Bernhard Grohl).

The 3 May 2023 drone attack on the Kremlin.

A Tu-22M3 bomber on fire at Soltsy-2 air base, 19 August 2023.[20]

____

20 Graeme Baker, "Ukrainian drone destroyed Russian supersonic bomber," *BBC*, 22 August 2023.

A destroyed Il-76 at Pskov air base, 31 August 2023 (Planet Labs PBC).[21]

____

21 Robert Greenall, "Ukraine war: Drone attack on Pskov airbase from inside Russia – Kyiv," *BBC News*, 1 September 2023.

DRONE AND MISSILE ATTACKS ON UKRAINE, FEBRUARY 2022 TO MAY 2025

These reports in this appendix come from the Air Force Command Facebook page.[1] No attempt has been made to cross-check them for accuracy. See Chapter 8 for the reports for June through September 2025.

February 2022 Intercepts:

	Total	Orlan-10 Drones	Cruise Missiles	Aircraft
24 February	39		24+	15
25 February	4		+1	2 planes & 1 helicopter
26 February	17			17 (6 planes & 11 helicopters)
27 February	2	1		1 Ka-52
28 February	5			5 planes
Total	**67**	**1**	**25**	**41**

---

1   https://www.facebook.com/kpszsu

Note that this is probably a gross underestimate of the amount of activity. These are only reported intercepts. A significant number of missiles were fired that were not intercepted. Counts of planes shot down have not been cross-checked with other sources. By nature, these tend to be inflated.

March 2022 Intercepts:

	Total	Forpost Drones	Cruise Missiles	Aircraft
1 March	2		+16	2 (plane & helicopter)
2 March	5			5 (3 planes & 2 helicopters)
3 March	3			3 Su-30, Su-34, Su-25
4 March	1			1 Su-25
5 March	12	1	2+	9 (5 planes & 4 helicopters)
6 March	No report		+8 fired	
7 March	4		?	4 (3 planes & 1 helicopter)
8 March	Included in the 9 March report			
9 March	8		2	6 (4 Su-25s, 2 helicopters)
10 March	4			4 planes
11 March	8	4		4 helicopters
12 March	9	2	3 *	4 (2 planes & 2 helicopters)
13 March	8	1		7 (4 planes & 3 helicopters)
14 March	5		+1 (fired on)	5 (1 plane & 4 helicopters)
15 March	9	3	2	4 (3 planes & 1 helicopter)

16 March	10	1		9 (6 planes * 3 helicopters)
17 March	14	3	3	8 (7 planes & 1 helicopter)
18 March	12	3	4	5 (2 planes * 3 helicopters)
19 March	3			3 helicopters
20 March	7	4	2	1
21 March	11	6	2 **	3 (1 plane & 2 helicopters)
22 March	No report			
23 March	11	1	2	8 (7 planes & a helicopter)
24 March	6	1	4	1 Su-34
25 March	12	3	5	4 (3 planes & a helicopter)
26 March	No report			
27 March	9	2	2	5 (4 planes & a helicopter)
28 March	17	4	2	11 (8 planes & 3 helicopters)
29 March	No report			
30 March	7	1	2	4
31 March	No report			
Total	**197**	**40**	**37**	**120**
Additional	+25		+25	

*"Three winged rockets of the Russians intercepted by air defense. However, most of them did hit the target."
** Report used the word missiles as plural.

The Air Force Command only started putting out daily summaries on 28 February 2022. They were still focused on what was intercepted and rarely addressed the total count of incoming missiles. This particularly undercounts cruise missiles, which were harder to intercept. A more rigorous count from multiple sources would probably result in a much higher count of cruise missiles fired.

Note that the claim of 122 airplanes and helicopters shot down is probably overstated. The Wikipedia listing on airplanes shot down in February is thirteen (vice 41 claimed by Ukrainian Air Defense), five jets and eight helicopters. In March the count is 36 (vice 120 claimed),18 jets and 18 helicopters.[2] We have not attempted to cross-check the veracity of the Wikipedia post or the Ukrainian Air Defense claims. Overclaiming by air defense has a long history by multiple nations in multiple wars.[3]

April 2022 Intercepts:

	Total[4]	Orlan-10 Drones	Kh-59 Kalibr Cruise Missiles	Aircraft
1 April	10	2		8
2 April	8	1	4	3 (2 planes & 1 helicopter)
3 April	6		2	4 (3 planes & 1 helicopter)
4 April	No report			
5 April	8		8	
6 April	3	1	1	1 Su-34
7 April	No report			
8 April	5	2	1	2 (helicopters)
9 April	13	5	4	4 (3 planes & 1 helicopter)
10 April	11	3	3	5 (1 plane & 4 helicopters)

---

2   See https://en.wikipedia.org/wiki/List_of_aviation_shootdowns_and_accidents_during_the_Russo-Ukrainian_War.

3   For example, see my book *Aces at Kursk*.

4   The General Staff report of cumulative losses were used for the 1st and 24th.

11 April	7	4		3 (1 plane & 2 helicopters)
12 April	No report			
13 April	2			2
14 April	No report			
15 April	7	3	2	2 planes & Ka-52
16 April	13	5	6	2 planes & helicopter
17 April	5	1		4 *
18 April	7	4	2	1 Su-30
19 April	9	6	1	2 Su-34 & Ka-52
20 April	4	3	1	
21 April	15	9		6 **
22 April	No report			
23 April	17	9	5	3 Su-34, Su-35, Su-25
24 April	11	9		2
25 April	10	4	3	3 Su-34, Su-35, Su-30
26 April	7	3	2	2 Su-25 & Ka-52
27 April	8	6	1	1 Su-34?
28 April	15	9	5	1 Su-34
29 April	10	9		1 Su-25
30 April	9	7		2 Su-25s
Total	**220**	**105**	**51**	**64**

*Su-type fighter, two Mi-24s and a Ka-52.
**Su-34, Su-35, Su-25, two Mi-8s and a Ka-52.

Again, it appears the claims of airplanes shot down it heavily inflated. The Wikipedia listing has ten aircraft shot down (vice 64 by the Air Force Command), three planes and seven helicopters.

May 2022 Intercepts:

	Total[5]	Forpost Grenade Orlan-10 Drones	Kh-59 Cruise Missiles	Aircraft
1 May	0			
2 May	8	8		
3 May	15	7	8	
4 May	9	4	3	2 Su-30s
5 May	15	14		1 Su-30
6 May	14	14		
7 May	14	11	2	1 helicopter
8 May	10	7	3	
9 May	21	17	2	2 helicopters
10 May	5	4?		1 Mi-24
11 May	10	10		
12 May	7	5	1	1 Ka-52
13 May	8	7	1	
14 May	8	7	?	1 Su-30/ Su-34
15 May	11	7	2	2: Ka-52 & Mi-28
16 May	5	3	1	1 Su-25
17 May	15	11	4	
18 May	2		1	1 Su-34
19 May	15	14	1	
20 May	5	3	1	Helicopter?

---

5   There are General Staff reports of cumulative losses posted this month on the Facebook page. These look to be lagged for a day, so are not used for this accounting unless there were no other reports. They were used on the 9th, 11th, 13th, 19th, 24th, 28th and 30th. We do suspect that these kill claims in these reports are overstated to some extent, but it does give a good indicator of the number of targets.

21 May	4	1	3	
22 May	5		4	1 Su-25
23 May	7	6	1	
24 May	6	4	2	
25 May	7	5	2	
26 May	8	5	2	1 Ka-52
27 May	2	1		1 Ka-52 *
28 May	1		1	
29 May	7	5	2	
30 May	5	3	2	
31 May	No report			
Total	**249**	**183**	**49**	**17**

*Note that Ukraine claims that one of its MiG-29s shot down a Russian Su-35.

June 2022 Intercepts:

	Total	Forpost Orlan-10 **Drones**	Kalibr **Cruise Missiles**	**Aircraft**
1 June	No report			
2 June	2	2		
3 June	15	14	1	
4 June	9	3	4	2 Su-34 & K-52
5 June	9	8	1	
6 June	6	3	3	
7 June	2	2		
8 June	No report			
9 June	3	3		
10 June	10	10		
11 June	No report			
12 June	No report			
13 June	3	3		
14 June	6	3	3?	

15 June	7	3	4	
16 June	No report			
17 June	2	2		
18 June	1	1		
19 June	5	4	1	
20 June	No report			
21 June	No report			
22 June	No report			
23 June	6	6		
24 June	2	2		
25 June	1	1		
26 June	1	1		
27 June	No report			
28 June	4		4	
29 June	No report			
30 June	No report			
Total	**94**	**71**	**21**	**2**

In May there were 17 aircraft reported shot down. The Wikipedia reports for June record only eight losses, four planes and four helicopters. In June the Air Force Command reported only two planes shot down. Wikipedia lists ten aircraft shot down in June, four planes and six helicopters.

June 2022 Activity:

	Total	Kh-22 Cruise Missiles	Kalibr **Ballistic Missiles**
25 June	+4	+2 *	+ 2*
27 June	+2	+2 *	
Additional	+6	+4	+2

*The word missiles was plural

Note that this is the first reported use of ballistic missiles.

July 2022 Intercepts:

	Total	Forpost Orlan-10 Drones	Cruise Missiles	Aircraft
1 July	4	4		
2 July	No report			
3 July	No report			
4 July	No report			
5 July	No report			
6 July	13	4	9	
6 July	5	3	2	
8 July	2	2		
9 July	No report			
10 July	3	2		1 helicopter
11 July	No report			
12 July	0			
13 July	2	2		
14 July	No report			
15 July	No report			
16 July	13	6	7	
17 July	No report			
18 July	2	2		
19 July	5	3	1	1 Su-35
20 July	10	10		
21 July	No report			
22 July	No report			
23 July	No report			
24 July	3		3	
25 July	10	5	4	1 Su-25
26 July	No report			
27 July	No report			
28 July	No report			

29 July	No report			
30 July	2	2		
31 July	No report			
Total	**74**	**45**	**26**	**3**

August 2022 Intercepts:

	Total	Orlan-10 Drones	Kalibr Kh-59 Cruise Missiles	Helicopters
1 August	No report			
2 August	3	3		
3 August	7	1	6	
4 August	No report			
5 August	No report			
6 August	No report			
7 August	No report			
8 August	No report			
9 August	No report			
10 August	9	9		
11 August	2		2	
12 August	No report			
13 August	1	1		
14 August	7	5		2 Ka-52s
15 August	3	2	1	
16 August	4	3		1 Ka-52
17 August	No report			
18 August	No report			
19 August	3	3		
20 August	5	1	4	
21 August	10	7	2	1 Ka-52
22 August	3	3		
23 August	6	5		1 Ka-52

24 August	9	8		1 Ka-52
25 August	9	9		
26 August	4	3		1
27 August	No report			
28 August	No report			
29 August	7	6	1	
30 August	3	3		
31 August	2	2		
Total	**97**	**74**	**16**	**7**

August 2022 Activity:

	Total	Shahed-type	Kalibr Kh-22 **Cruise Missiles**	Kh-47 **Ballistic Missiles**
7 August	+2			+2 *
8 August	+4		+4	
24 August	+8		+8	
Additional	+10		+8	2

*The word missiles was plural

September and October 2022 reports are presented in Chapter 6.

November 2022 Intercepts:

	Total	Shahed-type	Lancet Orion Orlan **Drones**	Kh-59 Kh-101 Kalibr **Cruise Missiles**	Mi-8	Ka-52	Su-25	Su-24M
1 Nov (03:00)	6	6						
1 Nov (12:00)	4	2	1		1			
2 Nov (01:00)	12	12 (out of 13)						

2 Nov (21:00)	4	4						
3 November	No report							
4 Nov (01:00)	9	9						
4 Nov (23:50)	18	11	3	2		2		
5 November	No report							
6 November	No report							
7 Nov (09:30)	1						1	
8 November	No report							
09 November	6	5	1 (Orlan-10)					
10 November	No report							
11 November	No report							
12 November	No report							
13 November	No report							
14 Nov (11:00)	2		2					
15 November	89	10	2	77				
16 November	No report							
17 Nov (13:00)	11	5		6 (out of 20)				

18 November	No report							
19 November	No report							
20 November	No report							
21 November	No report							
22 November	No report							
23 Nov (16:00)	56		5	51				
24 November	No report							
25 November	No report							
26 November	No report							
27 November	No report							
28 Nov (17:00)	2						1	1
29 November	No report							
30 November	No report							
Total	**220**	**64**	**14**	**136**	**1**	**2**	**2**	**1**
Average per day	7			Assuming "no report" = no activity				
Total (1-19)	162	64	9	85	1	2	1	0

November 2022 Activity:

	Total	Shahed-type	Kh-59 Kalibr Kh-101 **Cruise Missiles**	Drones
15 November	96	10	84?	2
17 November	25	5	20	
23 Nov (16:00)	75		70	5
Total	**196**	**15**	**174**	**7**
Additional	40		40	These are counts above and beyond the intercept counts
Average for day	9 (8.67)		Adding intercept and surplus activity reports	

December 2022 Intercepts:

	Total	Shahed-type	Orlan Drones	Kh-101 Cruise Missiles	Mi-8	Ka-52	Su-25	Su-24M
1 December	No report							
2 December	No report							
3 December	No report							
4 December	No report							
5 Dec (12:00)	60+			60+				
6 December	No report							
7 Dec (08:00)	17	14	3					

8 December	No report							
9 December	No report							
10 Dec (06:00)	10	10						
11 December	No report							
12 December	No report							
13 December	No report							
14 Dec (08:00)	10	10						
14 Dec (09:15)	3	3						
15 December	No report							
16 Dec (11:00)	60			60				
17 December	No report							
18 December	No report							
19 Dec (07:30)	30	30						
19 Dec (12:30)	2				2			
20 December	No report							
21 December	No report							
22 December	No report							
23 December	No report							
24 December	No report							
25 December	No report							
26 December	No report							

27 December	No report							
28 December	No report							
29 Dec (12:00)	74	11	4	58	1			
30 Dec (08:00)	16	16						
31 Dec (16:00)	13		1	12				
Total	**295**	**94**	**8**	**190**	**3**			
Average per day	9			Assuming "no report" = no activity and not including Mi-8s.				

December 2022 Activity:

	Total	Shahed-type	Kh-22 Kh-59 Kalibr Kh-101 Cruise Missiles	Kh-31P Air-to-surface	S-300 Other	Orlan-10 Drone
5 Dec (16:00)	70+		69	1		
16 December	103		76		27	
19 Dec (07:30)	35	35				
29 Dec (12:00)	89	11	70	2	2+	4
31 Dec (16:00)	21		20			1
Total	**318**	**47**	**235**	**3**	**29**	**5**
Additional	82	5	45	3	29	0

These are counts above and beyond the intercept counts
Average for day 12 Adding intercept and surplus activity reports

Totals for 2022 (intercepted or reported):

		Drones	Shahed-type	Cruise Missiles	Ballistic Missiles	Other Missiles	Helicopters & Planes
January	N/A						
February	67	1		25			41
March	197 + 25 = 222	40		62			120
April	220	105		51			64
May	249	183		49			17
June	94 + 6 = 100	71		25	2		2
July	74	45		26			3
August	97 + 10 = 107	74		24	2		7
September	137 + 15 = 152	57	24	46		1	24
October	42 + 403 = 445	6	243	168			28
November	220 + 40 = 260	14	64	176			6
December	295 + 82 = 377	8	99	235		32	3
2022	**2,273**	**604**	**430**	**887**	**4**	**33**	**315**

January 2023 Intercepts:

	Total	Shahed-type	Merlin Orlan Drones	Kalibr Kh-101 Kh-59 Cruise Missiles	Mi-8	Ka-52	Su-25	Su-24M
1 Jan (07:00)	45	45						
2 Jan (07:00)	42	39	2	1				
3 January	No report							
4 Jan (16:00)	3		1			1	1	
5 Jan (10:00)	2				1		1	
6 January	No report							
7 January	No report							
8 Jan (14:00)	2		1			1		
8 Jan (18:00)	2					2		

Date								
9 January	No report							
10 January	No report							
11 January	No report							
12 Jan (09:00)	2		1				1	
13 January	No report							
14 Jan (18:30)	25			25				
15 January	No report							
16 January	No report							
17 Jan (17:20)	1						1	
18 Jan (12:00)	1						1	
19 January	No report							
20 Jan (18:00)	2		2					
21 January	No report							
22 January	No report							
23 Jan (16:00)	6		1	2		1	2	
24 Jan (00:30)	3					3		
25 Jan (12:00)	2		1				1	
26 Jan (04:00)	24	24						
26 Jan (10:45)	47			47				
27 Jan (13:30)	1						1	
28 January	No report							
29 January	No report							
30 January	No report							
31 January	No report							
Total	**210**	**108**	**9**	**75**	**1**	**8**	**9**	

January 2023 Activity:

	Total	Shahed-type	Orlan Drones	Kalibr Kh-101 Kh-59 Cruise Missiles	Kh-31P Air-to-surface	S-300 Others
2 Jan (07:00)	42	39	2	1		

14 Jan (18:30)	38			38			
26 Jan (04:00)	24	24					
26 Jan (10:45)	55			55			
Total	**159**	**63**	**2**	**94**			
Additional	21			21			

These are counts above and beyond the intercept counts

February 2023 Intercepts:

	Total	Shahed-type	Orian Drones	Kh-101 Kh-59 Cruise Missiles	Mi-8	Ka-52	Su-25	Su-24M
1 February	No report							
2 February	No report							
3 February	No report							
4 February	No report							
5 February	No report							
6 February	No report							
7 February	No report							
8 February	No report							
9 Feb (15:00)	1		1					
10 Feb (05:00)	10	5		5				
10 Feb (10:30)	2			2				
10 Feb (11:30)	66	5		61				
10 Feb (23:55)	20	20						
11 Feb (21:30)	5	4	1					
12 February	No report							
13 Feb (12:00)	2					1	1	
14 February	No report							
15 February	2		1		1			
16 Feb (07:00)	16			16				
17 February	No report							

18 Feb (10:00)	2			2				
19 February	No report							
20 February	No report							
21 February	No report							
22 February	No report							
23 February	No report							
24 February	No report							
25 February	No report							
26 February	No report							
27 Feb (04:00)	11	11 (of 14)						
28 February	No report							
Total	**137**	**45**	**3**	**86**	**1**	**1**	**1**	

February 2023 Activity:

	Total	Shahed-type	Orlan Drones	Kalibr Kh-101 Kh-59 Cruise Missiles	Kh-31P Air-to-surface	S-300 Others
10 February	96+	25		71		
16 Feb (07:00)	32			32		
27 Feb (04:00)	14	14				
Total	**142**	**39**		**103**		
Additional	19	3		16		

March 2023 Intercepts:

	Total	Shahed-type	Granat Drones	Kh-59 Cruise Missiles	Su-24M	Su-34
1 March	4	4				
2 March	No report					
3 March (13:30)	1					1

4 March	No report					
5 March	No report					
6 March (08:00)	13	13				
7 March	No report					
8 March (00:00)	2	2				
9 March (09:00)	38	4		34		
10 March	No report					
11 March	No report					
12 March	No report					
13 March	No report					
14 March	No report					
15 March	No report					
16 March	No report					
17 March	No report					
18 March (01:30)	11	11 (of 16)				
19 March	No report					
20 March	No report					
21 March (19:45)	2			2		
22 March (04:00)	16	16 (of 21)				
23 March (21:30)	2			2		
24 March	No report					
25 March	No report					
26 March	No report					
27 March (23:40)	13	12	1			
28 March	No report					
29 March (01:30)	1				1	
30 March	No report					
31 March (01:30)	9	9 (of 10)				
Total	**112**	**71**	**1**	**38**	**1**	**1**

March 2023 Activity:

	Total	Shahed-type	Granat Drones	Kh-47 Kh-22 Kalibr Kh-101 Cruise Missiles	Kh-31P Air-to-surface	S-300 Others
9 March	89	8		66	2	13
18 March	5	5				
22 March	5	5				
27 March	15	12	1	2		
31 March	1	1				
Total	**115**	**31**	**1**	**68**	**2**	**13**
Additional	64	15		34	2	13

April 2023 Intercepts:

	Total	Shahed-type	Merlin-VR Lancet Orlan-10 Kh-101 Drones	Cruise Missiles	Su-24M	Su-34
1 April	No report					
2 April	No report					
3 April	No report					
4 April (03:00)	14	14 (of 17)				
5 April	No report					
6 April	No report					
7 April	No report					
8 April	No report					
9 April	No report					
10 April	2		2			
11 April	No report					

12 April	No report					
13 April	No report					
14 April	No report					
15 April	No report					
16 April	No report					
17 April	No report					
18 April (22:00)	7	6	1			
19 April (03:00)	10	10 (of 12)				
20 April (00:20)	10	10 (of 11)				
21 April (03:00)	8	8 (of 12)				
21 April (23:50)	4	4 (of 5)				
22 April	No report					
23 April (10:30)	4		4			
24 April (18:00)	9	6	3			
25 April	No report					
26 April (18:00)	6	5	1			
27 April	No report					
28 April (06:00)	23		2	21		
29 April	3	2	1			
30 April	No report					
Total	**100**	**65**	**14**	**21**		

April 2023 Activity:

	Total	Shahed-type		Drones	Kh-101 Cruise Missiles	Kh-31P Air-to-surface	S-300 Others
4 April	+3	+3					
19 April		+2	+2				
20 April		+1	+1				
21 April		+5	+5				
28 April (06:00)	25			2	23		
Total	**41**	**11**		**2**	**23**		
Additional	13	11			2		

May 2023 Intercepts:[6]

	Total	Shahed-type	Drones	Kalibr Kh-101 Cruise Missiles	Kh-47 Ballistic Missiles	Su-35
1 May	15			15		
2 May	No report					
3 May (06:00)	21	21				
3 May (17:00)	4		4			
4 May (02:30)	1			1		
4 May (06:00)	19	18	1			
5 May (08:00)	2	2				
5 May (08:00)	8	8				
6 May (18:00)	5		5			
7 May	No report					
8 May	35	35				
8 May (17:00)	3		3			
8 May (22:00)	8			8		
9 May (04:00)	15			15		
9 May (23:50)	3	3				
10 May	No report					
11 May	No report					
12 May	4		4			
13 May (06:00)	18	17	1			
14 May (07:00)	28	18	7		3	
14 May (18:00)	3		3			
14 May (23:50)	5	4	1			

6   The primary source for these statistics is the Ukrainian Air Force Command Facebook page. On the Facebook page for 2 June they include all the postings for May from the Telegram channel of the Commander of the Air Force. While there is no additional activity, but this chart has been posted to the photo section.

15 May	No report				
16 May (07:00)	27	6	3	12	6
17 May	No report				
18 May (05:30)	33	2	2	29	
19 May (06:00)	19	16		3	
20 May (06:00)	21	20	1		
20 May	5		5		
20 May (23:59)	4	4			
21 May (18:00)	3		3		
22 May (06:00)	25	20		4		1
23 May (06:00)	8	6	2		
24 May	No report				
25 May (07:00)	36	36			
26 May (07:00)	35	23	2	10	
27 May	No report				
28 May (07:00)	52	52			
29 May (05:00)	67	29	1	37	
29 May (12:00)	11			11	
30 May (07:00)	29	29			
31 May (18:00)	5	5			
Total	**577**	**374**	**48**	**148**	**6**	**1**

May 2023 Activity:

	Total	**Shahed-type**	**Drones**	**Iskander-K Kalibr Kh-101 Cruise Missiles**	**Iskander-M Kh-47 Ballistic Missiles**	**S-300 Others**
1 May	18			18		
3 May (06:00)	26	26				
4 May (06:00)	25	24	1			
8 May	35	35				

8–9 May(04:00)	25			25		
13 May (06:00)	22	21	1			
16 May (07:00)	27	6	3	12	6	
18 May (05:30)	34	2	2	30		
22 May (06:00)	36	20		9	2	5
25 May (07:00)	36	36				
26 May (07:00)	50	31	2	10		7
28 May (07:00)	54	54				
29 May (05:00)	76	35	1	40		
30 May (07:00)	31	31				
Total	**495**	**321**	**10**	**144**	**8**	**12**
Total	495 + 150 + 1 Su-35 = 646					
By type		321 + 86 = 407	10 + 38 = 48	144 + 26 = 170	8	12 + 1 airplane

Have filled in the total shot down on those reports where we don't
have totals flown.

June 2023 Intercepts:

	Total	Shahed-type	Orlan-10 Drones	Kalibr Kh-101 Iskander-K Cruise Missiles	Kh-47 Iskander-M Ballistic Missiles	Ka-52	Mi-8
1 June (06:00)	10			3	7		
2 June (06:00)	36	21		15			
3 June	No report						
4 June (07:00)	7	3		4			
5 June	No report						
6 June (04:00)	35			35			
7 June	No report						

8 June	No report						
9 June (07:00)	18	10	4	4			
10 June (07:00)	34	20	12	2			
11 June (09:00)	6	6					
12 June	No report						
13 June (08:00)	12	1		11			
14 June (08:00)	12	9		3			
15 June (06:00)	22	20	1	1			
16 June (07:00)	7	2	5				
16 June (12:00)	14		2	6	6		
16 June (21:00)	1					1	
17 June	No report						
18 June (07:00)	14	4	8			2	
18 June (19:00)	1					1	
19 June (07:00)	8	4		4			
19 June (23:00)	1					1	
20 June (07:00)	32	32					
21 June (07:00)	10	6	4				
21 June	1						1
22 June	3	3					
23 June (05:00)	1					1	
23 June (06:00)	14		1	13			
24 June (07:00)	43	2		41			
25 June	No report						
26 June (07:00)	13	7	4	2			
27 June	No report						
28 June (07:00)	6	6					
29 June	No report						
30 June (07:00)	10	10					
Total	**371**	**166**	**41**	**144**	**13**	**6**	**1**

June 2023 Activity:

	Total	Shahed-type	Drones	Kh-22 Kalibr Kh-101 Iskander-K Cruise missiles	Kh-47 Iskander-M Ballistic Missiles	Notes
1 June (06:00)	10			3	7	100% destroyed
2 June (07:00)	36	21		15		100% destroyed
4 June (07:00)	11	5		6		
6 June (04:00)	35			35		100% destroyed
9 June (07:00)	22	10	6	6		
10 June (07:00)	55	35	12	8		
13 June (08:00)	18	4		14		
14 June (08:00)	14	10		4		
15 June (08:00)	25	20	1	4		
16 June (12:00)	14		2	6	6	100% destroyed
19 June (07:00)	8	4		4		100% destroyed
20 June (07:00)	35	35			Some	
21 June (07:00)	10	6	4			
22 June	10	4		3	3	
23 June (06:00)	14		1	13		100% destroyed
24 June (07:00)	52	2		50		
26 June (07:00)	15	8	4	3		
30 June (07:00)	17	13				4 S-300s
Total	**401**	**177**	**30**	**174**	**16**	**4**
Total	401 + 38 = 439					
By type	177 + 18 = 195		30 + 13 = 43	174	16	4 + 7 helicopters

Have filled in the total shot down on reports when we don't have totals flown.

July 2023 Intercepts:

	Total	Shahed-type	Orlan-10 Zala Merlin-VR Lancet Drones	Iskander-K Kh-59 Kalibr Cruise Missiles	Ballistic Missiles	Helicopters
1 July	No report					
2 July	11	8		3		
3 July (08:00)	13	13				
4 July	No report					
5 July (20:00)	8		8			
6 July (08:00)	7			7		
7 July (07:00)	12	12				
8 July (07:00)	5	5				
9 July	No report					
10 July (per day)	8		7		1	
11 July (07:00)	27	26	1			
12 July (07:00)	11	11				
13 July (07:00)	22	20		2		
14 July (07:00)	23	16	7			
15 July (08:00)	10	4	6			
16 July	No report					
17 July	No report					
18 July (07:00)	38	31	1	6		
19 July (08:00)	37	23		14		
20 July (08:00)	18	13		5		
21 July	No report					
22 July (08:00)	14	5	9			
23 July	9			9		
24 July (07:00)	3	3				
25 July	No report					

26 July (16:00)	2			2		
26 July (21:00)	36			36		
27 July (08:00)	8	8				
28 July	No report					
29 July	No report					
30 July	8	4	4			
31 July	No report					
Total	**330**	**202**	**43**	**84**	**1**	

July 2023 Activity:

	Total	**Shahed-type**	**Drones**	Iskander-K Kalibr Kh-22 Onyx **Cruise Missiles**	Kh-47 Iskander-M **Ballistic Missiles**
23 July	19			17	2
26 July (16:00)	40			36	4
Additional	+14			+8	+6

August 2023 Intercepts:

	Total	**Shahed-type**	**Drones**	Kh-59 Kh-101 Kalibr **Cruise Missiles**	Kh-47 **Ballistic Missiles**	**Helicopters**
1 August	No report					
2 August (08:00)	23	23				
3 August (08:00)	22	15	7			
4 August	No report					

5 August	No report					
6 August (07:00)	57	27		30		
7 August	No report					
8 August	No report					
9 August	No report					
10 August	7	7				
11 August	1				1	
12 August (07:00)	3	3				
13 August	No report					
14 August (07:00)	24	15		8		1
15 August (07:00)	16			16		
16 August (08:00)	13	13				
16 August (09:00)	3	3	Destroyed by jet fighter and other units in Kharkiv region			
17 August (06:00)	1					1 Ka-52
18 August	No report					
19 August (07:00)	22	15 (of 17)	7			
20 August	No report					
21 August	No report					
22 August	No report					
23 August (07:00)	11	11 (of 20)				
24 August (02:30)	1			1		
25 August (07:00)	5	1		4		
26 August	No report					
27 August (08:00)	4			4 (of 8)		
27 August (00:00)	2	2				
28 August (07:00)	4			4		
29 August	No report					
30 August	43	15		28		
31 August	No report					
Total	**262**	**150**	**14**	**95**	**1**	**2**

August 2023 Activity:

	Total	Shahed-type	Drones	Kh-101 Kh-22 Kalibr Cruise Missiles	Kh-47 Ballistic Missiles	C-300 Others
6 August (07:00)	70	27		40	3	
10 August	10	10				
11 August	4				4	
14 August (07:00)	24	15		8		1 helicopter
15 August (07:00)	36			28		8
19 August (07:00)	+2	+2				
23 August (07:00)	+9	+9				
27 August (08:00)	+4			+4		
30 August (07:00)	+44	16		28		
Additional	+55	+15		+26	+6	+8

September 2023 Intercepts:

	Total	Shahed-type	Drones	Kh-101 Kalibr Cruise Missiles	Iskander-M Ballistic Missiles
1 Sep (07:00)	1			1 (of 2)	
2 September	No report				
3 Sep (07:00)	22	22 (of 25)			
4 Sep (08:00)	23	23 (of 32)			
5 September	No report				
6 Sep (07:00)	23	15 (of 25)	7	1	
7 Sep (07:00)	25	25 (of 33)			
8 Sep (07:00)	16	16 (of 20)			
9 September	No report				

10 Sep (08:00)	26	26 (of 33)			
11 Sep (08:00)	13	12	1		
12 September	No report				
13 Sep (08:00)	32	32 (of 44)			
14 Sep (07:00)	17	17 (of 22)			
15 Sep (08:00)	17	17			
16 September	No report				
17 Sep (08:00)	12	6		6 (of 10)	
18 Sep (08:00)	35	18		17	
19 Sep (08:00)	28	27 (of 30)	1		
20 Sep (08:00)	17	17			
21 Sep (08:00)	36			36 (of 43)	
22 September	No report				
23 Sep (08:00)	14	14 (of 15)			
24 September	No report				
25 Sep (07:00)	37	19	7	11 (of 12)	
26 Sep (08:00)	26	26 (of 38)			
27 September	No report				
28 Sep (08:00)	40	34 (of 44)	6		
29 September	No report				
30 Sep (08:00)	30	30 (of 40)			
Total	**490**	**396**	**15**	**78**	**1**

September 2023 Activity:

	Total	Shahed-type	Drones	Kalibr Cruise Missiles	Ballistic Missiles	Others
1 Sep (07:00)	+1			+1		
3 Sep (07:00)	+3	+3				
4 Sep (08:00)	+9	+9				
6 Sep (07:00)	+10	+10				

7 Sep (07:00)	+8	+8				
8 Sep (07:00)	+4	+4				
10 Sep (08:00)	+7	+7				
13 Sep (08:00)	+12	+12				
14 Sep (07:00)	+5	+5				
17 Sep (08:00)	+4			+4		
19 Sep (08:00)	+3	+3				
21 Sep (08:00)	+7	+7				
23 Sep (08:00)	+1	+1				
25 Sep (07:00)	+3			+1		+2 P-800
26 Sep (08:00)	+12	+12				
28 Sep (08:00)	+10	+10				
30 Sep (08:00)	+10	+10				
Additional	+109	+101		+6		+2

October 2023 Intercepts:

	Total	Shahed-type	Merlin-VR Drones	Kh-59 Iskander-K Cruise Missiles	Ballistic Missiles
1 Oct (08:00)	16	16 (of 30)			
1 October	3		3		
2 Oct (08:00)	4	4 (of 7)			
3 Oct (08:00)	30	29 (of 30?)		1	
4 October	No report				
5 Oct (08:00)	24	24 (of 29)			
6 Oct (08:00)	25	25 (of 33)			
7 October	No report				
8 October	No report				
9 October	No report				
10 Oct (08:00)	27	27 (of 36)			
11 October	No report				
12 Oct (06:00)	28	28 (of 33)			

13 October	No report				
14 October	No report				
15 October	No report				
16 Oct (08:00)	13	11 (of 12)		2 (of 5)	
17 Oct (07:00)	7	6		1	
18 October	No report				
19 Oct (08:00)	4	3		1	
20 October	No report				
21 October	No report				
22 Oct (08:00)	7	3	3	1	
23 Oct (08:00)	15	13	1	1	
24 Oct (08:00)	6	6			
24 Oct (09:00)	1			1	
25 Oct (08:00)	11	11			
26 October	No report				
27 Oct (08:00)	5	5 (of 6)			
27 Oct (17:00)	5		2	3	
28 Oct (08:00)	3			3 (of 4)	
29 Oct (07:00)	5	5			
29 Oct (17:00)	4		4		
30 Oct (07:00)	14	12		2	
31 October	No report				
Total	**257**	**228**	**13**	**16**	

October 2023 Activity:

	Total	Shahed-type	Drones	Kh-59 Iskander-K Kalibr Cruise Missiles	Iskander-M Ballistic Missiles	C-300 Others
1 Oct (08:00)	+14	+14				
2 Oct (08:00)	+3	+3				
3 Oct (08:00)	+1	+1				

5 Oct (08:00)	+5	+5				
6 Oct (08:00)	+8	+8				
10 Oct (08:00)	+9	+9				
12 Oct (06:00)	+5	+5				
16 Oct (08:00)	+5	+1		+3	+1	
19 Oct (08:00)	+13	+6		+1	+5	+1
22 Oct (08:00)	+10		+2			+8
27 Oct (08:00)	+1	+1				
28 Oct (08:00)	+1			+1		
29 Oct (08:00)	+1			+1		
Additional	+76	+53	+2	+6	+6	+9

November 2023 Intercepts:

	Total	Shahed-type	Mohajer-6 Orlan-10 Merlin VR Drones	Iskander-K Kh-59 Cruise Missiles	Iskander-M Ballistic Missiles
1 Nov (07:00)	19	18 (of 20)		1	
1 Nov (11:00)	2			2	
02 November	No report				
3 Nov (07:00)	25	24 (0f 48)		1	
4 Nov (07:00)	2	2			
4 Nov (19:00)	3			3	
5 November	No report				
6 Nov (07:00)	16	15 (of 22)		1 (of 2)	
7 November	No report				
8 November	No report				
09 November	No report				
10 Nov (08:00)	6	5 (of 6)			1 (of 2)
11 Nov (07:00)	19	19 (of 31)			
11 Nov (09:00)	1				1

12 November	No report				
13 Nov (13:00)	5		5		
14 Nov (07:00)	7	7 (of 9)			
15 November	No report				
16 November	17	16 (of 18)		1	
17 Nov (07:00)	9	9 (of 10)			
18 Nov (08:00)	29	29 (of 38)			
19 Nov (08:00)	15	15 (of 20)			
20 November	No report				
21 Nov (08:00)	10	9 (of 10)			1
21 Nov (17:00)	1		1		
22 Nov (07:00)	14	14			
23 November	No report				
24 Nov (07:00)	3	3			
25 November	72	71 (of 75)		1	
25 Nov (11:00)	3	3 (74 of 75)			
26 Nov (07:00)	8	8 (of 9)			
27 November	No report				
28 November	2	1	1		
29 Nov (07:00)	23	21		2 (of 3)	
30 Nov (07:00)	14	14 (of 20)			
Total	**325**	**303**	**7**	**14**	**1**

November 2023 Activity:

	Total	Shahed-type	Drones	Kh-59 Kh-22 Kh-31 Cruise Missiles	Iskander-M Ballistic Missiles	S-300 P-800 Others
1 Nov (07:00)	+2	+2				
3 Nov (07:00)	+24	+24				
6 Nov (07:00)	+10	+7		+1	+1	+1

10 Nov (08:00)	+2	+1		+1		
11 Nov (07:00)	+17	+12		+1	+2 *	+2
14 Nov (07:00)	+2	+2	Attacked Ukraine with strike drones, ballistic and controlled aviation missiles.			
16 November	+4	+2				+2 **
17 Nov (07:00)	+3	+1				+2 **
18 Nov (08:00)	+9	+9				
19 Nov (08:00)	+5	+5				
21 Nov (08:00)	+5	+1				+4
22 Nov (07:00)	+1			+1 Kh-22		
25 November	+1	+1				
26 Nov (07:00)	+1`	+1				
28 November	+1				+1	
29 Nov (07:00)	+1			+1		
30 November	+6	+6				
Additional	`+94	74		5	4	11

* "…Sneakily hit ballistics across the capital of Ukraine." It is plural so at least two.

** Unspecified number, but the word was plural.

December 2023 Intercepts:

	Total	Shahed-type	Drones	Iskander-K Kh-59 Cruise Missiles	Ballistic Missiles	Others
1 Dec (07:00)	19	18 (of 25)		1 (of 2)		
2 Dec (07:00)	11	10 (of 11)		1		
3 Dec (07:00)	10	10 (of 12)				
4 Dec (07:00)	19	18 (of 23)		1		
5 Dec (07:00)	10	10 (of 17)				
5 Dec (18:00)	1					1 Su-24SM
6 Dec (07:00)	41	41 (of 48)				

7 Dec (07:00)	15	15 (of 18)				
8 Dec (07:00)	5	5 (of 7)				
8 Dec (09:00)	14			14 (of 19)		
9 December	No report					
10 December	No report					
11 Dec (06:00)	26	18			8	
12 Dec (06:00)	11	9 (of 15)		2		
13 Dec (06:00)	20	10			10	
14 Dec (07:00)	41	41 (of 42)				
15 Dec (07:00)	14	14				
16 Dec (07:00)	30	30 (of 31)				
17 Dec (07:00)	21	20		1 (of 2)		
18 Dec (06:00)	5	5				3 Su-34s
19 Dec (07:00)	2	2				
20 Dec (07:00)	18	18 (of 19)				
21 Dec (06:00)	34	34 (of 35)				1 Su-34
22 Dec (07:00)	24	24 (of 28)				
22 Dec (12:00)	3					1 **
23 Dec (06:00)	9	9				
24 Dec (07:00)	14	14 (of 15)				
24 Dec (21:00)	1					
25 Dec (07:00)	32	28 (of 31)		1		3 *
26 Dec (07:00)	14	13 (of 19)				
26 December	2			2		
27 Dec (07:00)	32	32 (of 46)				
28 Dec (07:00)	7	7 (of 8)				
29 Dec (10:00)	114	27 (of 36)		87 (of 98)		
30 December	5	5 (of 10)				
31 Dec (07:00)	21	21 (of 49)				
Total	**645**	**508**		**110**	**18**	**9**

* A Kh-31P, an Su-34 and an Su-30SM.

** The landing ship *Novocherkask*

December 2023 Activity:

	Total	Shahed-type	Drones	Kh-101 Kh-59 Cruise Missiles	Ballistic Missiles	S-300 Others
1 Dec (07:00)	+8	+7		+1		
2 Dec (07:00)	+1	+1				
3 Dec (07:00)	+3	+2		+1		
4 Dec (07:00)	+5	+5				
5 Dec (07:00)	+13	+7				+6
6 Dec (07:00)	+7	+7				
7 Dec (07:00)	+3	+3				
8 Dec (07:00)	+8	+2				+6
8 Dec (09:00)	+5			+5		
12 Dec (06:00)	+6	+6				
14 Dec (07:00)	+3	+1				+2 *
16 Dec (07:00)	+1	+1				
17 Dec (07:00)	+1			+1		
20 Dec (07:00)	+3	+1				+2
21 Dec (06:00)	+1	+1				
22 Dec (07:00)	+4	+4				
24 Dec (07:00)	+1	+1				
25 Dec (07:00)	+3	+3				
26 Dec (07:00)	+6	+6				
27 Dec (07:00)	+14	+14				
28 Dec (07:00)	+1	+1				
29 Dec (10:00)	+44	+9		+12	+5	+18
30 December	+5	+5				
31 Dec (07:00)	+34	+28				+6
Additional	180	115		+20	+5	+40

*The word missiles was plural.

Totals for 2023 (intercepted or reported):

	Total	Shahed-type	Other Drones	Cruise Missiles	Ballistic Missiles	Others	Helicopters & Planes
January	210 + 21 = 231	108	9	96			18
February	137 + 19 = 156	48	3	102			3
March	112 + 64 = 176	86	1	72		15	2
April	100 + 13 = 113	76	14	23			
May	495 + 151 = 646	407	48	170	8	12	1
June	401 + 38 = 439	195	43	174	16	4	7
July	330 + 14 = 344	202	43	92	6		1
August	262 + 55 = 317	165	14	121	7	8	2
September	490 + 109 = 599	497	15	84	1	2	
October	257 + 76 = 333	281	15	22	6	9	
November	325 + 94 = 419	377	7	19	5	11	
December	645 + 180 = 825	623		130	23	41	7 + 1 ship
2023	**4,598**	**3,065**	**212**	**1,105**	**72**	**102**	**41 + 1**

January 2024 Intercepts (and suppressions):

	Total	Shahed-type	Drones	Kalibr Kh-101 Kh-59 Cruise Missiles	Kh-47 Ballistic Missiles	Others
1 Jan (08:00)	87	87 (of 90)				
1 Jan (19:00)	10	9 (of 10)		1		
2 Jan (06:00)	35	35				
2 Jan (11:00)	72			62 (of 70)	10	
3 January	No report					
4 Jan (08:00)	2	2				
5 Jan (11:00)	21	21 (of 29)				

6 January	No report					
7 Jan (07:00)	21	21 (of 28)				
8 Jan (11:00)	26	8		18 (of 24)		
9 January	No report					
10 January	No report					
11 January	No report					
12 January	No report					
13 Jan (11:00)	8			8		
14 Jan (22:00)	2					2 A-50 & Il-22
15 January	No report					
16 January	No report					
17 Jan (07:00)	19	19 (of 20)				
18 Jan (07:00)	22	22 (of 33)				
19 January	No report					
20 Jan (08:00)	7	7				
21 January	No report					
22 Jan (06:00)	8	8				
22 Jan (18:00)	1			1		
23 January	21			16	5 (of 12)	
24 January	No report					
25 Jan (06:00)	11	11 (of 14)				
25 Jan (16:00)	1			1		
26 January	No report					
27 Jan (07:00)	4	4				
28 Jan (06:00)	4	4 (of 8)				
28 January	1			1		
29 Jan (07:00)	8	8				
30 Jan (07:00)	15	15 (of 35)				
31 Jan (06:00)	14	14 (of 20)				
Total	**420**	**295**		**108**	**15**	**2**

January 2024 Activity:

	Total	Shahed-type	Drones	Kh-22 Kh-101 Kh-59 Cruise Missiles	Kh-47 Iskander-M Ballistic Missiles	Kh-31P S-300 Others
1 Jan (08:00)	+11	+3		+1		+7
1 Jan (19:00)	+1	+1				
2 Jan (11:00)	+27			+11	+12	+4
3 January						
4 Jan (08:00)	+3					+3
5 Jan (11:00)	+8	+8				
7 Jan (07:00)	+7	+7				
8 Jan (11:00)	+33			+14	+10	+9
13 January	+32	+3		+14	+6	+9
17 Jan (07:00)	+3	+1				+2
18 Jan (07:00)	+13	+11				+2
20 Jan (08:00)	+3					+3
23 January	+20			+9	+7	+4
25 Jan (06:00)	+7	+3				+4
27 Jan (07:00)	+1				+1	
28 Jan (06:00)	+9	+4			+2	+3
29 Jan (07:00)	+4				+1	+3
30 Jan (07:00)	+22	+20				+2
31 Jan (06:00)	+9	+6			+3	
Additional	+213	+67		+49	+42	+55

February 2024 Intercepts (and suppressions):

	Total	Shahed-type	Drones	Cruise Missiles	Kh-59 Kalibr Kh-101 Ballistic Missiles	Others
1 Feb (07:00)	2	2				
2 Feb (08:00)	18	18 (of 24)				
3 Feb (03:00)	9	9 (of 14)				
4 February	No report					
5 February	No report					
6 February	No report					
7 Feb (10:00)	44	15 (of 20)		29 (of 32)		
8 Feb (07:00)	11	11 (of 17)				
9 Feb (07:00)	10	10 (of 16)				
10 Feb (07:00)	23	23 (of 31)				
11 Feb (07:00)	40	40 (of 45)				
12 Feb (06:00)	15	14 (of 17)		1		
13 Feb (06:00)	16	16 (of 23)				
14 February	No report					
15 February	13			12 (of 18) 1 (of 6)		
16 February	No report					
17 February	4				1	3 (2 SU-34s, 1 SU-35)
18 Feb (07:00)	14	12 (of 14)		1		1 Su-34
19 Feb (07:00)	4	4				
19 Feb (10:00)	2					2 (Su-34 & Su-35)
20 Feb (07:00)	23	23				
21 Feb (07:00)	14	13 (of 19)		1		
21 F3b (07:30)	1					1 Su-34
22 Feb (07:00)	8	8 (of 10)				

23 Feb (07:00)	23	23 (of 31)				
23 Feb (19:00)	1					1 A-50 *
24 Feb (07:00)	14	12		2 (of 3)		
25 Feb (08:00)	16	16 (of 18)				
26 Feb (07:00)	12	9 (of 14)		3		
27 Feb (07:00)	13	11 (of 13)		2 (of 4)		
27 Feb (10:00)	1					1 Su-34
27 Feb (14:00)	1					1 Su-34 **
28 Feb (07:00)	10	10				
29 Feb (01:00)	1					1 Su-34
29 Feb (09:00)	2					2 Su-34s
Total	**365**	**299**		**52**	**1**	**13**

*Photo of crashed upside-down plane provided.

** Photo of crashing plane provided.

February 2024 Activity:

	Total	Shahed-type	Drones	Kh-22 Kh-101 Kh-59 Cruise Missiles	Iskander-M Ballistic Missiles	Kh-31 S-300 Others
2 Feb (08:00)	+6	+6				
3 Feb (03:00)	+7	+5		+2		
7 Feb (10:00)	+20	+5		7	+3	+5
8 Feb (07:00)	+6	+6				
9 Feb (07:00)	+6	+6				
10 Feb (07:00)	+8	+8				
11 Feb (07:00)	+5	+5				
12 Feb (07:00)	+5	3				+2 *
13 Feb (06:00)	+7	+7				
15 February	+13			+6	+5	+2
18 Feb (07:00)	+11	+2		+3		+6

20 Feb (07:00)	+3					+3
21 Feb (07:00)	+11	+6		+4		+1
22 Feb (07:00)	+3	+2				+1
23 Feb (07:00)	+14	+8		+2		+4
24 Feb (07:00)	+3			+1	+2	
25 Feb (08:00)	+2	+2				
26 Feb (07:00)	+8	+5			+1	+2
27 Feb (07:00)	+9	+2		+2	+4	+1
28 Feb (07:00)	+2					+2 *
Additional	+149	+78		+27	+15	+29

* The word missile was plural.

March 2024 Intercepts (and suppressions):

	Total	Shahed-type	Lancet Supercam Drones	Iskander-K Kh-59 Kh-101 Cruise Missiles	Kh-47 Iskander-M Ballistic Missiles	Others
1 March (08:00)	4	4				
2 March (08:00)	15	14 (of 17)				1 Su-34
2 March (18:00)	1					1 Su-34
3 March		No report				
4 March		No report				
5 March (06:00)	18	18 (of 22)				
6 March (07:00)	38	38 (of 42)				
7 March		No report				
8 March (07:00)	33	33 (of 37)				
9 March (08:00)	12	12 (of 15)				
10 March (07:00)	35	35 (of 39)				
11 March	59	59				
12 March	44	43		1		
13 March	23	22		1		
14 March	16	15		1		

Date	Total	Shahed-type	Drones	Cruise Missiles	Ballistic Missiles	Others
15 March (07:00)	27	27				
16 March (06:00)	2	2				
17 March (07:00)	14	14 (of 16)				
18 March (07:00)	17	17 (of 22)				
19 March		No report				
20 March (17:00)	2		2			
21 March (07:00)	31			29	2	
22 March	92	55 (of 63)		37		
23 March (08:00)	31	31 (of 34)				
24 March (08:00)	43	25 (of 28)		18 (of 29)		
25 March (08:00)	8	8 (of 9)				
25 March (10:30)	2				2	
26 March (07:00)	12	12				
27 March (08:00)	10	10 (of 13)				
28 March (07:00)	26	26				
29 March (08:00)	84	58 (of 60)		26		
29 March (15:00)	2			2		
30 March (07:00)	9	9 (of 12)				
30 March (day)	3		2	1		
31 March (08:00)	18	9 (of 11)		9 (of 14)		
Total	**731**	**596**	**4**	**125**	**4**	**2**

March 2024 Activity:

	Total	Shahed-type	Drones	Kh-22 Kh-59 Cruise Missiles	Kh-47 Iskander-M Ballistic Missiles	Kh-31P S-300 Others
1 March (08:00)	+5					+5
2 March (08:00)	+6	+3		+3		
5 March (06:00)	+4	+4				
6 March (07:00)	+9	+4				+5
8 March (07:00)	+7	+4		+2		+1
9 March (08:00)	+3	+3				

10 March (07:00)	+8	+4				+4
15 March (07:00)	+8			+1		+7
17 March (07:00)	+9	+2		+2		+5
18 March (07:00)	+12	+5		+2		+5
22 March	+59	+8		+10	+19	+22
23 March (08:00)	+7	+3				+4
24 March (08:00)	+14	+3		+11		
25 March (08:00)	+1	+1				
26 March (07:00)	+2					+2
27 March (08:00)	+3	+3				
28 March (07:00)	+5			+3		+2
29 March (08:00)	+15	+2		+8	+5	
30 March (07:00)	+7	+3				+4
31 March (08:00)	+9	2		+6	+1	
Additional	+193	+54		+48	+25	+66

April 2024 Intercepts (and suppressions):

	Total	Shahed-type	Zala Supercam Kh-59 Orlan-10 Kalibr Forpost Drones	Kh-101 Cruise Missiles	Ballistic Missiles	Others
1 April (18:00)	1		1			
2 April (08:00)	9	9 (of 10)				
3 April (07:00)	4	4				
4 April (07:00)	11	11 (of 20)				
5 April (07:00)	13	13				
6 April (08:00)	31	28 (of 32)		3		
6 April (12:00)	2		2			

7 April (08:00)	17	17				
8 April (07:00)	18	17 (of 24)		1		
8 April (16:00)	2		2			
9 April (06:00)	20	20				
9 April (18:00)	1		1			
10 April (07:00)	16	14 (of 17)		2		
11 April	57	39 (of 40)		18		
12 April (07:00)	16	16 (of 17)				
13 April	No report					
14-04-2024 (07:00)	10	10				
14 April (17:30)	2			2		
14 April (17:50)	1			1		
15 April	No report					
16 April (06:00)	9	9				
17 April	No report					
18 April	13	13				
19 April (08:00)	30	14		15		1 Tu-22M3
19 April (16:30)	1			1		
19 April (18:00)	4		4			
20 April (08:00)	5		3	2		
21 April	No report					
22 April (07:00)	6	5 (of 7)	1			
23 April (07:00)	15	15 (of 16)				
24 April	No report					
25 April	No report					
26 April (07:00)	2		2			
27-04-2024 (08:00)	21			21		
27 April (19:00)	4		4			
28-04-2024 (07:00)	5	4	1			
29 April	No report					
30 April	No report					
Total	**346**	**258**	**21**	**66**		**1**

April 2024 Activity:

	Total	Shahed-type	Drones	Iskander-K Kh-59 Cruise Missiles	Kh-47 Iskander-M Ballistic Missiles	Kh-31 S-300 Others
2 April (08:00)	+2	+1		+1		
3 April (07:00)	+3					+3
4 April (07:00)	+9	+9				
5 April (07:00)	+2					+2
6 April (08:00)	+7	+4				+3
7 April (08:00)	+2				+1	+1
8 April (07:00)	+7	+7				
9 April (06:00)	+4					+4
10 April (07:00)	+6	+3		+2	+1	
11 April	+25	+1		+6	+6	+12
12 April (07:00)	+2	+1		+1		
14 April(07:00)	+4					+4
19 April (08:00)	+7			+7		
20 April (08:00)	+5				+3	+2
22 April (07:00)	+5	+2				+3
23 April (07:00)	+3	+1			+2	
27 April (08:00)	+13			+7	+4	+2
28 April (07:00)	+1					+1
Additional	107	29		24	17	37

May 2024 Intercepts:

	Total	Shahed-type	Lancet Zala Orlan-10 Kh-59 Drones	Iskander-K Cruise Missiles	Ballistic Missiles	Others
1 May	No report					

2 May (08:00)	5	2	2	1		
3 May	No report					
4 May (06:00)	13	13				
5 May (07:00)	23	23 (of 24)				
6 May (06:00)	12	12 (of 13)				
7 May (16:00)	2			2		
8 May (08:00)	59	20 (of 21)		39		
9 May (06:00)	17	17 (of 20)				
10 May (07:00)	10	10				
10 May	1			1		
11 May	No report					
12 May (08:00)	5		5			
13 May	No report					
14 May (07:00)	18	18				
15 May	No report					
16 May	No report					
17 May (07:00)	20	20				
17 May (21:00)	8		5	3		
18 May (07:00)	13	13				
19 May (08:00)	37	37				
20 May (08:00)	29	29				
21 May (07:00)	28	28 (of 29)				
22 May (07:00)	24	24				
23 May	No report					
24 May	No report					
25 May	No report					
26 May (07:30)	43	31		12		
27 May	No report					
28 May (07:00)	3	3				
29 May (07:00)	13	13 (of 14)				
30 May (07:00)	39	32		7		
31 May (08:00)	5	4		1		
Total	**427**	**349**	**12**	**66**		

May 2024 Activity:

	Total	Shahed-type	Drones	Kh-59 Kh-101 Kalibr **Cruise Missiles**	Iskander-M Kh-47 **Ballistic Missiles**	S-300 **Others**
4 May (06:00)	+4					+4
5 May (07:00)	+1	+1				
6 May (06:00)	+1	+1				
8 May (08:00)	+17	+1		+13	+3	
9 May (06:00)	+3	+3				
10 May (07:00)	+2					+2
14 May (07:00)	+1				+1	
20 May (08:00)	+1				+1	
21 May (07:00)	+1	+1				
26 May (07:30)	+2				+2	
29 May (07:00)	+1	+1				
30 May (07:00)	+12			+4		+8
31 May (08:00)	+5					+5
Additional	+51	+8		+17	+7	+19

June 2024 Intercepts (and suppressions):

	Total	Shahed-type	Zala Orlan-10 Supercam Lantset **Drones**	Iskander-K Kalibr Kh-101 **Cruise Missiles**	Kh-47 **Ballistic Missiles**	Others
1 June (08:00)	81	46 (of 47)		35		
2 June (07:00)	24	24 (of 25)				

3 June	No report					
4 June (08:00)	4	2 (of 4)	2			
5 June (07:00)	22	22 (of 27)				
6 June (07:00)	17	17 (of 18)				
7 June (07:00)	53	48 (of 53)		5		
8 June (07:00)	10	9 (of 13)		1		
9 June	No report					
10 June	No report					
11 June	No report					
12 June (08:00)	29	24		4	1	
13 June	No report					
14 June (07:30)	24	17		7 (of 10)		
15 June	No report					
16 June	No report					
17 June	No report					
18 June (07:00)	10	10				
19 June (07:00)	19	19				
19 June (08:00)	11	7	4			
20 June (07:00)	32	27		5		
21 June (07:00)	4			4		
22 June (08:00)	25	13		12		
23 June (07:00)	2			2 (of 3)		
24 June (09:00)	2		1	1 (of 2)		
25 June	No report					
26 June	No report					
27 June (07:30)	28	23		5		
28 June	No report					
29 June (07:00)	10	10				
30 June	No report					
Total	**407**	**316**	**7**	**83**	**1**	

June 2024 Activity:

	Total	Shahed-type	Drones	Kalibr Iskander-K Kh-101 **Cruise Missiles**	Kh-47 Iskander-M **Ballistic Missiles**	S-300 **Others**
1 June (08:00)	+19	+1		+14	+4	
2 June (07:00)	+3	+1		+`1		+1
4 June (08:00)	+2		+2			
5 June (07:00)	+5	+5				
6 June (07:00)	+3	+1			+2	
7 June (07:00)	+5	+5				
8 June (07:00)	+4	+4				
12 June (08:00)	+1				+1	
14 June (07:30)	+7			+3	+4	
20 June (07:00)	+4			+1	+3	
22 June (08:00)	+4			+4		
23 June (07:00)	+1			+1		
24 June (09:00)	+1			+1		
27 June (07:30)	+1				+1	
Additional	+60	+17	+2	+25	+15	+`1

July 2024 Intercepts (and suppressions):

	Total	Shahed-type	Forpost Privet-82 Lantset Supercam Zala Orlan-10 **Drones**	Kh-59 Iskander-K **Cruise Missiles**	**Ballistic Missiles**	**Other**
1 July	No report					
2 July	No report					

3 July (11:00)	11	5	1	5	
4 July (08:00)	21	21 (of 22)			
5 July (07:30)	32	32			
5 July (19:00)	4			4	
5 July (22:00)	12		7	5	
6 July (07:30)	24	24 (of 27)			
7 July (08:00)	13	13			
8 July (07:30)	3			3 (of 4)	
8 July (14:00)	30			26	4
8 July (18:00)	5		5		
9 July	No report				
10 July (08:00)	14	14 (of 20)			
10 July (Odesa)	6	3		3	
11 July (07:00)	6	6			
12 July (08:00)	16	11 (of 19)		5	
13 July (07:00)	4	4 (of 5)			
14 July (08:00)	6		4	2	
15 July (10:00)	4		4 **		
16 July (11:00)	10	2	8		
17 July	No report				
18 July (08:00)	18	16		2	
18 July	7		7		
19 July	No report				
20 July (07:30)	13	12 (of 16)	1		
21 July (08:00)	35	35 (of 39)			
22 July (08:00)	16		16		
23 July (07:30)	8	7 (of 8)		1 ***	
23 July (08:00)	7		7		
24 July (08:30)	25	17 (of 23)	8		
25 July (08:30)	25	25 (of 38)			
26 July (07:30)	20	20 (of 22)			
27 July	13	4	8	1	
28 July (08:00)	8	7 (of 8)		1	

29 July (07:30)	10	9 (of 10)		1		
30 July (0800+)	7		7			
31 July (09:30)	90	89		1		
Total	**523**	**376**	**83**	**60**	**4**	

* The word missile was plural.

** Some duplicate reporting here.

*** Failed to reach target

July 2024 Activity:

	Total	Shahed-type	Drones	Kh-22 Kalibr Kh-101 3M22 Zircon Iskander-K Cruise Missiles	Iskander-M Ballistic Missiles	Others
3 July (11:00)	+2			+2		
4 July (08:00)	+1	+1				
5 July (19:00)	+2				+2 *	
6 July (07:30)	+3	+3				
7 July (08:00)	+2				+2	
8 July (07:30)	+3			+1	+2	
8 July (14:00)	+8			+7	+1	
10 July (08:00)	+11	+6		+4	+1	
11 July (07:00)	+2				+2	
12 July (08:00)	+8	+8 *				
13 July (07:00)	+1	+1				
16 July (11:00)	+2	+2 **				
18 July (08:00)	+1			+1 Kh-35		
20 July (07:30)	+8	+4		+1	+3	
21 July (08:00)	+9	+4		+2	+3	

23 July (07:30)	+1	+1				
24 July (08:30)	+7	+6			+1	
25 July (08:30)	+13	+13				
26 July (07:30)	+2	+2				
28 July (08:00)	+1	+1				
29 July (07:30)	+1	+1				
Additional	+88	+53		+18	+17	

* Location lost. They may have been decoys.
** Spotted over Belarus.

August 2024 Intercepts (and suppressions):

	Total	Shahed-type	Merlin Zala Lantset Supercam Orlan-10 Kh-59 Drones	Iskander-M Cruise Missiles	Ballistic Missiles	Others
1 August	7	7				
2 August (0800+)	11	1	10			
3 August (18:00)	5		5			
3 August (07:00)	24	24 (of 29)				
4 August (07:00)	5	5				
5 August (08:00)	24	24				
6 August (08:00)	19	15 (of 16)		2	2 (of 4)	
7 August	30	30				
8 August	6	4		2		
9 August (08:30)	27	27				
10 August	No report					
11 August (12:00)	53	53 (of 57)				
12 August	No report					
13 August (07:00)	30	30 (of 38)				

14 August (08:30)	17	17 (of 23)				
15 August (08:00)	29	29				
16 August (08:30)	5	3	2			
17 August (08:00)	14	14				
18 August	13	8		3	2	
19 August (07:00)	11	11				
20 August (08:00)	28	25 (of 26)		3		
21 August (11:15)	67	66 (of 69) *		1		
22 August (11:00)	4	4 (of 10) **				
23 August (08:00)	14	14 (of 16)				
24 August (08:00)	7		7			
25 August (07:30)	8	8 (of 9)				
26 August (18:00)	201	99 (of 109)		100	2	
27 August	75	70 (of 81) ***		5		
28 August	No report					
29 August (10:00)	76	74 (of 74) ****		2 (of 3)		
30 August (08:30)	16	16 (of 18) *****				
31 August (10:00)	49	49 (of 52) ******				
Total	**875**	**727**	**24**	**118**	**6**	

*16 "Lost – likely feel under the influence of radio electronic countermeasures"

** 2 "location lost (feel on their own)"

*** 10 "possibly fallen"

**** 14 "location lost (fallen)"

***** 4 "location lost (fell on their own)"

****** 25 "fell on their own – flew to Russia and Belarus":

August 2024 Activity:

	Total	Shahed-type	Drones	Kh-22 Iskander-K Kh-59 Cruise Missiles	Iskander-M Ballistic Missiles	Kh-31P S-300 Others
1 August	+2				+2 *	
2 August (18:00)	+3				+3	
3 August (07:00)	+9	+5				+4
4 August (07:00)	+4			2		+2
6 August (08:00)	+3	+1			+2	
8 August	+2				+2	
11 August	+8	+4				+4
13 August (07:00)	+10	+8			+2	
14 August (08:30)	+8	+6		+2		
15 August (08:00)	+3			+3		
16 August (08:30)	+3				+3	
17 August (08:00)	+1			+1		
18 August	+3			+2	+1	
20 August (08:00)	+3	+1			+2	
21 August (11:15)	+4	+3			+1	
22 August (11:00)	+10	+6			+2	+2 *
23 August (08:00)	+4	+2			+2	
24 August (08:00)	+4			+4		
25 August (07:30)	+9	+1		+7	+1	
26 August (18:00)	+35	+10		+18	+7	
27 August	+16	+11		+1	+4	
29 August	+1			+1		
30 August (08:30)	+3	+2			+1	
31 August (10:00)	+8	+3			+1`	+4
Additional	+156	+63		+41	+40	+12

*The word missile was plural

September 2024 Intercepts (and suppressions):

	Total	Shahed-type[7]	Drones	Kh-101 Cruise Missiles	Iskander-M Ballistic Missiles	Others
1 Sep (09:30)	8	8 (of 11)				
2 September	42	20 (of 23)		13 (of 14)	9 (of 16)	

---

7   Reporting in September is not consistent, but they are now tending to consistently report those Shahed drones that are shot down vice those that are affected by electronic countermeasures. Specifically:

3 Sep: Six "locationally lost," two "flew in the direction of Belgorod region and occupied Donetsk."

4 Sep: Six "location lost (allegedly suppressed REB, one flew to Belarus."

5 Sep: 15 lost location, two returned to Russia, one to Belarus.

6 Sep: 8 lost location, 1 returned to Donetsk.

7 Sep: 58 shot down. Six drones flew back to Russia, Belarus and Luhansk. Three lost location.

8 Sep: Two drones lost, three Kh-59 did not reach desired targets due to active resistance.

9 Sep: two drone location lost, possibly due to REB. On Kh-59 failed due to active resistance.

10 Sep: three left Ukraine airspace, three lost location (REB).

11 Sep: 5 drones lost location.

12 Sep: 44 drones shot down, three flew back to Russia, four lost location.

14 Sep: 72 shot down, two location, 2 returned to Russia.

17 Sep: 12 lost location, 2 returned to Russia.

18 Sep: 5 lost location, one flew to Russia.

21 Sep: 5 lost location.

22 Sep: 6 "were locally lost."

23 Sep: one drone and two Kh-59s "did not reach their targets due to the active resistance of the REB."

24 Sep: 13 drones lost location.

26 Sep: one drone returned to Russia.

27 Sep: one drones entered airspace of Romania, another "lost due to resistance of the REB Defense Forces"

28 Sep: one drone flew in direction of Russia, three more lost location.

3 Sep (08:00)	35	35 (of 35)				
4 Sep (09:30)	36	29 (of 29)		7		
5 Sep (10:30)	78	78 (of 78)				
6 Sep (08:00)	36	36 (of 44)				
7 September	67	67 (of 67)				
8 September	21	17 (of 23)		4		
9 Sep (08:00)	10	8		2 (of 3)		
10 Sep (08:00)	44	44 (of 46)				
11 Sep (08:00)	25	25 (of 25)				
12 September	51	51 (of 64)				
13 September	24	24 (of 26)				
14 Sep (08:00)	76	76 (of 76)				
15 Sep (08:00)	11	10 (of 14)		1		
16 Sep (08:00)	53	53 (of 56)				
17 Sep (08:00)	48	48 (of 51)				
18 Sep (09:30)	52	52 (of 52)				
19 Sep (08:00)	43	42 (of 42)		1		
20 Sep (09:30)	62	61 (of 70)		1		
21 Sep (08:30)	20	15 (of 16)		5		
22 Sep (08:30)	77	77 (of 80)				
23 Sep (08:00)	6	4		2		
24 Sep (08:00)	79	79 (of 81)				
25 Sep (07:00)	32	28 (of 32)		4		
26 September	71	67 (of 78)		4		
27 September	26	26 (of 32)				
28 Sep (08:30)	75	73 (of 73)		2		
29 Sep (08:30)	20	20 (of 22)				
30 Sep (08:30)	72	71 (of 73)		1		
Total	**1,300**	**1,244**		**47**	**9**	

29 Sep: five lost location.

30 Sep: one drone flew in the direction of Belarus, three lost location.

Those drones lost, deflected or turned back on the Russians are consider intercepted or suppressed.

September 2024 Activity:

	Total	Shahed-type	Drones	Iskander-K Kh-22 Kh-59 Kh-101 Cruise Missiles	Kh-47 Iskander-M Ballistic Missiles	Kh-31P S-300 Others
1 Sep (09:30)	+4	+3			+1	
2 September	+16	+3		+1	+7	+5
3 Sep (08:00)	+4			+1	+3	
4 Sep (09:30)	+13	+7		+4	+2	
5 Sep (10:30)	+1				+1	
6 Sep (08:00)	+10	+8		+1		+1
8 September	+6	+6				
9 September	+1			+1		
10 Sep (08:00)	+4	+2			+1	+1
11 Sep (08:00)	+9				+1	+8
12 September	+18	+13		+3	+2	
13 September	+2	+2				
15 Sep (08:00)	+6	+4			+2	
16 Sep (08:00)	+3	+3				
17 Sep (08:00)	+3	+3				
19 Sep (08:00)	+3					+3
20 Sep (09:30)	+9	+9				
21 Sep (08:30)	+4				+4	
22 Sep (08:30)	+5	+3		+2		
24 Sep (08:00)	+6	+2		+2	+1	+1
25 Sep (07:00)	+8	+4				+4
26 September	+13	+11				+2
27 September	+9	+6		+2	+1	
28 Sep (08:30)	+2				+2	

29 Sep (08:30)	+2	+2			
30 Sep (08:30)	+4	+2			+1	+1
Additional	+165	+93		+17	+29	+26

Drones and Missiles Fired (October 2024):

Note: the format of these charts has changed because of more consistent reporting. The data contained in these charts is the same. The intercept reports have placed later in this appendix.

	Total	Shahed-type	Kh-31 Air-to-surface	P-800 Onyx Kh-22, Kh-35 Kh-59/69, Kh-101 Kalibr, Iskander-K Cruise Missiles	Kh-47M2 Iskander-M Ballistic Missiles	3M22 unknown S-300 S-400 Others
1 Oct (08:30)	32	32				
2 October	32	32				
3 Oct (08:30)	105	105				
4 October	19	19				
5 Oct (07:00)	16	13		3		
6 October	91	87		2	2	
7 Oct (11:00)	81+	78			3	
8 Oct (08:30)	21	19			2	
9 Oct (08:00)	25	22			3	
10 Oct (11:00)	70	62	1	2	2	3
11 Oct (11:00)	68	66	1	1		
12 October	28	28				
13 Oct (08:30)	72	68		2	2	
14 October	No report					
15 Oct (08:30)	26	17		2		7

Date	Total	Shahed-type	Air-to-surface	Cruise Missiles	Ballistic Missiles	Others
16 Oct (07:00)	138	136		1		1
17 Oct (08:00)	57	56		1		
18 Oct (08:30)	135	135				
19 Oct (12:00)	104	98		6		
20 Oct (10:00)	51	49			2	
21 Oct (08:30)	119	116	1	1	1	
22 October	60	60				
23 October	82	81	1			
24 Oct (08:30)	54	50		4		
25 Oct (10:00)	63	63				
26 Oct (12:00)	98	91		2	3	2
27 Oct (09:30)	80	80				
28 Oct (10:30)	100	100				
29 October	49	48			1	
30 Oct (07:00)	62	62				
31 Oct (08:00)	53	43		8	2	
Total	**1,991**	**1,916**	**4**	**35**	**23**	**13**
Average per day:	64					

Drones and Missiles Fired (November 2024):

	Total	Shahed-type	Air-to-surface	Cruise Missiles	Ballistic Missiles	3M22 S-300 Others
1 November	51	48		3		
2 November	No report					
3 November	97	96		1		
4 Nov (08:30)	81	80			1	
5 Nov (08:30)	81	79		2		
6 Nov (07:30)	65	63		2		

7 Nov (12:00)	106	106				
8 November	97	92		4	1	
9 Nov (08:00)	51	51				
10 Nov (09:30)	145	145				
11 Nov (09:30)	76	74		2		
12 Nov (11:00)	113	110		2		1
13 Nov (10:00)	96	90		2	2	2
14 Nov (08:30)	59	59				
15 Nov (08:30)	31	29		2		
16 Nov (08:30)	84	83				1
17 Nov (12:00)	210	90		110	9	1
18 November	14	11		1	2	
19 November	87	87				
20 Nov (11:00)	128	122		5		1
21 November	No good report		*1*	7		
22 Nov (17:30)	114	114				
23 November	No report					
24 November	73	73				
25 Nov (11:00)	145	145				
26 November	192	188			4	
27 November	89	89				
28 Nov (10:30)	188	97		88		3
29 November	132	132				
30 Nov (09:30)	10	10				
Total	**2,615**	**2,363**	**0**	**224**	**19**	**9**
Average per day:	87					

Figures in italics are not used.

Drones and Missiles Fired (December 2024):

	Total	Shahed-type	Air-to-surface	Cruise Missiles	Ballistic Missiles	Others
1 Dec (09:30)	78	78				
2 Dec (08:30)	110	110				
2 Dec (20:30)	3			3		
3 December	28	28				
4 December	51	50		1		
5 Dec (08:30)	46	44			2	
6 Dec (07:00)	53	53				
7 Dec (08:30)	15	14				1
8 Dec (08:30)	74	74				
9 Dec (08:00)	39	37		2		
10 December	No report					
11 Dec (17:00)	2			2		
12 December	No report					
13 Dec (11:30)	287	193		87	7	
14 December	132	132				
15 Dec (08:30)	109	108				1
16 Dec (08:30)	49	49				
17 Dec (12:00)	31	31				
18 December	81	81				
19 Dec (08:30)	88	85		1	2	
20 Dec (10:00)	71	65		1	5	
21 December	114	113				1
22 Dec (10:00)	104	103			1	
23 December	72	72				
24 Dec (10:00)	60	60				
25 Dec (12:00)	184	106		66	2	10
26 Dec (08:30)	31	31				
27 December	26	24			2	
28 Dec (08:30)	16	16				
29 December	16	10				6

30 December	43	43				
31 Dec (12:00)	61	40		14	7	
Total	**2,074**	**1,850**		**177**	**28**	**19**
Average per day:	67					

Totals for 2024 (intercepted or reported):

	Total	Shahed-type	Other Drones	Cruise Missiles	Ballistic Missiles	Other Missiles	Helicopters & Planes
January	420 + 213 = 633	362		157	57	55	2
February	365 + 149 = 514	377		79	16	29	13
March	731 + 193 = 924	650	4	173	29	66	2
April	346 + 107 = 453	287	21	90	17	37	1
May	427 + 51 = 478	357	12	83	7	19	
June	407 + 60 = 467	333	9	108	16	1	
July	523 + 88 = 611	429	83	78	21		
August	875 + 156 = 1,031	790	24	159	46	12	
September	1300 + 165 = 1,465	1,337		64	38	26	
October	1,991	1,916	4	35	23	13	
November	2,615	2,363		224	19	9	
December	2,074	1,850		177	28	19	
2024	**13,256**	**11,051**	**157**	**1,427**	**317**	**286**	**18**

Drones and Missiles Fired (January 2025):

	Total	Shahed-type	Air-to-surface	Cruise Missiles	Ballistic Missiles	Others
1 Jan (09:30)	111	111				
2 Jan (08:30)	72	72				
3 Jan (09:00)	93	93				
3 Jan (20:00)	40	32			3	5
4 Jan (09:00)	81	81				
4 Jan (20:00)	30	30				
5 January	103	103				
6 January	130	128		2		
7 January	38	38				
8 January	64	64				
9 Jan (09:00)	70	70				
9 Jan (17:00)	3			3		
10 January	72	72				
11 January	74	74				
12 January	94	94				
13 January	110	110				
14 January	80	80				
15 Jan (10:30)	117	74		42	1	
16 January	55	55				
17 January	52	50			2	
18 Jan (08:00)	43	39			4	
19 January	61	61				
20 Jan (08:00)	141	141				
21 January	135	131			4	
22 Jan (10:00)	99	99				
23 Jan (09:30)	96	92			4	
24 January	58	58				
25 Jan (09:30)	63	61		2		
26 January	72	72				

27 January	104	104				
28 Jan (09:30)	100	100				
29 January	57	57				
30 January	81	81				
31 January	102	102				
Total	**2,701**	**2,629**		**49**	**18**	**5**
Average per day:	87					

Drones and Missiles Fired (February 2025):

	Total	Shahed-type	Air-to-surface	Cruise Missiles	Ballistic Missiles	Others
1 Feb (15:00)	165	123	2	33	7	
2 February	55	55				
3 February	71	71				
4 February	65	65				
5 February	106	104			2	
6 February	77	77				
7 February	112	112				
8 February	139	139				
9 February	151	151				
10 February	83	83				
11 Feb (10:00)	143	124		18	1	
12 Feb (08:30)	130	123			7	
13 February	140	140				
14 Feb (08:30)	133	133				
15 February	70	70				
16 February	143	143				
17 February	147	147				
18 February	176	176				
19 February	169	167			2	
20 Feb (10:00)	175	161		13	1	

21 Feb (08:00)	162	160			2	
22 Feb (08:00)	162	162				
23 Feb (08:00)	270	267			3	
24 Feb (08:00)	185	185				
25 Feb (11:00)	220	213		7		
26 February	177	177				
27 February	166	166				
28 February	208	208				
Total	**4,000**	**3,902**	**2**	**71**	**25**	
Average per day:	143					

Drones and Missiles Fired (March 2025):

	Total	Shahed-type	Air-to-surface	Cruise Missiles	Ballistic Missiles	Others
1 March (08:30)	154	154				
2 March (08:30)	79	79				
3 March (08:30)	83	83				
4 March	99	99				
5 March (09:30)	185	181			3	1
6 March	114	112			2	
7 March (10:00)	252*	194	51		3	4
8 March	148	145	1		2	
9 March	119	119				
10 March (08:00)	176	176				
11 March (08:00)	127	126			1	
12 March (09:30)	136	133			3	
13 March	118	117			1	
14 March	27	27				
15 March (08:30)	178	178				
16 March	90	90				
17 March	174	174				

18 March	137	137			
19 March (08:00)	151	145			2	4
20 March (08:30)	171	171			
21 March (09:30)	214	214			
22 March (08:30)	179	179			
23 March (08:30)	147	147			
24 March	99	99			
25 March	140	139			1
26 March	117	117			
27 March	86	86			
28 March	163	163			
29 March (08:30)	172	172			
30 March	112	111			1
31 March	133	131			2
Total:	**4,280**	**4,198**	52		**21**	9
Average per day:	138				

* Numbers don't add up. Ukraine states 67 rockets were launched, but only lists 58.

Drones and Missiles Fired (April 2025):

	Total	Shahed-type	Air-to-surface	Cruise Missiles	Ballistic Missiles	Others
1 April	2			2		
2 April	74	74				
3 April	39	39				
4 April (08:30)	78	78				
5 April	92	92				
6 April	132	109		17	6	
7 April	No report					
8 April (08:00)	47	46			1	
9 April	55	55				
10 April	145	145				

11 April	39	39				
12 April	88	88				
13 April (08:30)	55	55				
14 April (09:00)	62	62				
15 April (12:00)	53	52			1	
16 April (09:30)	97	97				
17 April (10:00)	80	75			2	3
18 April (09:30)	43	37		5	1	
19 April (09:00)	95	87	3	2	3	
20 April	No report					
21 April (09:00)	99	96	2	1		
22 April (09:00)	54	54				
22 April (18:00)	77	77				
23 April	134	134				
24 April	215	145		59	11	
25 April	103	103				
26 April	117	114	2	1		
27 April	149	149				
28 April	166	166				
29 April	100	100				
30 April	108	108				
Total	**2,598**	**2,476**	**7**	**87**	**25**	**3**
Average per day:	93					

Drones and Missiles Fired (May 2025):

	Total	Shahed-type	Air-to-surface	Cruise Missiles	Ballistic Missiles	Others
1 May	175	170			5	
2 May	150	150				
3 May	185	183			2	

4 May	165	165				
5 May	118	116			2	
6 May	136	136				
7 May	192	187			5	
8 May	31	31				
9 May	No report					
10 May	No report					
11 May	108	108				
12 May	108	108				
13 May	10	10				
14 May	146	145			1	
15 May	110	110				
16 May	112	112				
17 May	62	62				
18 May	273	273				
19 May	112	112				
20 May	108	108				
21 May	76	76				
22 May	129	128			1	
23 May	176	175			1	
24 May	264	250			14	
25 May	367	298		60	9	
26 May	364	355		9		
27 May	60	60				
28 May	94	88		1	5	
29 May	90	90				
30 May	92	90			2	
31 May	114	109		3		2
Total	**4,127**	**4,005**		**73**	**47**	**2**
Average per day:	142					

The tables for June, July, August and September are in Chapter 8.

Totals for 2025:

	Total	Shahed-type	Other Drones	Cruise Missiles	Ballistic Missiles	Other Missiles	Helicopters & Planes
January	2,701	2,629		49	18	5	
February	4,000	3,902		71	25	2	
March	4,280	4,198		52	21	9	
April	2,598	2,476		87	25	10	
May	4,127	4,005		73	47	2	
June	5,677	5,438		172	59	8	
July	6,438	6,240		118	56	24	
August	4,288	4,132	(12)	98	50	8	
September							
October							
November							
December							

Note: We do not think they Ukraine quit shooting down "other drones," we just think they quit reporting it by the Air Command Staff.

Intercepted Missile Counts:

Air Defense Efforts (October 2024):

	Total	Failed to Reach Target	Percent Failed
1 Oct (08:30)	32	29	
2 October	32	25	
3 Oct (08:30)	105	102	
4 October	19	16	
5 Oct (07:00)	16	13	
6 October	91	83	Four UAVs were still in the air.

7 Oct (11:00)	81+	71	One UAV was still in the air.
8 Oct (08:30)	21	18	
9 Oct (08:00)	25	21	
10 Oct (11:00)	70	55	
11 Oct (11:00)	68	62	Four UAVs were still in the air.
12 October	28	26	
13 Oct (08:30)	72	67	One UAV was still in the air.
14 October	No report		
15 Oct (08:30)	26	16	One UAV was still in the air.
16 Oct (13:00)	138	132	
17 Oct (08:00)	57	51	
18 Oct (08:30)	135	124	
19 Oct (12:00)	104	92	
20 Oct (10:00)	51	46	
21 Oct (09:30)	119	104	
22 October	60	56	One UAV was still in the air.
23 October	82	81	
24 Oct (08:30)	54	50	
25 Oct (10:00)	63	52	
26 Oct (12:00)	98	89	One UAV was still in the air.
27 Oct (09:30)	80	74	
28 Oct (10:30)	100	94	
29 October	49	47	
30 Oct (07:00)	62	58	
31 Oct (08:00)	53	45	
Total	**1,991**	**1,799**	**90%**

Air Defense Efforts (November 2024):

1 November	51	51	100%	
2 November	No report			
3 November	97	95		
4 Nov (08:30)	81	77		
5 Nov (08:30)	81	80		
6 Nov (07:30)	65	60		Two UAVs still in the air.
7 Nov (12:00)	106	99		
8 November	97	94		One UAV was still in the air.
9 Nov (08:00)	51	50		
10 Nov (09:30)	145	139		
11 Nov (09:30)	76	74		
12 Nov (11:00)	113	96		
13 Nov (10:00)	96	92		Two UAVs still in the air.
14 Nov (08:30)	59	59	100%	
15 Nov (08:30)	31	26		
16 Nov (08:30)	84	83		
17 Nov (12:00)	210	187		
18 Nov (08:00)	14	11		
19 November	87	82		One UAV was still in the air.
20 Nov (11:00)	124	122		
21 November	No report			
22 November	114	111		Four UAVs still in the air.
24 November	73	73	100%	Four UAVs still in the air.
25 November	145	143		
26 November	192	176		
27 November	89	89	100%	
28 Nov (10:30)	188	176		Based upon 13:30 report
29 November	132	130		
30 Nov (09:30)	10	10	100%	
Total	**2,611**	**2,485**	**95%**	

Air Defense Efforts (December 2024):

	Total	Failed to Reach Target	Percent Failed	
1 Dec (09:30)	78	78	100%	One UAV was still in the air.
2 Dec (08:30)	110	109		One UAV was still in the air.
2 Dec (20:30)	3	3	100%	
3 December	28	25		
4 December	51	48		
5 Dec (08:30)	46	43		
6 Dec (07:00)	53	50		
7 Dec (08:30)	15	14		
8 Dec (08:30)	74	74	100%	
9 Dec (08:00)	39	39	100%	One UAV was still in the air
10 December	No report			
11 Dec (17:00)	2	2	100%	
12 December	No report			
13 Dec (11:30)	287	266		
14 December	132	132	100%	
15 Dec (08:30)	109	108		
16 Dec (08:30)	49	49	100%	Three UAVs were still in the air.
17 December	31	31	100%	One UAV was still in the air.
18 December	81	81	100%	
19 Dec (08:30)	88	85		
20 Dec (10:00)	71	65		
21 December	114	113		
22 Dec (10:00)	104	96		

23 December	72	72	100%	
24 Dec (10:00)	60	60	100%	One UAV was still in the air.
25 Dec (12:00)	184	113+		
26 December	31	31	100%	
27 December	26	24		
28 Dec (08:30)	16	16	100%	
29 December	16	9		
30 December	43	43	100%	
31 Dec (12:00)	61	46		
Total	**2,074**	**1,925**	**93%**	

Air Defense Efforts (January 2025):

	Total	Failed to Reach Target	Percent Failed	
1 Jan (09:30)	111	110	100%	
2 Jan (08:30)	72	72	100%	One UAV was still in the air
3 Jan (09:00)	93	86		
3 Jan (20:00)	40	35		
4 Jan (09:00)	81	81	100%	
4 Jan (20:00)	30	30	100%	
5 January	103	103	100%	
6 January	130	130	100%	
7 January	38	38	100%	
8 January	64	63		
9 Jan (09:00)	70	70	100%	
9 Jan (17:00)	3	3	100%	
10 January	72	67		
11 January	74	74	100%	
12 January	94	94	100%	
13 January	110	109		

14 January	80	79		
15 Jan (10:30)	117	104+		
16 January	55	52		
17 January	52	43		
18 Jan (08:00)	43	40		
19 January	61	58		
20 Jan (08:00)	141	140		
21 January	135	131		
22 Jan (10:00)	99	95		
23 Jan (09:30)	96	84		
24 January	58	52		
25 Jan (09:30)	63	62	100%	
26 January	72	59		
27 January	104	96		
28 Jan (09:30)	100	93		
29 January	57	43		
30 January	81	76		
31 January	102	96		
Total	**2,701**	**2,568**	**95%**	

Air Defense Efforts (February 2025):

	Total	Failed to Reach Target	Percent Failed
1 Feb (15:00)	165	117+	
2 February	55	53	
3 February	71	63	
4 February	65	65	100%
5 February	106	99	
6 February	77	74	
7 February	112	112	100%
8 February	139	138	
9 February	151	144	

10 February	83	83	100%
11 Feb (10:00)	143	123	
12 Feb (08:30)	130	117	
13 February	140	137	
14 Feb (08:30)	133	131	
15 February	70	70	100%
16 February	143	141	
17 February	147	142	
18 February	176	170	
19 February	169	162	
20 Feb (10:00)	175	158	
21 Feb (08:00)	162	157	
22 Feb (08:00)	162	157	
23 Feb (08:00)	270	257	
24 Feb (08:00)	185	184	
25 Feb (11:00)	220	218	
26 February	177	176	
27 February	166	162	
28 February	208	204	
Total	**4,000**	**3,814**	**95%**

Air Defense Efforts (March 2025):

	Total	**Failed to Reach Target**	**Percent Failed**
1 March (08:30)	154	154	100%
2 March (08:30)	79	79	100%
3 March (08:30)	83	77	
4 March	99	97	
5 March (09:30)	184	170	
6 March	114	111	
7 March (10:00)	252	230	
8 March	148	133	

9 March	119	110	
10 March (08:00)	176	172	
11 March (08:00)	127	114	
12 March (09:30)	136	118	
13 March	118	112	
14 March	27	25	
15 March	178	168	
16 March	90	80	
17 March	174	160	
18 March	137	127	
19 March (08:00)	151	128	
20 March (08:30)	171	138	
21 March (09:30)	214	195	
22 March (08:30)	179	163	
23 March (08:30)	147	122	
24 March (08:00)	99	93	
25 March	140	112	
26 March	117	104	
27 March	86	68	
28 March	163	140	
29 March (08:30)	172	163	
30 March	112	100	
31 March	133	102	
Total	**4,279**	**3,865**	**90%**

Air Defense Efforts (April 2025):

	Total	Failed to Reach Target	Percent Failed
1 April	2	2	
2 April	74	61	
3 April	39	35	
4 April	78	64	
5 April	92	82	

6 April (10:00)	132	106	
7 April	No report		
8 April (08:00)	47	40	
9 April (08:30)	55	40	
10 April	145	134	
11 April	39	37	
12 April	88	80	
13 April (08:30)	55	55	
14 April (09:00)	62	51	
15 April (12:00)	53	45	
16 April (09:30)	97	91	
17 April (10:00)	80	55	
18 April (09:30)	43	36	
19 April (09:00)	95	69	
20 April	No report		
21 April (09:00)	99	89	
22 April (09:00)	54	54	
22 April (18:00)	77	69	
23 April	134	114	
24 April	215	180	
25 April	103	81	
26 April	117	97	
27 April	149	124	
28 April	166	114	
29 April	100	84	
30 April	108	72	
Total	**2,598**	**2,161**	**83%**

Air Defense Efforts (May 2025):

	Total	Failed to Reach Target	Percent Failed
1 May	175	142	

2 May	150	126	
3 May	185	150	
4 May	165	149	
5 May	118	63	
6 May	136	124	
7 May	192	147	
8 May	31	26	
9 May	No report		
10 May	No report		
11 May	108	101	
12 May	108	85	
13 May	10	10	
14 May	146	122	
15 May	110	91	
16 May	112	109	
17 May	62	42	
18 May	273	216	
19 May	112	76	
20 May	108	93	
21 May	76	63	
22 May	129	112	
23 May	176	150	
24 May	264	251	
25 May	367	311	
26 May	364	297	
27 May	60	43	
28 May	94	71	
29 May	90	56	
30 May	92	56	
31 May	114	72	
Total	**4,127**	**3,354**	**81%**

Air Defense Efforts (June 2025):

	Total	Failed to Reach Target	Percent Failed
1 June	479	385	
2 June	84	52	
3 June	112	75	
4 June	95	61	
5 June	104	74	
6 June	452	406	
7 June	215	174	
8 June	52	40	
9 June	499	479	
10 June	322	284	
11 June	86	49	
12 June	63	49	
13 June	59	43	
14 June	58	43	
15 June	194	167	
16 June	138	125	
17 June	472	428	
18 June	58	30	
19 June	104	88	
20 June	86	70	
21 June	280	260	
22 June	50	28	
23 June	368	354	
24 June	97	78	
25 June	71	52	
26 June	41	24	
27 June (09:30)	371	365	
28 June	23	22	
29 June (08:30)	537	475	

30 June	107	74	
Total	**5,677**	**4,854**	**86%**

Air Defense Efforts (July 2025):

	Total	Failed to Reach Target	Percent Failed
1 July	52	47	
2 July	118	79	
3 July	52	40	
4 July (08:00)	550	478	
5 July (09:30)	322	292	
6 July (08:30)	161	117	
7 July (09:30)	105	75	
8 July (08:00)	58	34	
9 July (08:30)	741	718	
10 July (10:00)	415	178	
11 July (13:00)	79	60	
12 July (10:00)	623	602	
13 July	60	40	
14 July (08:30)	140	108	
15 July (13:00)	267	244	
16 July (08:30)	401	343	
17 July (08:30)	64	41	
18 July (08:30)	35	17	
19 July (10:30)	379	344	
20 July	No report		
21 July (09:30)	450	427	
22 July	42	33	
23 July	71	45	
24 July (11:30)	107	91	
25 July	63	54	
26 July (09:30)	235	200	

27 July (10:30)	83	78	
28 July (09:30)	331	311	
29 July	39	32	
30 July	78	51	
31 July	317	291	
Total	**6,438**	**5,470**	85%

UKRAINIAN ATTACKS ON RUSSIA, 25 FEBRUARY 2022 TO 31 AUGUST 2025

This is a list of incidents based upon multiple open news sources. The number of drones and missile fired are often based upon Russian sources and in many cases based upon their claims of drones and missiles intercepted. The losses are often based upon Russian claims and have not been independently verified. This listing is only of attacks on Russia, the territory that was under their control as of 2013. Attacks on Crimea or the Donbas or other occupied areas of Ukraine are not listed here.

Abbreviations: K-C = Karachay-Cherkessia Republic; N.N. = Nizhny Novgorod; St. P. = Saint Petersburg

Date	Target	Oblast	Type of Attack	Russian losses
25 February 2022	Millerovo air base	Rostov	Missiles (Tochka-U)	1 Su-30SM
1 March	Taganrog air base	Rostov	Explosion	
23 March	Zhuravlyovka	Belgorod	Shelling	
24 March	Nekhoteyevka	Belgorod	1 BM-30 Smerch	1 chaplain
29 March	Belgorod	Belgorod	Explosions	
1 April	Belgorod Oblast	Belgorod	Air (two Mi-24s)	Fuel depot

Date	Location	Oblast	Attack	Effect
13 April	Bryansk Oblast	Bryansk	Mortar fire	2 cars damaged
14 April	Klimovo	Bryansk	6 missiles	7 wounded, 1 Ukrainian Mi-8 lost
19 April	Golovchino	Belgorod	Shelling	3 wounded
25 April	Zhuravlyovka	Belgorod	Shelling	2 wounded
25 April	Bryansk	Bryansk	2 explosions	2 oil facilities
29 April	near Krupets	Kursk	Shelling	
30 April	near Krupets	Kursk		
30 April		Bryansk	Shelling	
11 May	Solokhi	Belgorod	Shelling	1 killed, 7 wounded
15 May	Sereda	Belgorod	Shelling	1 wounded
17 May	Bezymeno	Belgorod	Shelling	1 wounded
17 May	Tyotkino	Kursk	Shelling	
18 May	Solokhi	Belgorod	Shelling	1 wounded
18 May	Alekseevka	Kursk	Shelling	
19 May	Tyotkino	Kursk	Shelling	1 killed, 1 wounded
25 May	Zhuravltovka	Belgorod	Shelling	
26 May	Zhuravlyovka, et al	Belgorod	Shelling	1 killed
26 May	Vorozhba	Kursk	Shelling	1 wounded
6 June	Tyotkino	Kursk	Shelling	Bridge damaged
12–14 June	Klintsy	Bryansk	Shelling	
13 June	Klintsy	Bryansk	Shelling	
14 June	Klintsy	Bryansk	Shelling	5 wounded
14 June	Klintsy	Bryansk	Heli. fired missiles	1 wounded
22 June	Oil refinery	Rostov	Drone	
25 June	Rail line	Moscow	Sabotage	
3 July	Belgorod	Belgorod	Missiles (Tochka-U)	5 killed, 4 wounded

20 August	Car	Moscow	Sabotage	1 killed (Darya Dugina)
15 September	Valuyki	Belgorod	Shelling	1 killed
11 October	Shebekino	Belgorod	Explosion	
15 October	Belgorod	Belgorod	Explosions	Oil deport caught fire
16 October	Belgorod airport	Belgorod	Missiles	2 wounded
1 November	Krasnooktyabrsky	Kursk	Shelling	
2 November	Guyevo	Kursk	Shelling	5 wounded
14 November		Belgorod	Several blasts	
15 November	Shebekino	Belgorod	Shelling	2 killed, 3 wounded
16 November	Salnoy Kon, oil depot	Oryol	UAV	
5 December	Engel-2 air base	Saratov	Drones	2 Tu-95s damaged
5 December	Dyagilevo air base	Ryazan	Drones	3 killed, 4 wounded, 1 oil truck
6 December	Khalino air base	Kursk	Drone	Old reservoir caught Fire
17 December	Belgorod	Belgorod	Explosions	Car damaged
18 December	Belgorod	Belgorod	Explosions	1 killed, 4 wounded
18 December		Belgorod	Explosions	2 killed, 3 wounded
25 December	Engel-2 air base	Saratov		3 killed
Total for 2022	**49 attacks**		**15+ missiles 6+ drones**	**22 killed, 49 injured/ wounded**

Date	Target	Oblast	Type of Attack	Russian losses
4 January 2023	Rail line	Krasnoyarsk	Sabotage	
11 February	Shebekino	Belgorod	Missiles (Grad)	3 wounded
22 February	Shebekino	Belgorod		2 wounded
28 February	Tuapse, oil depot	Krasnodar	2 drones	
28 February	Observation tower	Bryansk	UAV	
4 March	Oil pipeline	Belgorod	Drone	
6 March	Novy Oskol	Belgorod	3 missiles	1 wounded
6 March	Iskra	Kursk		
15 March	Belgorod	Belgorod	2 missiles	
27 March	Gas station	Belgorod	Drone	
2 April	Café	St. P.	Sabotage	1 killed (Vladlen Tatarsky)
6 April	Khimki	Moscow	Drone	
9 April	Vozesenovka	Belgorod	Shelling	
10 April	Airfield	Belgorod	Drone	
16 April	Electrical substation	Belgorod	Drone	
3 May	Kremlin	Moscow	2 drones	
3 May	Taman	Krasnador	Drones	
3 May	Military airfield	Bryansk	5 drones	An-124 slightly damaged
4 May	Unit No. 45117	Voronezh	Drone	
4 May	Oil refinery	Rostov	Drone	
6 May	Car	N.N.	AT mine	1 killed, 1 wounded (Zakhar Prilepin)

10 May	Starodub	Bryansk	Drone	
11 May	Oil depot	Bryansk	Drone	
14 May	Military warehouse	Bryansk	Drone	
15 May	Border post	Bryansk	Drone	5 wounded
15 May	Excavator	Kursk	Drone	1 wounded
22 May		Belgorod	Raid by FRL and RVC	
30 May	Moscow	Moscow	8 to 25 drones	
1 June	Shebekino	Belgorod	Raid by FRL and RVC	
9 June	Voronezh	Voronezh	Drone	3 wounded
19 June	Valuyki	Belgorod	Shelling	7 wounded
2 July	Air base	Krasnodar	Missile	
4 July	Moscow	Moscow	5 drones	
8–9 July		Belgorod	4 missiles	4 missiles across 3 provinces
8–9 July		Bryansk	See above	
8–9 July		Rostov	See above	
11 July	Jogger	Krasnodar	Assassination (gun)	1 killed (Captain Stanislav Rzhitsky)
16 July	Shebekino	Belgorod	Shelling	1 killed
28 July	Taganrog	Rostov	Missile	
28 July	Azov	Rostov	Missile	14 wounded
28 July	Oil refinery	Samara	Bomb detonated	
30 July	Moscow	Moscow	3 drones	
31 July	Police station	Bryansk	Drone	
1 August	Moscow	Moscow	Drones	
1 August	St. Petersburg	St. P.	Sabotage	

Date	Target	Location	Method	Notes
4 August	Landing ship	Krasnodar	Boat drones	*Oenegorsky Gornyak* severely damaged
4 August	Kursk	Kursk	Drones	
16 August		Bryansk	Sabotage	Ukrainian saboteurs eliminated
18 August	Moscow	Moscow	Drone	Expocentre crashed into
19 August	Soltsy-2 air base	Novgorod	Drone	Tu-22M destroyed
20 August	Kursk	Kursk	Drone	5 wounded
20 August		Rostov	Drones	
20 August		Belgorod	Drones	
20 August	Moscow	Moscow	Drones	
21 August	Moscow	Moscow	Drone	2 injured
21 August	Shaykovka air base	Kaluga	Drone	
22 August		Moscow	2 drones	
22 August		Bryansk	2 drones	
23 August	Lavy	Belgorod	Drone	3 killed
23 August	Moscow	Moscow	Drone	
25 August	Shaykovka air base	Kaluga	S-200 missile	
25 August		Tula	Explosions	
26 August		Moscow	Drone	
26 August	Shchetinovka	Belgorod	Drone	1 killed
26 August	Urazovo	Belgorod	Shelling	
27 August	Air base	Kursk	16 drones	Claimed 4 Su-30 and 1 MiG-29
30 August	Pskov airport	Pskov	Drones	2 Il-76s destroyed, 2 Il-76s damaged

30 August	Fuel depot	Kaluga		
30 August	Factory	Bryansk		
1 September	Factory	Moscow	Drone	
1 September	Kuchatov	Kursk	Drones	
2 September	Urazovo	Belgorod	Shelling	1 killed
7 September	Rostov-on-Don	Rostov	2 drones	
7 September	Military base	Volgograd	Drone	
7 September	Bryansk	Bryansk	Drone	
17 September	Oil depot	Oryol	Drone	
18 September	Chkalovsky air base	Moscow		An-148, Il-20 and Mi-8 damaged
20 September	Sochi airport	Krasnodar	Drone	Fuel storage tank caught Fire
24 September	Kursk	Kursk	Drone	Government building damaged
24 September	Khalino air base	Kursk	Drone	1 killed, 4+ wounded
29 September	Electrical substation	Kursk	Drones	
29 September		Belgorod	Drones	
29 September	Radar station	Kursk	Drones	
29 September		Kaluga	Drones	
1 October	Adler air base	Krasnodar	Drones	
1 October	Factory	Smolensk	Drones	
4 October				
4 October		Belgorod	31 drones	
7 October	Urazovo	Belgorod	Drone	
7 October		Belgorod	Shelling	
7 October	Moscow	Moscow	3 Tochka-U missiles	
12 October		Belgorod	Drone	2 killed

Date	Target	Location	Means	Result
15 October		Kursk	27 drones	27 drones over two provinces
15 October	Energy facility	Belgorod	See above	
18 October		Kursk	28 drones	28 drones over two provinces
18 October		Belgorod	See above	
18 October	Khalino air base	Kursk	Drones	
18 October	Russian Mi-8	Crimea	Russian air defense	3 killed, friendly fire
26 October	Nuclear power plant Kursk	3 drones		
26 October		Tver	Shootout	1 Ukrainian agent killed
29 October	Oil refinery	Krasnodar	Drone	
3 November	Car	N. N.	Sabotage	Car set on fire
11 November	Valuyki	Belgorod	Drones and missiles	
11 November	Rybnoye	Ryazan	IED	Freight train derailed
14 November	Factory	Bryansk	Drone	
14 November		Moscow	Drone	
14 November		Tambov	Drone	
14 November		Oryol	Drone	
16 November	Car	Belgorod	Sabotage	1 killed (Oleksandr Slisarenko)
26 November		Moscow	24 drones	Total of 24 drones over five provinces
26 November		Tula	See above	1 wounded
26 November		Kaluga	See above	
26 November		Smolensk	See above	

26 November		Bryansk	See above	
29 November	Warehouse	Bryansk	Drones	Warehouse storing Shahed drones was attacked
30 November	Railway	Buryatia	4 explosions	
30 November	Railway	Moscow	Sabotage	
30 December	Belgorod	Belgorod	Shelling	25 killed, 108 wounded
Total for 2023	**118 attacks**		**21+ missiles 232+ drones**	**42 killed, 157 injured/ wounded**

Date	Target	Oblast	Type of Attack	Russian losses
1 January 2024	Belgorod	Belgorod	Explosions	
1 January	Belgorod	Belgorod	Shelling	
3 January	Chelyabinsk air base	Chelyabisk	Sabotage	1 Su-34 set on fire
5 January	Grayvoronsky area	Belgorod	Raid	
9 January	Fuel depot, et al	Oryol	3 drones	3 wounded
9 January	Gornal	Kursk		1 killed
18 January	Oil terminal	St. P.	Drone	
18 January	Valday	Novgorod	Drone	
18 January		Moscow	Drone	
19 January	Oil depot	Bryansk	Drone	
19 January	Factory	Tambov	Drone	
21 January	Gas terminal	St. P.	Drone	
21 January	Factory	Tula	Drone	
21 January	Factory	Smolensk	Drone	
21 January		Oryol	Drone	
25 January	Oil terminal	Krasnodar	Drones	

31 January	Oil refinery	St. P.	Drone	
3 February	Oil refinery	Volgograd	Drone	
9 February			Black Sea	19 drones over five locations
9 February	Oil refinery	Krasnodar	See above	Fire in Ilsky oil refinery
9 February		Kursk	See above	
9 February		Bryansk	See above	
9 February		Oryol	See above	
15 February	Belgorod	Belgorod	14 missiles	7 killed, 18 injured
15 February	Oil refinery	Kursk	Drone	Set on fire
23 February	Beriev A-50	Krasnodar		A-50 shot down and crashed. Ten airmen killed.
23 February	Factory	Lipetsk	Drones	
26 February	Pochaevo	Belgorod	Drone	3 killed
29 February	Golovchino	Belgorod		
2 March	St. Petersburg	St. P.	Drone	
4 March	Railway bridge	Samara		
5 March	Oil deport	Belgorod	Drone	
6 March	Factory	Kursk	Drones	
8 March	Rozhdestvenka	Belgorod	Drones	2 killed, 1 wounded
9 March		Rostov	47 drones over four locations	Beriev aircraft company in Taganrog damaged
9 March		Volgograd	See above	
9 March		Belgorod	See above	
9 March		Kursk	See above	
10 March	Kulbaki	Kursk	Shelling	1 killed, 1 wounded
10 March		Leningrad	Drone	

11 March	Belgorod	Belgorod	Drone	
11 March	Oil depot	N.N.	Drone	
11 March	Oil depot	Oryol	Drone	
11 March		Moscow	Drone	
11 March		Leningrad	Drone	
11 March		Bryansk	Drone	
11 March		Kursk	Drone	
11 March		Tula	Drone	
11 March		Voronezh	Drone	
12 March		Belgorod	Raid by FRL and RVC	
12 March		Kursk	Raid by FRL and RVC	
13 March	Oil refinery	Ryazan	30 drones over three locales	
13 March	Oil refinery	Leningrad	See above	
13 March		Voronezh	30 drones	
13 March		Belgorod	See above	
2 April	Factory	Tatarstan	Drones	12 injured
2 April	Oil refinery	Tatarstan	Drones – converted light aircraft	
5 April	Air base	Rostov	44 drones	20 killed or injured (or 8 injured)
5 April	Engels-2 air base	Saratov	1 drone	(Claimed 7 killed – not accepted)
5 April	Yeysk air base	Krasnodar	6 drones	(Claimed 4 killed – not accepted)
5 April	Air base?	Kursk	1 drone	
5 April		Belgorod	1 drone	
7 April	Ship	Kaliningrad	Sabotage	Russian corvette *Serpukhov*

9 April		Crimea	Neptune missile	
9–10 April	Klimovo	Bryansk	Shelling	2 killed
9–10 April	Korenevsky district	Kursk	Drone	3 killed
16 April		Bryansk	Drone	
17 April		Mordovia	Drone	
17 April		Tatarstan	Drone	
19 April	Tu-22M3	Stavropol	S-200 missile	Tu-22M3 crashed, 2 killed.
26 April	Ka-52	Moscow	Sabotage	Ka-32 destroyed
27 April	Two oil refineries	Krasnodar	Drones	
6 May	Berezovka	Belgorod	Drones	8 killed, 25 wounded
9 May	Belgorod	Belgorod	Airstrike	8 injured
9 May	Fuel depot	Krasnodar	Drone	
9 May	Oil refinery	Bashkortostan		Drone – converted light aircraft
11 May	Belgorod		Drone	5 killed, 9 wounded at two oblasts
11 May	Kursk		Drone	See above
12 May	Belgorod	Belgorod	Tochka-U missile?	16 killed, 27 wounded
14 May	Freight train	Volgograd	Drone	
23 May		Krasnodar	Drone	
26 May		Orenburg	Drone	
31 May	Oil depot	Krasnodar	Neptune missiles and drones	2 injured

1 June		Belgorod		10 HIMARS
2 June		Belgorod		HIMARS
6 June	Oil refinery	Rostov	Drone	
8 June	Air base	Astrakhan	10 drones?	2 Su-57s damaged
8 June		Voronezh	25 drones	
8 June	Air base	North Ossetia	3 drones	
8 June	Facility	Chuvashia		2 drones
14 June	Air base	Rostov	70 drones	6 killed, 10 wounded, 2 Su-34s damaged
14 June	Power plant	Rostov	See above	
14 June	Power plant	Voronezh	6 drones	
14 June	Belgorod		2 drones	
14 June		Kursk	6 drones	
14 June		Crimea	1 drone	
14 June		Volgograd	2 drones	
15 June	Shebekino	Belgorod	Shelling	5 killed
17 June	Factory	Belgorod	Drone	
17 June	Factory	Voronezh	Drone	
17 June	Factory	Lipetsk	Drone	
20 June	Oil refinery	Krasnodar	Drone	
20 June	Oil depot	Tambov	Drone	
20 June	Oil deport	Adygea	Drone	
21 June		Crimea	70 drones	
21 June		Krasnodar	43 drones	1 killed, 6 wounded
21 June	Yeysk air base	Krasnodar		
21 June	Shahed drone depot	Krasnodar	Neptune missile	
21 June		Volgorod	1 drone	
25 June	Ammunition depot	Voronezh		

25 June		Belgorod	Drone	1 killed
28 June	Oil depot	Tambov	Drone	
29 June	Gorodishche	Kursk	Drone	5 killed
9 July		Belgorod	38 drones over six oblasts 1 killed, 2 injured	
9 July		Voronezh	See above	
9 July	Facility	Astrakhan	See above	
9 July		Kursk	See above	
9 July		Rostov	See above	
9 July	Oil depot	Volgograd	See above	
13 July	Oil depot	Rostov	Drone	
17 July	Tserkovny	Belgorod	Drone	2 killed
18 July	Airfield	Perm	Sabotage	2 KAMAZ trucks burned
20 July	Millerovo air base	Rostov	26 drones	16 explosions
21 July	Air base	Moscow	Sabotage	2 helicopters damaged
21 July	Air base	Samara		1 Mi-8 destroyed
23 July	Ferry	Krasnodar	Drone	1 killed
24 July	Car	Moscow	Sabotage	2 wounded
25 July	Shebekino	Belgorod	Shelling	1 killed, 2 wounded
27 July	Olenya air base	Murmansk	Drones	2 Tu-22M3s damaged
27 July	Engels-2 air base	Saratov	Drones	
27 July	Dyagilevo air base	Ryazan	Drones	
27 July	Oil refinery	Ryazan	Drones	

Date				
27 July		Kursk	12 drones shot down in five oblasts	
27 July		Belgorod	See above	
27 July		Rostov	See above	
27 July		Bryansk	See above	
27 July		Lipetsk	See above	
28 July	Oil depot	Kursk	Drone	Fire
31 July		Belgorod	19 drones and 1 Neptune missile over five oblasts	
31 July		Bryansk	See above	
31 July	2 facilities	Kursk	See above	Fires
31 July		Kaluga	See above	
31 July		Rostov	See above	
3 August	Morozovsk air base	Rostov	Drones	Fire
3 August		Oryol		Drone
8 August	Lipetsk air base	Lipetsk	See below (drones)	6 injured
8 August				75 drones over six oblasts and Crimea
8 August	Shebekino	Belgorod	4 drones	4 drones hit apartment building
11 August		Kursk	14 drones and four Tochka-U missiles	13 injured
11 August		Voronezh	16 drones	
11 August		Belgorod	3 drones	
11 August		Bryansk	1 drone	

11 August		Oryol	1 drone	
13 August	Savaslevka air base	N.N.	Drones	
14 August	Savasleyka air base	N.N.	11 drones	11 drones hit air base
14 August	Khalino air base	Kursk	37 drones and 4 missiles (Tochka-U)	
14 August		Voronezh	37 drones	
14 August		Belgorod	17 drones	
14 August	2 air bases	Volgograd	9 drones	
14 August		Bryansk	3 drones	
14 August		Oryol	2 drones	
14 August		Rostov	1 drone	
18 August	Oil depot	Rostov		Fire
21 August		Moscow	11 drones	
22 August	Marinovka air base	Volgograd	Drones	Fire
23 August	Oil depot	Rostov		
24 August		Kursk	Military campaign	Continued until March 2025
26 August	Refinery	Omsk		Fire
28 August	Oil depot	Rostov	Drones	Fire
28 August	Oil depot	Kirov	Drones	
31 August	Belgorod	Belgorod	Missile	5 killed
1 September	Refinery	Moscow	Over 100 drones over two or more oblasts	
1 September	Power station	Tver	See above	
10 September	Moscow	Moscow	20 drones	1 killed and 8 injured
10 September		Bryansk	72 drones	

10 September		Kursk	14 drone	
10 September		Kaluga	7 drones	
10 September		Tula	13 drome	
10 September		Belgorod	8 drones	
10 September		Oryol	1 drone	
10 September		Voronezh	5 drones	
10 September		Lipetsk	4 drones	
18 September	Ammunition depot	Tver	Drone	Fire – 13 injured
21 September	Ammunition depot	Tver	Drone	
21 September	Ammunition depot	Krasnodar	Drone	
21 September	Tikhoretsk air base	Krasnodar	drone	
3 October	Borisoglebsk air base	Voronezh	Drones	
10 October	Khanskaya air base	Adygea	Drone	Fire
6 November	Naval base	Dagestan	An-22 drone	Ships damaged
8–9 November	Chemical plant	Tula	13 drones	Fire
10 November	Moscow	Moscow	34 drones	
14 November	Krymsk air base	Krasnodar	51 drones	
17 November	Factory	Udmurtia	Drones	
20 November	Arsenal	Novgorod	Drones	
22 November	Maryino	Kursk	Storm Shadow missiles 1 wounded	
22 November	Oil depot	Kaluga	2 missiles and 27 drones	Fires

Date	Target	Location	Weapon	Result
25 November	Oil depot	Kaluga	Drones	Fires
1 December		Bryansk	Drones	
1 December		Kaluga	Drones	
14 December	Oil depot	Oryol	Drones	Fire
17 December		Moscow	Assassination	1 killed (Lt. General Igor Kirillov)
19 December	Oil refinery	Rostov	Neptune missiles and drones	
21 December		Saratov	Drones	
23 December	Millerovo air base	Rostov	Drones	
24 December	Millerovo air base	Rostov	Drones	
25 December		Chechnya	Drone	
25 December		N. Ossetia	Drones	
25 December	Command post	Kursk	???	
27 December	Sochi	Krasnodar	Drone	
27 December	Kazan	Tatarstan	Drone	
27 December	Samara	Samara	Drone	
27 December	Grozny	Chechnya	Drone	
27 December	Makhachkala	Dagestan	Drone	
27 December	Volgograd	Volgograd	Drone	
27 December	Astrakhan	Astrakhan	Drone	
31 December	Lgov	Kursk	Storm Shadow missiles 8 killed, 22 wounded	
Total for 2024	**213 attacks**	**49+ missiles**	**99 killed, 210+ injured/ wounded**	
				1,252+ drones

Date	Target	Oblast	Type of Attack	Russian losses
2 January 2025	Command post	Kursk	???	
4 January	Ust-Luga	Leningrad	4 drones	
4 January		Leningrad	72 drones and 8 ATACMs	
4 January		Belgorod	See above	
4 January		Kursk	See above	
5 January		Several	103 drones	61 shot down, 42 were "decoys"
7 January	HQ	Kursk	???	810th Guards Naval Infantry Brigade
8 January	Oil depot	Saratov	11 drones	2 firefighters killed. @ 800,000 tons of jet fuel reported destroyed.
8 January		???	21 drones	
10 January	Ammunition depot	Rostov	Drones and Neptune missile	
10 January		Leningrad	Drones	Fire
11 January	Apartment	Tambov	Drone	3 injured from crash
11 January	Novorossiysk	Krasnodar	Drones	Fire
11 January	Oil process-ing plant	Tatarstan	Drones	
12 January		Kherson	Drones	1 killed, 3 injured
13 January	Gas pipeline	Krasnodar	9 drones	
13 January	Missile system		Russian drone	Friendly fire incident
14 January	Aleksin	Tula	Drones	10 explosions heard
14 January		Bryansk	Drone	
14 January		Belgorod	Drone	
14 January		Crimea	Drone	
14 January	Chemical factory	Tatarstan	Drones	Fire

14 January	Engels-2 Air Base	Saratov	Drones	
14 January	Oil depot	Saratov	Drones	Fire
14 January	Distillery	Tambov	Drones	
15 January	Oil refinery	Volgograd	Explosion	Fire
15 January	Oil depot	Voronezh	Drone	Fire
16 January	Factory	Tambov	Drones (aircraft-type)	
16 January	Oil depot	Voronezh	Drone	
16 January	S-400 system	Belgorod	???	
17 January	Oil depot	Kaluga	Drones	Fire
17 January	Towers	Krasnodar	Partisans	
18 January	Oil depot	Tula	Drones	
20 January	Oil depot	Voronezh	Drones	4 explosions
20 January	Aviation factory	Tatarstan	31 drones in six regions	Explosions. This is where the Tu-160s are built
20 January		Bryansk	14 drones and 4 HIMARs	
21 January	Oil depot	Voronezh	6 drones	
21 January		Bryansk	22 drones	
21 January		Rostov	12 drones	
21 January	Factory	Smolensk	10 drones	7 explosions
21 January		Saratov	4 drones	
21 January		Kursk	1 drone	
23 January			49 drones	
23 January	Oil refinery	Ryazan	10 drones	
23 January		Kursk	See above	
23 January		Bryansk	See above	
23 January		Belgorod	See above	
23 January		Crimea	See above	
24 January		Moscow	7 drones	
24 January		11 regions	77 drones	

24 January	Power station	Kursk	See above	
24 January	Power plant	Ryazan	See above	
24 January	Factory	Bryansk	37 drones[1]	
26 January		5 regions	32 drones	
26 January	Oil refinery	Ryazan	See above	Fire. Ceased operations[2]
26 January	Warehouse	Oryol	See above	200 Shahed drones claimed destroyed
26 January		Belgorod	See above	
26 January		Tver	See above	
26 January		Kursk	See above	
29 January			87 drones	A total of 104 drones over 9 regions
29 January	Oil refinery	N.N.	4 drones	All struck? Fires
29 January	Nuclear power plant	Smolensk	11 drones	
29 January		Kursk	See above	"Nearly half" the 104 drones fired were sent to this locale
29 January		Tver	See above	
29 January		Bryansk	See above	
29 January		Belgorod	See above	2 killed, 2 injured
29 January		Murmansk	2 drones	
29 January		Tartanstan	???	Flights suspended
29 January		St. P.	???	Flights suspended
29 January	Port	Leningrad	Fixed wing UAVs dropped bombs	
31 January	Oil refinery	Volgograd	8 drones	Fire

1   "Major Russian microchip factory halts production after Ukrainian drone strikes," *The Moscow Times*, 24 January 2025.

2   Abby Fenbert, "Russia's Ryazan oil refinery suspends operations after drone strike, Reuters reports," *The Kyiv Independent*, 28 January 2025. The Ryazan oil refinery was attack on 24 and 26 January 2025 and had previously been attacked in May 2024.

31 January		Rostov	25 drones	
31 January		Kursk	6 drones	
31 January		Yaroslav	4 drones	
31 January		Krasnodar	2 drones	
31 January		Voronezh	2 drones	
31 January		Belgorod	2 drones	
Total for January:	**74 attacks**		**721 drones and 13 missiles**	**5 killed, 8 injured/ wounded**
1 February	Boarding school	Kursk	Air strike	4 killed
2 February	Malinovka, etc.	Belgorod	Drones	2 killed
3 February	Oil refinery	Volgograd	25 drones	Fire
3 February	Gas process-ing plant	Astrakhan	7 drones	Fire
3 February		Rostov	27 drones	
3 February	Command post	Kursk	Air strike?	
3 February		???	11 drones	
3 February		Moscow	Bomb (assassination)	1 killed (Armen Sargsyan)
4 February	Drone operator	Belgorod	Sabotaged goggles	1 wounded[3]
5 February	Oil depot	Krasnodar	4 drones?	Fire
6 February	Logachevka	Belgorod	Drone	3 killed
6 February	Air base	Krasnodar	30 drones	Fires[4]

---

3   Seven others later reported injured, but not sure if they were inside Russia or not.

4   Stefan Korshak and Christopher Stewart, "US Spy Planes Flew Over Black Sea Just Before Ukraine Hit Russian Airbase," *Kyiv Post*, 6 February 2025. The count of 30 drones is based upon Russian claims to shot down 13 incoming drones over the Sea of Azov, another six over dry land and 11 reported explosions near the air base (this assumed one drone per explosion).

6 February	Radar systems	Moscow	Sabotage	Explosion[5]
7 February	2 Valdai radars	Moscow	Explosions	
8 February	Oil refinery	Volgograd	11 drones	
8 February		Krasnodar	2 drones	
8 February		Belgorod	5 drones	
8 February	S-400 missiles	Rostov	18 drones	
8 February	Airfield	Rostov	See above	
9 February		Rostov	Drones	14 buildings damaged
10 February	Oil refinery	Krasnodar	Drones	10 explosions
11 February	Engels-2 air base	Saratov	18 drones	
11 February	Oil refinery	Saratov	See above	
11 February		4 regions	22 drones	
13 February	Steel mill	Lipetsk	12 drones	1 injured
13 February		Bryansk	37 drones	
13 February		Kursk	12 drones	
13 February		Tver	9 drones	
13 February		Belgorod	3 drones	
13 February		Kaluga	3 drones	
13 February		Smolensk	3 drones	
13 February		Voronezh	3 drones	
13 February		???	1 drone	Math error?[6]
14 February	Kukuyevka	Belgorod	Drone	1 killed
14 February	Drone base	Kursk	Air force	

---

5   David Axe, "It seems a Ukrainian agent traveled 300 miles across Russia to plant explosives under a high-tech Russian drome-jammer near Moscow," *Forbes*, 13 February 2025. It is claimed that two Valdai radar systems were destroyed.

6   Tim Zadorozhnyy, "Russia's largest steel mill reportedly targeted by 'massive' Ukrainian drone strike," *The Kyiv Independent*, 13 February 2025. Not sure that twelve drones is "massive." Total drones given is 83, yet the totals for each Oblast only equals 82.

Date	Target	Location	Drone(s)	Source:[7]
15 February	Oil depot	Belgorod	Drone(s)	
15 February	Factory	Kaluga	12 drones	Fire[8]
15 February	Oil refinery	Volgograd	17 drones	
15 February		Rostov	9 drones	
15 February		Saratov	2 drones	
16 February	Cars near border	Belgorod	2 drones?	4 civilians killed[9]
17 February	Oil refinery	Krasnodar	17 drones	1 injured
17 February	Oil pumping station	Krasnodar	7 drones	Pumping station on oil pipeline
17 February		Azov Sea	38 drones and Neptune cruise missile	
17 February		Crimea	15 drones	
17 February		Black Sea	7 drones	
17 February		Kursk	2 drones	
17 February		Rostov	2 drones	
17 February		Bryansk	1 drone	
17 February		Belgorod	1 drone	
19 February	Oil refinery	Samara	Drones	Three explosions, fire
20 February		Saratov	Assassin plot	Thwarted by FSB
20 February	Oil pumping station	Krasnodar	2 drones	Fire
24 February	Oil refinery	Ryazan	2 drones	Five explosions, fire
24 February		Other regions	20 drones	Intercepted
26 February	Oil refinery	Krasnodar	85 drones	At least 40 explosions

7   Kateryna Serohina, "How many oil refineries in Russia were attack since beginning of 2025," *RBC-Ukraine*, 18 February 2025.

8   "Wave of Drone Attacks Hits Russia, Igniting Fire at Industrial Facility", *Defense Express*, 15 February 2025 and Alona Mazurenko, Drones Attack Russia Overnight: Explosion near oil refinery, industrial facility catches fire – video," *Ukrainska Pravda*, 15 February 2025.

9   "Four killed in Ukrainian drone attacks in Russia's Belgorod region, governor says," *Reuters*, 16 February 2025.

26 February		Crimea	30 drones	
26 February		Azov Sea	8 drones	
26 February		Black Sea	5 drones	
26 February		Bryansk	1 drone	
26 February		Kursk	1 drone	
27 February	Car in Graivoron	Belgorod	3 drones	1 killed, 1 wounded
27 February		???	16 drones	
27 February	Ammunition dump	Kursk	24 drones?	Fire
28 February		Oryol	8 drones	
28 February		Kursk	7 drones	
28 February		Bryansk	4 drones	
28 February		Krasnodar	2 drones	
28 February		Smolensk	1 drone	
28 February		Six regions	17 drones[10]	
Total for February:	**71 attacks**		**640 drones 1 cruise missile**	**16 killed, 4 injured/ wounded**
1 March		Tver	21 drones	
1 March		Crimea	11 drones	
1 March		Bryansk	5 drones	
1 March		Belgorod	3 drones	
1 March		Rostov	3 drones	
1 March		Smolensk	2 drones	
1 March		Lipetsk	2 drones	
1 March		Kursk	1 drone	
3 March	Oil refinery	Bashkortostan	Drones	Fire
4 March	Oil refinery	Samara	18 drones in six regions	Fire

---

10 Some of these may overlap with other reports, especially in Bryansk. The 17 drones were downed over Bryansk, Belgorod, Voronezh, Smolensk, Tver and Crimea. See: "Russian air defenses down 17 drones in six Russian regions," *Reuters*, 28 February 2025.

4 March	Factory	Rostov	See above	
4 March	Oil pipeline	Rostov	See above	
8 March	Oil refinery	Leningrad	2 drones	
9 March	Railway	Crimea	Partisans	Burned a relay cabinet
9 March	Oil refinery	Chuvashia	Drones	
9 March		Belgorod	52 drones	
9 March		Lipetsk	13 drones	
9 March		Rostov	9 drones	
9 March		Voronezh	8 drones	
9 March		Astrakhan	3 drones	
9 March		Ryazan	1 drone	
9 March		Kursk	1 drone	
9 March		Krasnodar	1 drone	
10 March	Oil refinery	Samara	Drones	
11 March	Oil refinery	Moscow	91 drones	3 killed, 20 injured. Largest drone attack against Moscow[11]
11 March		Kursk	126 drones	Total of 337 drones fired[12]
11 March		Bryansk	38 drones	

11   Tim Zadorozhnyy, "Ukrainian drones strike Tuapse oil refinery in Russia's Krasnodar Kai, governor says," *The Kyiv Independent*, 14 March 2025.

12   Largest Ukrainian attack to date and significantly larger than any previous attack. Moscow claimed it shot down 337 drones. The seven other regions are Belgorod, Ryazan, Kaluga, Lipetsk, Oryol, Voronezh and Nizhny Novgorod. See: Volodymyr Ivanyshyn and Martin Fornusek, "Moscow targeted by largest drone strike in war, over 300 UAVs downed across Russia, authorities claim," *The Kyiv Independent*, 11 March 2025. Note that several source say 343 drones including: Jessie Yeung, Edward Szekeres and Kosta Gak, "Russia says it was hit by 'massive' drone attack ahead of crucial talks between US and Ukraine," *CNN World*, 11 March 2025. Also see Aryna Balachuk, "Moscow claims hundreds of drones targeted Russia overnight: 337 UAVs reported downed – photos," *Ukrainska Pravda*, 11 March 2025 for drone counts by province.

11 March		Belgorod	25 drones	
11 March		Ryazan	22 drones	
11 March		Kaluga	10 drones	
11 March		Lipetsk	8 drones	
11 March	Oil pipeline	Oryol	8 drones	
11 March		Voronezh	6 drones	
11 March		N. Novgorod	3 drones	
12 March	Feed mill	Kursk	2 drones?	4 killed, 2 injured
12 March		Rostov	Drones	
12 March		Voronezh	5 drones	
13 March		Kursk	6 drones	
13 March		Voronezh	6 drones	
13 March		Rostov	5 drones	
13 March		Belgorod	5 drones	
13 March		Bryansk	30 drones	
13 March	Drone factory	Kaluga	25 drones	
14 March	Oil refinery	Krasnodar	Drones	Fire until 17 March
14 March		Moscow	4 drones (R-360 Neptune)	
14 March		5 regions	23 drones	
14 March		Black Sea	1 drone	
14 March	Gas compressor	Tambov	See above	
14 March	Gas compressor	Saratov	See above	
14 March	S-300	Belgorod	See above	
15 March			126 drones	Ukraine downs 130 drones while Russian downs 126[13]
15 March		Volgograd	See above	
15 March		Voronezh	See above	

<hr>

13   "Ukraine says 130 drones launched by Russia downed: Moscow days 126 fired by Ukraine intercepted," *The Times of Israel*, 15 March 2025.

16 March		Voronezh	16 drones	
16 March		Belgorod	9 drones	
16 March		Rostov	5 drones	
16 March		Kursk	1 drone	
17 March		8 regions	59 drones	
17 March	Oil refinery	Astrakhan	13 drones	Fire. 1 injured
18 March	Command post	Belgorod	???	3rd Motorized Rifle Division
18 March		Belgorod	Raid	Incursion by Ukrainian armed forces
18 March		4 regions	46 drones	
18 March		Belgorod	See above	1 seriously wounded
18 March		Bryansk	See above	
18 March		Kursk	See above	5 wounded
18 March		Orlov	See above	
19 March		Kursk	35 drones	
19 March		Other regions	22 drones	
19 March	Oil pumping station	Krasnodar	See above	Fire
20 March			82 drones	Russia claimed it shot down 132 drones
20 March	Pontoon truck	Kursk	GBU-39 SBD	Fired from an Su-27[14]
20 March	Engels-2 air base	Saratov	50 drones	2 killed, 3 wounded, 5 civilians injured
21 March		Kursk	4 drones	
21 March		Other regions	38 drones	Detected over Russia

---

14 "Ukrainian Su-27 Strikes Russian Pontoon in Kursk with US-Made FBU-29 Glide Bombs," *Kyiv Post*, 18 April 2025. Followed up with HIMARS strikes.

21 March	Gas pumping station	Kursk	Shelled?	Shelled by Russia? Fire[15]
21 March	Dobrino	Belgorod	Drone	1 killed
22 March	Explosives factory	Samara	Drones	
23 March	Oil refinery	Volgograd	3 drones	
23 March	Car	Belgorod	Drone	1 killed, 1 wounded
23 March	Transformer	Smolensk	Sabotage	Atesh partisan group
23 March		Rostov	29 drones	1 killed
23 March		Astrakhan	20 drones	
23 March		Voronezh	3 drones	
23 March		Crimea	2 drones	
23 March		Kursk	1 drone	
23 March		Saratov	1 drone	
24 March	Landing site	Belgorod	Missiles (inc. HIMARS)	Two Ka-52s, 2 Mi-8s destroyed
24 March		Bryansk	12 drones	
24 March		Rostov	12 drones	
24 March		Crimea	2 drones	
24 March		Krasnodar	1 drone	
24 March		Azov Sea	1 drone	
25 March	Kondratovka	Kursk	"Precise strike"	30 soldiers killed?
26 March	Car	Belgorod	Landmine	1 killed, 1 wounded
27 March	Command post	Kursk		Bn commander killed, 9th Motorized Rifle Rgt
27 March	Border checkpoint	Bryansk	Airstrike	15–40 Russian soldiers killed?
28 March	Gas pumping station	Kursk	Shelled?	Shelled by Russia?

---

15   Alisa Orlova, "Key Russian Gas Hub Supplying Europe Ablaze as Kyiv and Moscow Trade Blame," *Kyiv Post*, 21 March 2025.

Date	Target	Location	Count	Notes
28 March	Oil refinery	Saratov	19 drones	Not sure the oil refinery was attacked
28 March		Voronezh	32 drones	A total of 78 drones intercepted over six regions
28 March		Kursk	17 drones	
28 March		Belgorod	6 drones	
28 March		Lipetsk	2 drones	
28 March		Rostov	1 drone	
28 March		Tambov	1 drone	
31 March	Air base	Kaluga	Drones	One Tu-22M3 destroyed
Total for March:	**104 attacks**		**1,292 drones 2 missiles 1 glide bomb**	**58 killed? 39 injured/wounded**
4 April		Kursk	34 drones	
4 April		Oryol	30 drones	
4 April		Lipetsk	18 drones	
4 April		Kaluga	7 drones	
4 April		Rostov	4 drones	
4 April		Azov Sea	4 drones	
4 April		Tambov	3 drones	
4 April		Moscow	3 drones	
4 April		Bryansk	2 drones	1 killed, 1 injured
4 April		Voronezh	1 drone	
4 April		Tula	1 drone	
5 April	Fiber-optics factory	Mordovia	Drones	
5 April	Explosives factory	Samara	Drones	

5 April	Tu-22M3	Samara	Drone	At Engels. At least one Tu-22M3 damaged[16]
7 April	BUK missile launcher	Kursk	Drones	Three launchers destroyed
7 April		Azov Sea	13 drones	
7 April		Krasnodar	@ 2 drones	
7 April		Bryansk	@ 2 drones	
7 April		Crimea	@ 2 drones	
8 April		Kursk	GBU-39[17]	
9 April		Russia	158 drones	Russia claimed it destroyed 158 drones
9 April		Moscow	See above	Russian helicopter shot down by Russian air defenses
9 April		Krasnodar	67 drones	
9 April		Rostov	29 drones	
9 April		Voronezh	11 drones	
9 April		Kursk	10 drones	
9 April	Mozdok air base	N. Ossetia	15 drones	
9 April		Belgorod	5 drones	
9 April		Penza	2 drones	
9 April		Saratov	1 drone	
9 April	Engels-2 air base	Samara	Unspecified drones	
9 April		Oryol	1 drone	
9 April		Stavropol	1 drone	

---

16   Stanislav Pohorilov, "Ukrainian drone shot down Russian long-range bomber worth U.S. $100 ml – Ukraine's Commander-in-Chief," *Ukrainska Pravda*, 9 April 2025.

17   "Ukrainian Su-27 Strikes Russian Pontoon in Kursk with US-Made FBU-29 Glide Bombs," *Kyiv Post*, 18 April 2025.

Date	Target	Location	Type	Casualties
9 April		Crimea	3 drones	
9 April	Orenburg air base	Orenburg	Unspecified drones	
9 April		Azov Sea	7 drones	
9 April		Black Sea	6 drones	
14 April	Drone unit	Kursk	Bombed	
15 April	Apartment	Kursk	109 drones	1 killed, 9 injured
15 April	448th Missile Bde	Kursk	Strike	
15 April		???	6 drones	
16 April	112th Missile Bde	Ivanovo	7 drones	2 minor injuries
17 April	112th Missile Bde	Ivanovo	Drones	Fire
18 April	Car	Bryansk	Assassination	1 killed. Car bomb
19 April	Drone launch site	Kursk	Missile	Up to 20 killed
22 April	Depot	Vladimir	Drones	4 injured
23 April	Shahed factory	Tatarstan	Drones	
24 April	Mokraya Orlovka	Belgorod	Drone	1 killed
25 April	Car	Moscow	Bomb (assassination)	1 killed (Lt. General Yaroslav Moskalik)
26 April	820th Gds NI Bde	Kursk	Raid	Some killed. Two POWs
27 April	Command post	Kursk	Strike	1 killed
28 April		St. P.	Drone	
28 April		Leningrad	2 drones	
28 April		Novgorod	2 drones	
28 April	Electronics plant	Bryansk	102 drones	1 killed, 1 injured
29 April	Car	Belgorod	Drone	2 killed
30 April	Factory	Vladimir	Drones	

Total for April	**56 attacks**		**692 drones** **1 missile** **1 glide bomb**	**11 killed, 17 injured/wounded**
2 May	S-300V system	Crimea	Drones	
2 May	2 Su-30s	Krasnodar	HUR Magura 7	2 killed. Two Su-30s shot down
3 May				14 drone boats 170 UAVs 8 Storm Shadows 3 Neptunes
3 May	Port	Krasnodar	See above	Neptune and Storm Shadow missiles. 4 people injured
3 May		Crimea	See above	Two fighter jets claimed destroyed on ground
5 May		Moscow	4 drones	
5 May		Kursk	Drones	3 killed
5 May		Bryansk	17 drones	
5 May		Kaluga	5 drones	
6 May		Moscow	19 drones	
6 May		Other regions	86 drones	
7 May			507 drones	Total 524 less 17 for Moscow. These are shoot-down claims
7 May	Factory	Mordovia	See above	
7 May	Factory	Tula	See above	
7 May	Air base	Kaluga	See above	
7 May	Air base	Moscow	17 drones (of the 524)	
7 May		N. N.	See above	
7 May		Kirov	See above	
7 May		Yaroslavl	See above	
7 May		Tartarstan	See above	
12 May		Kursk	Missiles	3 injured

16 May	Railway track	Smolensk	Sabotage	Atesh set fire to track
16 May		Black Sea	6 drones	
19 May	Shebekino	Belgorod	Drone	1 killed
21 May			106 drones	Out of 159 over 9 regions
21 May		Tula	See above	
21 May		Ryazan	See above	
21 May	Factory	Oryol	53 drones	
21 May		Moscow	See above	
22 May			65- drones	105 drones over 10 regions[18]
22 May		Bryansk	Drone	1 killed, 1 injured
22 May		Tula	Drones	2 injured
22 May		Moscow	40+ drones	
22 May	Factory	Tula	Drones[19]	
23 May			66 drones	
23 May		Crimea	22 drones	
23 May	Factory	Lipetsk	See above	
23 May		Moscow	24 drones	
23 May		Kursk	See above	
23 May		Oryol	See above	
23 May		Tula	See above	

18   Moscow claimed they shot down 485 Ukrainians drones over the last three days, from 20 May to 22 May, including 63 over Moscow. We currently count 159 drones shot on 21 and 105 on 22 May for a total of 264. See: Kateryna Denisova, "Mass Ukrainian drone strikes targets Moscow, Russia claims, multiple airports closed," *The Kyiv Independent*, 22 May 2025. Other reports claim an additional 100 drones were shot down during the day on 21 May. See: Tetyana Oliynyk, "Lage-scale Ukrainian drone attack reported in Russia – video," *Ukrainska Pravda*, 21 May 2025. We do not have a good count for 20 May.

19   Iryna Balachuk, "Drone attack on Russia: explosions heard in Tula and near Moscow, armes factories targeted – video," *Ukrainska Pravda*, 11 July 2025.

23 May		Bryansk	See above	
23 May		Ryazan	See above	
23 May		Belgorod	See above	
23 May	Ivanova-S air base	Ivanonvo	See above	1 A-50 damaged
23 May		Vladimir	See above	
23 May		Voronezh	See above	
23 May	Factory	Lipetsk	See above	8 injured. Fire
23 May	Lgov	Kursk	Rocket strike	16 injured
24 May			3 drones	104 drones claimed shot down that night
24 May	Factory	Tula	1 drones	
24 May	Factory	Lipetsk	2 drones	
24 May		Belgorod	74 drones	
24 May		Bryansk	24 drones	
25 May	Air base	Tver	Drones	Fire and smoke
25 May	Factory	Tula	Drones[20]	
26 May	Shahed factory	Tartarstan	See above	
26 May	Factory	Ivanovo	See above	
26 May		Other regions	98 drones	
26 May		Moscow	10+ drones	
27 May	Rail relay cabinet	Tula	Sabotage	Atesh partisans
27 May			39 drones over several regions	
27 May		Belgorod	56 drones	
27 May		Tartarstan	See above	
27 May	Factory	Ivanovo	See above	

---

20   Iryna Balachuk, "Drone attack on Russia: explosions heard in Tula and near Moscow, armes factories targeted – video," *Ukrainska Pravda*, 11 July 2025.

Date	Target	Location	Count	Result
28 May	Technopark	Moscow	33 drones	Fire
28 May		Bryansk	59 drones	
28 May		Belgorod	19 drones	
28 May		Tula	13 drones	
28 May		Kursk	10 drones	
28 May		Oryol	8 drones	
28 May		Kaluga	3 drones[21]	
30 May	Car	Belgorod	Drone	1 killed
31 May		Kursk		10 injured
Total for May	**68 attacks**		**1,674 drones, 14 sea drones, 14 missiles**	**8 killed, 94 injured/ wounded**
1 June	Olenya air base	Murmansk	117 drones at 4 locales	See Chapter 1
1 June	Belaya air base	Irkutsk	See above	See Chapter 1
1 June	Dyaghalev air base	Ryazan	See above	See Chapter 1
1 June	Ivanovo air base	Ivanovo	See above	See Chapter 1
1 June	Ukrainka air base	Amur	Attempted	See Chapter 1, 1 killed
1 June	Railway bridge	Bryansk	Sabotage	7 killed, 66 injured
1 June	Railway bridge	Kursk	Sabotage	1 injured
3 June	Kerch Strait Bridge	Crimea	2 sea drones	
5 June	Iskander launcher	Bryansk	Missiles	8 killed?
5 June		Belgorod	15 drones	
5 June		Rostov	11 drones	

---

21 Another sources give a higher total of 296 (vice 112). They also report 42 drones in the Moscow Region (vice 33). See: "Ukraine fires massive drone barrage at Moscow," *Alarabiya English*, 28 May 2025.

5 June		Voronezh	3 drones	
6 June			174 drones	Intercepted in Crimea and 12 regions
6 June	Oil refinery	Saratov	See above	
6 June	Fuel depot	Saratov	See above	Englee-2
6 June	Factory	Tambov	See above	3 injured
6 June	Dyagilevo air base	Ryazan	See above	
6 June	Airport	Bryansk	See above	1 Mi-8 destroyed, 1 Mi-35 damaged
6 June	Military site	Ryazan	FPV drone	Perpetrator killed
7 June	Su-35	Kursk	Missile	Shot down by F-16 using AMRAAM
7 June	Factory	Tula	Drones	
7 June	Factory	N.N.	Drones	Fire
8 June		Moscow	10 drones	
8 June	Factory	Tula	Drones	Fire, 2 injured
8 June		Kaluga	7 drones	
9 June	Duty station	Kursk	4 HIMARS	1 killed
9 June	Air base	N.N.	Drones	2 planes damaged
9 June	Factory	Chuvasia	Drones	Fire
10 June		Bryansk	46 drones	Total of 102 drones reported (counted 103)
10 June		Belgorod	20 drones	1 killed
10 June		Voronezh	9 drones	
10 June		Kaluga	4 drones	
10 June	Shahed factory	Tatarstan	4 drones	
10 June	Shahed factory	Tatarstan	See above	2 factories targets in Tatarstan
10 June		Leningrad	2 drones	
10 June		Moscow	3 drones	
10 June		Oryol	2 drones	

Date	Target	Location	Means	Outcome
10 June		Kursk	2 drones	
10 June		Smolensk	1 drone	
10 June		Crimea	10 drones	
11 June	Factory	Tambov	Drones	
11 June		Novgorod	Car bomb	Failed. Agent arrested
12 June	Factory	Moscow	Drones	
12 June		Belgorod	38 drones	
12 June	Borisovka	Belgorod	See above	1 killed
12 June		Bryansk	4 drones	
12 June		Crimea	2 drones	
13 June	Air base	Voronezh	Drones	15 blasts reported
14 June	Factory	Samara	Drones	
14 June	Factory	Stavropol	Drones	
14 June	Power substation	Kaliningrad	Sabotage	Fire
15 June	Factory	Tatarstan		1 killed
16 June	Oil depot	Oryol	11 drones	
16 June		Kursk	Drones	
17 June		Tambov	Drones	10 explosions reported
18 June	Factory	Tula	Drones	
19 June		Bryansk	19 drones	
19 June		Kursk	17 drones	
19 June		Smolensk	13 drones	
19 June		Volgograd	7 drones	
19 June		Oryol	6 drones	
19 June		Rostov	5 drones	
19 June		Crimea	5 drones	
19 June		Belgorod	3 drones	
19 June		Astrakhan	3 drones	
19 June		Ryazan	2 drones	
19 June		Moscow	1 drone	

19 June		Ropstov and Tula	4 drones	
19 June		Saratov	???	Airport closed
19 June		Kaluga	???	Airport closed
20 June	Factory	Tula	Drones[22]	
23 June	Factory	Rostov	Drones	Fire
24 June	Moscow	Drones	2 injured	
25 June	Factory	Rostov	7 drones	
25 June			33 drones	Intercepted in several areas and Crimea
25 June		Unspecified	11 drones	After 22:40?
25 June		Belgorod	13 drones	
25 June		Tatarstan	4 drones	
25 June		Ulyanovsk	2 drones	
25 June		Saratov	1 drone	
25 June		Bryansk	1 drone	
25 June		Crimea	1 drone	
26 June		Kursk	24 drones?	1 injured
26 June	Fuel depots	Bryansk	Drones	Fire
26 June		Moscow	3 drones	
26 June		Elsewhere	21 drones?	
27 June		Rostov	19 drones	
27 June	Bridge	Volgograd	13 drones	Fire
27 June	Air base	Volgograd	See above	Claimed 2 Su-34 destroyed and two damaged
27 June		Crimea	4 drones	
27 June		Belgorod	1 drone	
27 June		Bryansk	1 drone	

---

22   Source for reports for 18 and 20 June: Iryna Balachuk, "Drone attack on Russia: explosions heard in Tula and near Moscow, armes factories targeted – video," *Ukrainska Pravda*, 11 July 2025.

Date	Target	Location	Weapon	Result
27 June	Oil refinery	Samara	1 drone	Fire
28 June	120th Arsenal	Bryansk	Drones	
Total for June	**92 attacks**		**777 drones** **2 sea drones** **7 missiles**	**20 killed, 75 injured/wounded**
1 July	Electric plant	Udmurtia	2 drones	3 killed. Fire. 1,300km from Ukraine border
1 July		Saratov	4 drones	
1 July		Rostov	16 drones	
1 July		Kursk	5 drones	
1 July		Belgorod	2 drones	
1 July		Voronezh	1 drone	
1 July		Oryol	1 drone	
1 July		Crimea	17 drones	
1 July		Azov Sea	11 drones	
1 July		Black Sea	3 drones	
3 July		Kursk	HIMARS	2 to 22 killed
3 July		Lipetsk	10 drones	1 killed, 2 injured
3 July		St. P.	Car bomb	Woman (perpetrator) arrested
3 July		Moscow	Car bomb	1 killed
3 July	Arsenal	Kursk	8 drones	Explosion
3 July		Belgorod	27 drones	
3 July		Voronezh	22 drones	
3 July		Crimea	2 drones	
4 July	Power substation	Moscow	Drones	4 explosions
4 July	Shahed factory	Moscow	Drones	
4 July		Rostov	Drones	1 killed
5 July	Warehouse	Chuvashia	Drones	
5 July		Engels	Drones	
5 July		Saratov		Flights cancelled

5 July		Ulyanovsk		Flights cancelled
5 July		St. P.		Flights cancelled
5 July	Air base	Voronezh drones		Fire. 8–10 explosions
5 July	Gas pipeline	Primorsky	Sabotage	
6 July		Bryansk	30 drones	
6 July		Kursk	29 drones	
6 July		Oryol	18 drones	
6 July		Belgorod	17 drones	
6 July		Tula	13 drones	
6 July		Kaluga	4 drones	
6 July		Leningrad	3 drones	
6 July		Smolensk	2 drones	
6 July		Novgorod	2 drones	
6 July		Tver	1 drone	
6 July		Azov Sea	1 drone	
7 July	Ammunition plant	Moscow	Drones	
7 July	Oil refinery	Krasnodar	Drones	
7 July		Moscow	Suicide	Transport Minister committed suicide
8 July		Kursk	Drones	4 killed
10 July	Shebekino	Belgorod	Drones	2 killed
10 July	Railway infrastructure	Volgograd	Sabotage	Atesh
11 July	Factory	Kursk	53 drones	Fire
11 July	Shebekino	Belgorod	Shelling	1 killed
11 July		Lipetsk	4 drones	1 killed, 1 wounded
11 July	3 factories	Tula	13 drones	1 killed, 1 wounded
11 July	Gas pipeline	Tyumen	Sabotage	Fire
11 July	Factory	Moscow	11 drones	
11 July		Bryansk	19 drones	
11 July		Smolensk	15 drones	

11 July		Belgorod	14 drones	
11 July		Oryol	11 drones	
11 July		Rostov	2 drones	
11 July		Kaluga	2 drones	
11 July		Crimea	7 drones	
11 July		Black Sea	4 drones	
15 July	Factory	Lipetsk	Drones	1 injury, fire
16 July	Pervomaysky	Belgorod	Drone	1 killed
17 July			106 drones	126 drones total for the day
17 July		Leningrad	See above	
17 July		Moscow	3 drones	
17 July		Kaluga	3 drones	1 injured
17 July		Belgorod	See above	2 killed, 7 injured
17 July		Smolensk	14 drones	1 injured
17 July		Voronezh	See above	3 injured
17 July		Bryansk	See above	
17 July		Kursk	See above	
18 July		Moscow	10 drones	
18 July		Oryol	17 drones	4 blasts
18 July		Rostov	Drones	Fire
18 July		Bryansk	31 drones	
18 July		Crimea	4 drones	
18 July		Azov Sea	3 drones	
18 July		Smolensk	2 drones	
18 July	Industrial area	N.N.	2 drones	
18 July		Belgorod	1 drone	
18 July		Kaluga	1 drone	
18 July		Voronezh	1 drone	
18 July		Black Sea	1 drone	
19 July		Moscow	13 drones	
19 July		Rostov	8 drones	

19 July		Bryansk	48 drones[23]	
19 July		Oryol	12 drones	
19 July		Kaluga	10 drones	
19 July		Tula	1 drone	
19 July		Kursk	1 drone	
19 July		Smolensk	1 drone	
19 July		Voronezh	1 drone	
20 July	Railway infrastructure	Tula	Sabotage	Atesh
20 July			158 drones	Intercepted 230+ drones[24]

23 These reports dated 19 July were posted to Telegram by the Russian Ministry of Defense at 17:10 18 July. It is possible that they could be additional strikes and updated reports that apply to 18 July. See: https://t.me/mod_russia/54796. They were supposed to have been intercepted between 18:15 and 23:05 Moscow time. The counts for 18 July were taken from Stanislav Pohorilov, "Over 70 drones attack Moscow Oblast and eight other regions – videos," *Ukrainska Pravda*, 18 July 2025 (at 0833). The counts for 19 July were taken from Olha Hlushchenko, "Almost 90 drones attack Russia in one evening," *Ukrainska Pravda*, 19 July 2025 (at 00200).

24 Note that another article has 40 drones intercepted between 20:00 and 23:30 on 19 July. Not sure if these are included in the 230+ count. See Ivan Diakonov, "Russia claims 40 Ukrainian drones downed in seven regions overnight," *Ukrainska Pravda*, 20 July 2025. They specially record 21 drones over Bryansk, 9 over Kaluga, four over Moscow, two over Kursk, two over the Black Sea, one over Tula and one over Belgorod. They then record another 93 drones shot down the night of 19/20 July, including 38 over Bryansk, 19 over Moscow, 21 over Kaluga, 8 over Tula, 5 over Oryol, 5 over Nizhny Novgorod, 3 over the Black Sea, 2 over Kursk, one over Belgorod and one over Ryazan. See: Roman Petrenko, "Russia claims 93 Ukrainian drones downed in overnight attacks," *Ukrainska Pravda*, 20 July 2025. Again, it is not certain if the previous report of 40 drones is also part of this report and if this report is part of the count of 230+ drones. Adam Schrader, "Russia faces intense barrage of drones, shutting down Moscow airports," UPI, 20 July 2025, reports that "The Russian Defense Ministry said in a series of statements that between 7:45 a.m. local times on July 19 and 5:40 p.m. on July 20, its air defense systems reportedly shot down at least 272 Ukrainian fixed-wing drone across more than a dozen regions." They report 55 drones intercepted over Kalua, 46 over Moscow and

Date	Target	Location	Count	Notes
20 July		Moscow	27 drones	
20 July		Kaluga	45 drones	
20 July	S-300P and Nebo-M	Belgorod	"Long-range firepower"	
21 July		Moscow	5 drones	
21 July	Railway station	Rostov	Drones	Fire
23 July	Power plant	Rostov	Drones	3 injured, fires
24 July	Fuel depot	Krasnodar	Drones	2 killed
25 July	Facility	Bryansk	Guided bombs	French AASM Hammer
25 July		Belgorod	26 drones	
25 July		Bryansk	25 drones	
25 July		N. Ossetia	Drones	
25 July		Chechnya	Drones	
25 July		Ingushetia	Drones	
25 July		Stavropol	5 drones	
25 July	Chemical factory	Stavropol	30 drones	These 30 are in addition to 105 Russia claimed to have intercepted
25 July		K-B	Drones	
25 July	Train station	Krasnodar	8 drones	
25 July		Tambov	Drones	
25 July	Train station	Rostov	23 drones	
25 July		Kursk	3 drones	
25 July		Tambov	3 drones	
25 July		Voronezh	2 drones	
25 July		Oryol	1 drone	
25 Juily		Azov Sea	9 drones	A total of 105 reported intercepted

drones intercepted over Tula, Kursk, Oryol, Smolensk, Belgorod, Nizhny Novgorod, Tver, Ryazan and Crimea. This reporting appears to overlap with the previous day.

26 July	Facility	Stavropol	Drones	Fire
26 July	Su-27UB	Krasnodar	Sabotage	Fire. Su-27UB destroyed
26 July		Bryansk	24 drones	
26 July		Rostov	12 drones	
26 July		Oryol	2 drones	
26 July		Tula	2 drones	
26 July		Belgorod	1 drone	
26 July		Azov Sea	4 drones	
26 July		Black Sea	3 drones	
26 July		Crimea	6 drones	
27 July	Railway power station	Volgograd	9 drones	Loss of power to rail services
27 July		Bryansk	36 drones	Total of 99 drones intercepted[25]
27 July		Smolensk	21 drones	
27 July		Kaluga	10 drones	
27 July		Rostov	9 drones	
27 July		Crimea	Drones	
27 July		Voronezh	Drones	
27 July		Kursk	Drones	
27 July		Moscow	Drones	
27 July		N. N.	Drones	
27 July		Oryol	Drones	
27 July		Tambov	Drones	
27 July		Black Sea	Drones	
27 July		Leningrad	12+ drones	1 injured

25 Reuters reported that 291 "Air defense systems downed two guided aircraft bombes, three projectiles of Czech-made Vampire multiple rocket launch systems and 291 fixed-wing drones. No further detailed provided. It is not known if these figures include operations inside of Ukraine." See "Russia says 291 Ukrainian drones downed," *Reuters*, 27 July 2025.

29 July	Train station	Rostov	Drones	1 freight train set on fire
31 July	Railway substation	Volgograd	Drones	
31 July	Drone operation base Belgorod	MiG-29	JDAM-ER	
31 July	Factory	Penza	Drones	
Total for July	**143 attacks**		**1,272 drones and 2 missiles**	**22 killed, 22 injured/wounded**
1 August		Rostov	Helicopters	Explosions
2 August		?	78 drones	
2 August		Rostov	34 drones	1 killed
2 August	Oil refinery		Ryazan	See above
2 August	Oil refinery		Samara	See above. 1 killed
2 August	Factory	Penza	See above	1 killed, 2 injured
2 August	Fuel storage base	Voronezh	See above	According to the Ukrainian General Staff[26]
2 August	Oil depot	Krasnodar	See above	Fire. According to *The Kyiv Independent*
3 August		Voronezh	Drones	1 injured
3 August	Oil depot	Krasnodar	Drones	Massive fire
3 August	Oil refinery	N. N.	Drones	
4 August	Railway station	Volgograd	Drones	Fire
5 August	Railway station	Rostov	Drones	
6 August		3 regions	35 drones	3 regions including Crimea
6 August	Railway station	Rostov	16 drones	

---

26 "Ukraine war latest: Ukrainian drones target Shahed storage site, industrial facilities in Russia; Strikes hit oil depot in Sochi," *The Kyiv Independent*, 3 August 2025.

6 August	Mi-28	Tver	Partisans	1 Mi-28 destroyed. Partisans = People's Resistance of Ukraine
7 August	Oil refinery	Krasnodar	Drones	
7 August	Military base	Krasnodar	Drones	
7 August	2 train stations	Volgograd	Drones	Fire
8 August	90th AA Krasnodar Missile Bde	Explosions	2 killed?	
10 August		Tula	11 drones[27]	
10 August		Bryansk	7 drones	
10 August		Oyrol	5 drones	
10 August		Kaluga	2 drones	
10 August		Moscow	1 drone	
10 August		Ryazan	1 drone	
10 August	Oil refinery	Saratov	Drones	1 killed. Multiple explosions and fire
10 August	Oil refinery	Komi	Drones[28]	
11 August		Black Sea	20 drones	20 drones over 4 regions
11 August		Kaluga	See above	
11 August		Bryansk	See above	

27   Drone intercept counts for 10 through 13 August and 29 to 31 August taken from daily reports from *Izvestiya*, among other sources. See: "The air defense forces repelled an attack by Ukrainian drones on the Rostov region," 13 August 2025" at https://en.iz.ru/en/1935971/2025-08-13/air-defense-forces-repelled-attack-ukrainian-drones-rostov-region and Russia's special operation in Ukraine | Footage | News. The reporting is not always systematically presented. Only use those reports that summarize for the day and record details as to regions the drones were intercepted in.

28   Yulia Akymova and Bohdan Babaiev, "Ukrainian drones launch historical 2,000 km strikes to cripple Russian oil refinery." Sources, *RBC-Ukraine*, 10 August 2025.

Date	Target	Location	Drones	Notes
11 August		Moscow	See above	
11 August		Crimea	4 drones	
11 August		N. N.	2 drones	
11 August		Belgorod	1 drone	
11 August	Factory	Stavropol	Drones	
11 August	Helium factory	Orenburg	Drones	
12 August		Bryansk	12 drones	
12 August		Kursk	9 drones	
12 August		Belgorod	3 drones	
12 August		Voronezh	1 drone	
12 August		Orel	1 drone	
13 August	Pipeline	Bryansk	15 drones	Oil pumping station on Druzhba pipeline
13 August		Volgograd	11 drones	
13 August	Pipeline?	Rostov	7 drones	
13 August	Oil refinery	Krasnodar	5 drones	Oil refinery at Slavansk-on-Kuban[29]
13 August		Belgorod	2 drones	
13 August		Voronezh	2 drones	
13 August		Crimea	2 drones	
13 August		Sea of Azov	2 drones	46 fixed-wing drones intercepted overnight
14 August			35 drones	Total of 44 drones intercepted
14 August	Oil refinery	Volgograd	9 drones	
14 August		Rostov	See above	16+ injured
14 August		Belgorod	See above	
14 August	Pristen	Belgorod	See above	1 killed

---

29   Anna Fratsyvir, "Ukraine strikes oil facility in western Russia in overnight drone attack, Kyiv confirms," *The Kyiv Independent*, 13 August 2025.

15 August	Ship	Astrakhan		
15 August	Oil refinery	Samara	Drones	
15 August	Factory	Ryazan	Explosion	*23 killed, 154 injured. May have been an accident*
16 August			19 drones	
16 August		Rostov	10 drones	
16 August	Military convoy	Kursk		Lt. General Abatchev seriously wounded
16 August	Chemical plant	Stavropol	Drones	9–10 explosions
17 August	Railway station	Voronezh	Drones	
18 August	Oil pumping station	Tambov	Drones	Druzhba pipeline
20 August		Bryansk	Saboteurs intercepted	3 Ukrainians killed, 3 captured
21 August	Oil refinery	Rostov	Drones	
21 August	Pipeline	Rostov	2 drones (fixed wing)	Large fire
21 August	Oil pumping station	Bryansk	Drones	Fire. Druzhba pipeline
22 August		Krasnodar	Sea drone	5 killed
23 August		St. P	1 drone	
23 August		Leningrad	4 drones	
23 August		Kursk	Raid	Raised Ukrainian flag
24 August			85 drones	95 drones intercepted over more than a dozen regions
24 August	Nuclear power plant	Kursk	Drone	
24 August	Gas terminal	Leningrad	10 drones	Fire
24 August	Railway line	K-C	Sabotage	Atesh

Date	Target	Location	Weapon	Notes
24 August	Oil refinery	Samara	Drones[30]	
25 August		Estonia	Drone	Ukrainian drone diverted to Estonia
26 August	Pipeline	Ryazan		Explosion
28 August	Oil refinery	Krasnodar	Drones	Large fire
28 August	Oil refinery	Samara	Drones	
29 August		Crimea	15 drones	
29 August		Rostov	13 drones	
29 August		Krasnodar	11 drones	
29 August		Black Sea	30 drones	
29 August		Bryansk	5 drones	Note this does not match other reports for Bryansk
29 August		Belgorod	4 drones	
29 August		Smolensk	2 drones	
29 August		Kaluga	2 drones	
29 August		Tver	2 drones	
29 August		Tula	1 drone	
29 August		Kursk	1 drone	Total of 86 drones reported as intercepted this day
29 August	Pumping station	Bryansk	18 drones (fixed wing)	
30 August		Smolensk	18 drones	
30 August		Crimea	2 drones	
30 August	Oil refinery	Krasnodar	Drones	Fire
30 August	Oil refinery	Samara	Drones	
30 August	Chemical plant	Tula	Drones	
31 August		Volgograd	11 drones	

---

30   "Ukraine strikes Syzran oil refinery in Russia, General Staff confirms," *UKRINFORM*, 24 August 2025.

31 August		Rostov	8 drones	
31 August		Belgorod	1 drone	
31 August		Bryansk	1 drone	
31 August		Belgorod	2 drones	Headline says 136, which we are not sure of[31]
31 August			32 drones	Destroyed over Black Sea and Crimea
Total for August	**102 attacks**		**693 drones 1 sea drone**	**22 killed, 19 injured/wounded**
Total for 2025 (through August)	**711 attacks**		**12,455 drones 39 missiles**	**161 killed, 285 injured/wounded**

Note: While this listing is fairly comprehensive, it is not exhaustive. Furthermore, not every one of these incidents has been exhaustively researched. More can be done to develop this list, especially for 2025.

Abbreviations:

K-C = Karachay-Cherkessia Republic

N.N. = Nizhny Novgorod

St. P. = Saint Petersburg

---

31 "During the day, 136 USAVs of the Armed Forces of Ukraine attacked nine municipalities of the Belgorod region" at https://en.iz.ru/en/1946067/2025-08-31/during-day-136-uavs-armed-forces-ukraine-attacked-nine-municipalities-belgorod-region.

SELECT BIBLIOGRAPHY

Books

Church, Peter, *A Short History of South-East Asia* (John Wiley & Sons, Singapore, 2006).

Clausewitz, Carl von, *On War* (Princeton University Press, Princeton, New Jersey, 1976).

Dupuy, Colonel Trevor N., *Elusive Victory: The Arab-Israeli Wars 1947-1974* (HERO Books, Fairfax, VA, USA, 1984).

Fox, Roger P., *Air Base Defense in the Republic of Vietnam, 1961-1973* (Office of Air Force History, Washington D.C., 1979).

Khruschev, Nikita, *Khruschev Remembers: The Last Testament* (Little, Brown and Company, New York, 1974).

Lawrence, Christopher A., *Aces at Kursk: The Battle for Aerial Supremacy on the Eastern Front, 1943* (Air World, Barnsley, UK, 2024).

Lawrence, Christopher A., *America's Modern Wars: Understanding Iraq, Afghanistan and Vietnam* (Casemate Publishers, Philadelphia & Oxford, 2015).

Lawrence, Christopher A., *Kursk: The Battle of Prokhorovka* (Aberdeen Books, Sheridan, CO, 2015).

The Military Balance 2022 (Routledge, UK, February 2022).

The Military Balance 2025 (Routledge, UK, February 2025).

Strange, Lt-Col. Louis Arbon, *Recollections of an Airman* (Casemate, Philadelphia & Oxford, 2016, originally published in 1933).

Selected Articles and Websites

Mystics & Statistics blog, www.dupuyinstitute.org

War Mapper @War_Mapper on X (twitter).

INDEX

BIOGRAPHY

Christopher A. Lawrence is a professional historian and military analyst. He is the Executive Director and President of *The Dupuy Institute*, an organization dedicated to scholarly research and objective analysis of historical data related to armed conflict and the resolution of armed conflict. *The Dupuy Institute* provides independent, historically-based analysis of lessons learned from modern military campaigns.

Mr. Lawrence was the program manager for the Ardennes Campaign Simulation Data Base, the Kursk Data Base, the Modern Insurgency Spread Sheets and for a number of other smaller combat data bases. He participated in studies on casualty estimates (including estimates for Bosnia and Iraq) and studies of air campaign modeling, enemy prisoner of war capture rates, medium weight armor, urban warfare, situational awareness, counterinsurgencies, and other subjects for the U.S. Army, Department of Defense, the Joint Staff, and the U.S. Air Force. He has also directed a number of studies related to the military impact of banning antipersonnel mines for the Joint Staff, the Los Alamos National Laboratories, and the Vietnam Veterans of America Foundation.

His published works include papers and monographs for the Congressional Office of Technology Assessment and Vietnam Veterans of America Foundation, in addition to over 40 articles written for limited distribution newsletters and over 60 analytical reports prepared for the Department of Defense. He is the author of *America's Modern Wars: Understanding Iraq, Afghanistan and Vietnam* (Casemate Publishers, Philadelphia & Oxford, 2015); *Kursk: The Battle of Prokhorovka* (Aberdeen Books, Sheridan, CO, 2015); *War by Numbers: Understanding Conventional Combat* (Potomac Books, Lincoln, NE, 2017); *The Battle of Prokhorovka* (Stackpole Books, Mechanicsburg, PA, 2019); *Aces at Kursk: The Battle for Aerial Supremacy on the Eastern Front, 1943* (Air World, Barnsley, UK, 2024); *Hunting Falcon: The Story of WWI German Ace Hans-Joachim Buddecke* (Pen and Sword Books, Barnsley,

UK, 2025), *The Battle for Kyiv: The Fight for Ukraine's Capital* (Frontline Books, Barnsley, UK, 2023) and *The Siege of Mariupol: The Azovstal Steel Plant and Ukraine's Battle for Survival* (Frontline Books, Barnsley, UK, 2025)

Mr. Lawrence lives in northern Virginia near Washington, D.C., with his wife and son.